BOOKS BY JAMES A. PIKE

The Other Side: An Account of My Experiences with Psychic Phenomena

If This Be Heresy

You and the New Morality

What Is This Treasure

A Time for Christian Candor

Teen-agers and Sex

Beyond the Law

A New Look in Preaching

Our Christmas Challenge

Facing the Next Day

Doing the Truth: A Summary of Christian Ethics

If You Marry Outside Your Faith

Beyond Anxiety

Cases and Other Materials on the New Federal and Code Procedure

CO-AUTHOR OF

Administrative Law

The Faith of the Church

Man in the Middle

The Church, Politics and Society

Roadblocks to Faith

EDITOR OF

Modern Canterbury Pilgrims

THE OTHER SIDE

THE OTHER SIDE

An Account of My Experiences with Psychic Phenomena

by

JAMES A. PIKE

with

DIANE KENNEDY

Garden City, New York
DOUBLEDAY & COMPANY, INC.

The author is grateful to the following for permission to use copyrighted material:

DeVorss & Co. for material from Plato's *Republic* which appears in *Breakthrough to Creativity* by Shafica Karagulla.

Harper & Row, Publishers, Incorporated, for material from *If This Be Heresy* by James A. Pike.

Saturday Review for material from a review by James A. Pike of "The Swan in the Evening: Fragments of an Inner Life," by Rosamond Lehmann. Copyright © 1968 Saturday Review, Inc.

Library of Congress Catalog Card Number 68–29044

Printed in the United States of America

To
JIM

FOREWORD

The title of this book is a *double-entendre.* The other side of death will immediately come to the mind of any reader who encountered some of the unsought-for but widespread publicity about some of my experiences since the death of my eldest son. That aspect of the two-and-a-half year period since my son died is more fully spelled out here. However, because of the way in which my experiences were all too often reported—and, especially, headlined—I am equally concerned that this book will also present *the other side* of credulity and naïveté.

What measure of understanding I have gained in these matters I owe in large part to others. There are the people who were connected in one way or another with the empirical data themselves, and most of these will be identified in the pages that follow. I am also indebted to a number of scientists whom I have consulted or who have shared materials with me, such as J. B. Rhine, Ph.D., Director of the Institute of the Study of Man; Ian Stevenson, M.D., Professor of Psychiatry and Neurology, University of Virginia Medical School; Karlis Osis, Ph.D., Director of Research, American Society for Psychical Research; Gardner Murphy, Ph.D., Director of Research, Menninger Foundation and President of the American Society for Psychical Research; Mr. Chester Carlson, inventor of Xerox and member of the boards of the Center for the Study of Democratic Institutions and the American Society for Psychical Research; Mr. Irving Laucks, colleague at the Center and author of a work in this field; and the many, many persons who have written me, whether to inquire, to criticize, to seek pastoral help or to share experiences.

Of the latter, quite a few have told of experiences which appeared to be connected in some way with the persons and data here treated. With no reflection on the credibility of these reports, by and large I have had to exclude occasions on which I have not been personally present (as well as from when I have); but I am nonetheless grateful to all who have thus shared of themselves—especially my good friends Mr. and Mrs. Phil Dick, Ann Borg and Michael Hackett.

The thinking through and writing of this book in the midst of other responsibilities has been possible only due to the collaboration from start to finish of Miss Diane Kennedy, Director of New Focus Foundation, the board of which has given support and encouragement and whose secretaries, Joyce Duncan and especially Gertrude Platt, have devoted much time to the manuscript. I appreciate, too, the assistance outside of regular hours of my secretary at the Center, Miss Myrtle Goodwin, and the help of Mr. Scott Kennedy, student at the University of California at Santa Cruz.

I hope that with the help of so many who have made varied contributions both to what is written about and to the writing, both imports of *The Other Side* will come through adequately.

✠ JAMES A. PIKE

Jerusalem, Israel
Ascension Day, 1968
(the tenth anniversary of my consecration as a bishop)

1

Let me show in an allegory how far our nature is enlightened or unenlightened. Imagine human beings living in an underground cave, which has a mouth open toward the light and reaching all along the cave. Here they have been from childhood. They have their legs and necks chained so that they cannot move and can only see the wall of the cave before them, being prevented by the chains from turning their heads. Above and behind them at a distance the fire of the sun is blazing, and between the sun and the prisoners there is a raised way and a low wall built along the way. And do you see men passing along the way carrying all sorts of vessels and statues and figures of animals made of wood and stone and various materials which appear as shadows on the wall of the cave facing the prisoners? Some of them are talking, others silent.

"You have shown me a strange image and they are strange prisoners," Glaucon replies.

Like ourselves, and they see only their own shadows, or the shadows which the sun throws on the opposite wall of the cave, of the men and the objects which are being carried. If they were able to converse with one another, would they not suppose that they were seeing as realities what was before them? And suppose further that the prison had an echo which came from the other side. Would they not be sure to fancy when one of the passers-by spoke that the voice which they heard came from the passing shadow?

To them the truth would be literally nothing but the shadows of images.

At first when any one of the prisoners is liberated and compelled suddenly to stand up and turn around and walk and look towards the light he will suffer sharp pain and he will be unable to see the reality of which in his former state he had seen the shadow. Conceive of someone saying to him that what he saw before was an illusion. Would he not be perplexed? Would he not fancy that the shadows which he formerly saw are truer than the objects which are now shown to him? If he is compelled to look straight at the light, will he not have a pain in his eyes which will make him turn away? He will take refuge in the shadows which he can see and which he will conceive to be in reality clearer than the things which are now being shown to him?

He will require to grow accustomed to the sight of the upper world. Last of all, he will be able to see the sun. He will then proceed to argue that the sun is he who gives the seasons and the years and is the guardian of all that is in the visible world, and in a certain way the cause of all things which he and his fellows have been accustomed to behold.

When he remembered his old habitation and the wisdom of the cave and his fellow prisoners, do you suppose that he would congratulate himself on the change and pity them? Imagine once more such an individual coming suddenly out of the sun to be replaced in his old situation. Would he not be certain to have his eyes full of darkness?

If there were contests and he had to compete in measuring the shadows with the prisoners who had never moved out of the cave, while his sight was still weak, would he not seem ridiculous? Men would say of him, "Up he went and down he came without his eyes," and that it was better not even to think of ascending. If any one tried to loose another and lead him up to the light, let them only catch the offender and they would put him to death.

—*Plato,* THE REPUBLIC

As I entered my bedroom in Cambridge, England, on Sunday evening, February 20, 1966, there on the floor lay two postcards, face up—in such a way as to form a 140° angle in front of the nightstand between the twin beds. This would not have been so surprising if the postcards had been mine—but I had never seen them before. Also, I had been away from Cambridge for a long weekend and in my absence the cleaning woman was to have gone over the whole apartment. Up to then she had been most thorough and reliable and it seemed strange that she would have left anything lying on the floor.

"Hey, look at this!" I called out. Two colleagues came into the room and together we began examining and discussing the first of a long and complicated series of events more astonishing than anything I had ever before experienced. Entirely unexpectedly I soon became involved as a reluctant student in what for me was quite a new field of analysis and study.

Just sixteen days before that event, the older of my two sons, Jim, had died at the age of twenty. In the early hours of Friday, February 4, 1966, he took his own life in a New York City hotel room. It goes without saying that in any case his death would have left a very deep impression on my mind and spirit. But fitting the pieces together into a composite picture which would help explain his suicide was made far more complex by the strange phenomena which began to occur that frosty Sunday evening in Cambridge.

Immediately prior to his suicide Jim and I had spent about four and a half months together in Cambridge—the closest period of our father-son relationship. We were able to get acquainted on a person-to-person basis at levels for which unbroken periods of time had not been available at home. There was much happiness in what we shared; but in the course of those months, I came to see as never before the depth and complexity of the problems which burdened Jim. Consequently, when his death came I had more reason, by virtue of sheer evidence and acquired insight, to understand it and less reason, because of the relationship we had by then established, to expect it.

Ψ

I am sure that much of my son's story is also that of many, many young people today. Some might wonder why a father would reveal the inner life of his son during a crucial period when much of it was characterized by unresolved turmoil. I can only say that I have for the past year carried a feeling of guilt over and above that which virtually any parent would feel who had lost a child by suicide. This particular sense of compunction was awakened by the example of the mother of a boy who had been a close friend of Jim's. Immediately upon learning of the death of her son by suicide while under the effects of LSD, she went on television and radio to indicate the circumstances of his death as a warning to other young people who might be following the same path.

In my own case there were many factors to be weighed in considering whether or not to reveal any of the inner side of what happened. Further, as we shall see, the events both preceding and following Jim's death were so complicated as to require not only time but also a great deal of study and reflection to sort out. But now I am convinced that the full story ought to be told.

From my considerable and varied pastoral experience, I feel sure that some of what is related here will be of help to at least a few young persons, and their parents, who have similar difficulties to surmount. From my study of other works in the whole realm of extrasensory perception and psychic phenomena, I am confident that students and scientists in this field will find this account, and the analyses thereof, of some interest and use. For those who fall into neither of these categories, the story addresses itself to the age-old question of the survival of death, and there is reason to believe that it will offer an added basis of hope in that realm.

What is put forth here, then, is a slice out of the lives of two persons. To understand what happened during this period when our lives were so interwoven requires not only autobiographical material, but also a rather frank portrayal of how things were with my son Jim.

The happier aspects of Jim's life, thoughts and personality were characteristic of many in his generation. He had a great disdain for sham in any form and was quick to puncture clichés and platitudes of any and every variety. He had a refreshing openness to the new, and a corresponding honesty, wanting to know things as they are and to say it as it is. In addition, he could find great joy in life and had an ability to celebrate it.

The less positive aspects, likewise, were characteristic of many in his generation. He had little motivation for "accomplishing" in relation to the future; he was highly critical of adult society and largely rejected it, adopting instead the "drop out" culture as the one he identified with; he was confused about his identity and found life relatively meaningless, in long-range—or even medium-range—terms. These things will be spoken of frankly because silence about them would make irrelevant some of the most striking phenomena after his death. What is significant in and of itself is not what was characteristic of Jim while he was living, nor the corresponding occurrences afterward, but rather the degree of correlation observable between them. And more than all that, I am convinced that unless those who have been personally close to them begin to speak more openly about some of the disturbing—as well as the heartening—inclinations of youth in our society, the generation gap will only widen and understanding in any depth will be very slow to come indeed.

Some will be critical of such candor by a father about his son. There is a popular assumption in our society that to speak of a person's unresolved problems is to condemn that person as "bad," or to indicate that he is not loved. Though I have no way to guarantee that some readers will not make such as assumption, I trust that many will not. I say this not in naïve optimism or sentimentality, but rather because I myself—whatever other faults I might have—have been able to be fairly consistent in viewing persons realistically without judging them, and I find that more and more people are like this in our time. This is an important example of what, happily, is an increasing psychological sophistication and moral sensitivity in our society.

Ψ

It was really not until the summer before I left for a six-month sabbatical in Cambridge that my concern for Jim's well-being grew beyond the bounds of that which is characteristic of most parents of contemporary college-age young people. Though Jim was not a top student, he had attended good schools—St. Hilda's, then Trinity, in New York City; Town, a day school in San Francisco; Webb, a boarding school in southern California; and then, as a senior, Lowell, a limited-enrollment college-preparatory public high school in San Francisco—and had completed his work with acceptable marks. He was potentially capable of much better work scholastically, but he had developed a cool disinterest in his studies, except for a course now and again which happened to interest him—in which case he would do quite well in it. So, in spite of his spotty record—by and large he just scraped by—he had more than enough A's and B's to enroll in San Francisco State College.

It had not been with great enthusiasm for the educational opportunities open to him, however, that Jim had started San Francisco State. It probably never occurred to him that it was possible *not* to go on to higher education, since both of his parents had pursued advanced degrees and the vast majority of his friends talked of college—and more—as being taken for granted in much the same way high school is. In any case, he never raised the question as to *whether* to go; but the reason *why* was far from evident to him.

For Jim the first year of college seemed to offer, as its principal advantage, an opportunity to get out "on his own." He was eager for this independence, as most young people are, and we cooperated in his having it—with, I must admit, modified rapture. He and a fellow student rented a modest apartment quite near a locale which has since become very widely known: the Haight-Ashbury district. The location was chosen—at least ostensibly—because it was nearer the college than the Bishop's House and thus was more convenient for the pursuit of his studies. Unfortunately, however—as would be easier now to anticipate than it was then—the atmosphere was far from conducive to academic pursuits. The end result was most distressing.

Ψ

Sometime that fall Jim began having sessions with a psychiatrist in San Francisco who specialized in the problems of young people. His problems seemed to lie primarily in two realms. One was his lack of motivation with regard to his studies: by this time he had fallen into a state of virtual disinterest in learning of any kind. The other principal area of concern was that of personal relationships: he felt unable fully to enter into such meaningfully and in depth. There were, fortunately, some exceptions to this, but he had a growing concern about his ability to love.

It was somewhat uncharacteristic of Jim to seek help of this kind, and his indication that he wanted to see a psychiatrist in itself revealed the apparent seriousness of his difficulties. Yet his mother and I were not clear about the nature of his problems. Moreover, once he had begun therapy, even less could be discerned as to what was going on, for he grew more and more withdrawn and uncommunicative. This was accepted as a necessary part of the therapeutic process, since he now had a confidant in his psychiatrist and thus would have less need of sharing with his parents. But it did increase the feeling of being out of touch with his thoughts and concerns.

Nor did the psychiatrist reveal the content of his sessions with Jim: obviously an important element in therapy is the confidential nature of the relationship. It did become necessary, however, for the doctor to consult with us about an important decision which needed to be made about the course that Jim and his doctor would pursue.

It seemed that both of them felt that there were two bottlenecks in communication which were blocking progress toward the analysis and resolution of the problems being dealt with: from the unconscious level of Jim's mind to the conscious, and from Jim's conscious mind to the therapist.

It was Jim himself who suggested the use of LSD under the supervision of his therapist as a possible means of breakthrough. But such would have been impossible without parental approval.

This was during the period when LSD was still being used both therapeutically and experimentally by professionals. Since then, of course, it has been outlawed in most states—though such laws have not dramatically curtailed the use of LSD except by those who are best qualified to control and regulate it. In any case, Jim's psychiatrist had a lengthy personal consultation with us as parents. We in turn each consulted psychiatrist friends and after lengthy deliberation—and with less than a sense of certainty—gave our consent.

The day came. I remember quite vividly that evening when Jim "reported in." It seemed that he had had what is called a "good trip" and it had apparently been useful, but more than that he seemed reluctant to tell us. He continued, instead, to be both subdued and withdrawn. I remember wondering whether the trip had served the purpose intended; but I was not gravely concerned about any *ill* effects because I knew the trip had been carefully supervised and I understood that psychedelic drugs were not addictive. Moreover, there was less data available about hallucinogenics at that time, and thus I was not fully aware of the dangers.

Ψ

This venture into the realm where chemistry and depth psychology merge did not occur in a vacuum. Any college young person today, especially in California, and more especially in Haight-Ashbury, is very close to—if not a part of—the psychedelic subculture. There is a lot of talk about trips, and a variety of hallucinogenics are readily available to those who wish to experiment on their own.

Because the influence of such a subculture is powerful, it would appear that any introduction to the use of psychedelic drugs was probably not a good idea—even if properly supervised. Yet for the same reason, one can almost assume that if Jim had not had this particular initiation into the use of consciousness-expanding drugs, it is likely that he would have been otherwise introduced to them before very long.

In fact, he was already living in two worlds, with two sets of acquaintances. There were those from San Francisco and its environs whom he had known at Town and Webb and who had dispersed to various colleges, but whom he saw during holidays and in the summer. Then there were those he had met at Lowell and at San Francisco State, and some others (whom he had met through mutual acquaintances) who lived in Haight-Ashbury or Berkeley. I learned later that those in the first category were by no means entirely free of awareness of—or even involvement with—drugs. But it was in the second group that the smoking of marijuana and the taking of psychedelic drugs were quite to the fore; and Jim was already spending a great deal of time in their company.

So, though the session with his therapist was innocuous, I'm sure, Jim was involved in the life and activities of the group we have come to describe as the drop-out subculture, and he began to experiment with drugs on other occasions as well.

Ψ

A parent can't be a policeman for a young man that age—particularly one living away from home—and for the major part of the school year I had relatively few opportunities even to observe his behavior, let alone influence it. But during the summer following Jim's first year in college circumstances fell out in such a way that I was in a better position than usual to know what was going on. In order to pay his rent, and thus to perpetuate his new pattern of independence, Jim had taken a half-time job with a bank in downtown San Francisco. To save the cost of parking, he left his car each day in the parking lot on the Cathedral close.

Things were not going at all well for Jim personally. He was moving deeper into a pattern of drug use and the effects were beginning to show. He took to dropping in at my office in Diocesan House, sometimes en route to work and sometimes on the way home. From time to time he stopped because I left a note under the windshield wiper of his car, suggesting he drop in. Our visits became longer and longer and more and more frequent as the summer went on, and the better acquainted we became, the more my concern increased.

I was grateful for the opportunity to get to know Jim on an adult basis, and from that standpoint I relished our time together. Yet the better acquainted we became, the more candid his conversation grew.

"Tonight I'm trying a trip on Romilar," I remember his saying one Friday.

"What is Romilar?" I asked in genuine innocence.

"Here—look," he responded, pulling a rather large bottle of cough syrup out of his pocket.

"That looks like cough medicine," was my all too obvious observation. "Can you get high on that?"

"You sure can—and it's cheap, too. You just drink three or four tablespoons and you're off—on a long trip, just like LSD, only different," Jim explained.

"What do you mean?" I queried, sincerely puzzled.

"Well, I mean you're high—but it feels different. You are less aware of your surroundings than on LSD and more aware of what's happening to you. I mean the physical sensations are intense and you see vivid scenes. You don't gain much insight like you do on LSD, but it's great while it lasts. Each bottle is good for three or four trips. Wild."

I listened carefully, not knowing exactly how to approach the whole matter so as to indicate my concern without foreclosing further revelations of this kind. The fact that Jim was not only stepping up the frequency of the trips he took but also experimenting with growing numbers of hallucinogenics ("pot," or marijuana; "acid," or LSD; peyote and its synthetic form, mescaline; and now Romilar) indicated a great need for caution, I felt.

"I think I'd cool it some, Jim," I said, looking at him steadily. "I'm interested in your experiences; but they worry me."

"Oh, come off it, Dad. What's the harm? Life is to be lived—experienced—enjoyed. Why cool it?" he said, dismissing my concern.

"Nevertheless," I cautioned, "I don't like it."

Ψ

Although not many scientific facts were then available as to the danger of such drugs, I was readily drawing my own conclusions.

Jim looked less and less well physically as the summer wore on. Over him fell a pall of vagueness which is not easy to describe but not hard to identify when one is observing it. There were also signs of the kind of dissipation which accompanies a pattern of too little sleep and too much alcohol.

Yet while he may have been getting too little sleep, he was not drinking, I knew. As a matter of fact very few persons on acid and pot use hard liquor, and many don't even drink wine or beer.

The overriding question was, of course, what could I do? I knew it was important not to disturb the openness which had begun to characterize our conversations—especially in the light of the mounting problem—and I had gone as far as I felt I dared, without engendering antagonism, in articulating my growing concern and in flashing an amber light. But I felt some positive step needed to be taken. At some point it occurred to me that perhaps the solution lay in capitalizing on the relationship we had begun to build while also getting Jim out of Haight-Ashbury and into new—and, hopefully, more wholesome—surroundings.

I was due to leave for England the last week in September for a six-month sabbatical leave, having served seven years as the fifth Bishop of California. A diocesan strategy committee and the Standing Committee had made it possible for me to have this period of spiritual and intellectual refreshment and renewal at Cambridge University.

It occurred to me that I could take Jim along. He could continue his schooling in a completely new and different atmosphere, and by breaking out of the scene in which he seemed to be at least temporarily absorbed, he might well catch a vision of some alternatives for his life.

Of course I took up the idea with his mother first. While we both recognized there were some elements of gamble in my proposal, the alternative seemed to offer little hope of any change: Jim was steadily moving into even deeper involvement in the psychedelic scene. Moreover, Jim's level of academic motivation seemed to be at an all-time low. We hoped that by a radical change, a new college, new surroundings, etc., new interest might be sparked, a pattern broken and new possibilities opened up.

So, with Esther's concurrence, I put it to Jim. Of course I let him know how much I would enjoy having him along just as a companion for me in study and travel—and everyday living. I also stressed how interesting it could be for him to have a period of academic experience abroad. But I was frank about what was the principal motive: to provide at least a long recess in—if not a graduation from—his pattern of drug-taking. I came out with the latter because I was sure that he would suspect that it was a hidden agendum, knowing of my worry in that regard. It was reassuring—and somewhat surprising—that, while also warming to the other considerations, he promptly latched onto this special reason as of great importance to him, too. "I'd really like to get out of all this," I remember his saying, giving me a sense of relief.

Ψ

The time was very short for making arrangements for Jim to go. Fortunately, a Cambridge professor happened through at just the crucial moment, and he was able to give the information I needed: there was an institution right in the city of Cambridge which would serve very well for Jim's level of education. An exchange of cables and a trans-Atlantic call firmed up Jim's admission to Cambridgeshire College of Arts and Technology, which offered, among its curricula, a British equivalent to our lower-division level of college study, in which Jim had a year yet to go. A necessary corollary was permission from Jim's draft board to leave the country, and that also was procured without difficulty since there was to be no break in the continuity of his academic work.

So, with all arrangements made, we prepared to leave. Jim

was frank to indicate that he had begun to feel anxious about going. Even though he could see—and indeed felt—the value of getting "out of all this," nevertheless he had a growing fear that he might have a tremendous urge to take a trip or feel high and that there would be no drugs available over there. (I *hoped* not.) Just before we were to leave he asked me what I would think of his tucking into a suitcase a hunk of raw peyote. Since enough for a trip would be a sizable piece of a plant I explained that carrying it out of one country and into another would not be permitted even if it did not have psychedelic properties—and the fact that it did would certainly not help the chances of getting it through.

He did give up on the peyote, but as it turned out he went armed for the contingency in two other ways. Two rather innocent-looking packs of cigarettes in his jacket pocket were in fact the carriers of rolled marijuana, and in the back of his pocket diary he had written the names of some contacts in both New York and London. Unfortunately, it turned out that neither precaution was necessary on his part.

We were all going on the rather naïve assumption that acid and pot would not be available in Cambridge. In fact, we doubted that such would have been so much as heard of there. It was only after Jim's death that we learned that much of the impetus for the psychedelic movement had come from England anyway. Had we known, we would have been less cheerful about the prospects of escaping the hallucinogenic influence of Haight-Ashbury and Berkeley.

2

Unless all existence is a medium of revelation, no particular revelation is possible.

—*Archbishop William Temple*

Man cannot afford to be a naturalist, to look at Nature directly, but only with the side of his eye. He must look through and beyond her.

—*Henry David Thoreau*

The declared aim of modern science is to establish a strictly detached, objective knowledge. Any falling short of this ideal is accepted only as a temporary imperfection, which we must aim at eliminating. But suppose that tacit thought forms an indispensable part of all knowledge, then the idea of eliminating all personal elements of knowledge would, in effect, aim at the destruction of all knowledge. The ideal of exact science would turn out to be fundamentally misleading and possibly a source of devastating fallacies.

—*Michael Polanyi*

Things got off to a good start.

When we arrived in London we put into the Great Eastern, a comfortable, old-fashioned hotel which was part of the Liverpool Street Station, out of which the train proceeds northeast an hour and a half to Cambridge. Jim spent his time poking around and buying postcards—practically the first thing he did on arrival at any new place. He always had good intentions of mailing them off to family and friends, but usually they just accumulated. I, meanwhile, was busy with such things as finding out about various methods of acquiring the use of a car for the six months in Cambridge.

Our arrival in Cambridge itself was at the beginning of the Michaelmas Term and there was little promising housing left. But just as things were most discouraging, an unexpected cancellation of plans by an American university professor opened up for us an almost brand-new, modern, two-bedroom flat. It was located on Carlton Way in a pleasant residential area and was about ten minutes both from the University and from Cambridgeshire College. By midmorning the next day we were moved in, bag and baggage. No. 9 Carlton Court had all the features we Americans now tend to take for granted but which in England are far from common outside of major cities: central heating, wall-to-wall carpeting, drapes and Venetian blinds, ultramodern furniture in light woods, picture windows and private garage. All of this was well worth the third-floor walk-up and what for that part of England was somewhat higher than average rent.

But much to the surprise of both of us, complete as everything seemed, moving ourselves in was just the beginning of it. We found that there was a host of things to do (and to find out *how* to do). Together, we went about doing these things with real zeal. We rapidly equipped ourselves with a car (on a guaranteed repurchase plan), applied for insurance, procured license plates, signed up in person with each of the government-owned utilities (gas, electricity and telephone), formally notified "The Constabulary of Cambridgeshire and the Isle of Ely" of the fact of our residence, purchased linens and other household necessities, arranged for "British Relay" (linkage of a rented TV set with a single area-wide antenna), shopped for a bargain-priced stereo record-player (records meant a great deal to Jim), provided for milk delivery and laundry pick-up service and laid in a supply of staples, as well as enough perishables for the next few meals.

Though we both had traveled in foreign countries before, this business of setting ourselves up for living in an apartment, rather than in a hotel or motel, was an entirely new experience for each of us. It immediately gave us a feeling of "belonging," as though we were becoming citizens of England. In fact, before long we found ourselves, often as not, referring to "our problem in Rhodesia" and "their problem in Vietnam." And far more importantly, sharing the experience brought us, in very short order, closer to one another as two adults.

All these external activities automatically provided a rather full and variegated subject matter for mutual involvement of father and son—with less self-consciousness on the part of either of us than would have been so in the case of just talking. But talk we did.

Ψ

I remember especially the first evening Jim really opened up to me on the subject of his problems. I had never raised with Jim the matter of his sessions with his psychiatrist, beyond asking him from time to time how, generally, it was going. But to this question, which could have been an opener for his sharing had he wanted to, there had never been a response which provided any illumination. However, that evening after dinner, when we actually sat down in our new living room for the first time, he introduced the subject in a very easy way.

He told me of what I would call his "identity crisis." He explained that he wanted very much to be a loving, caring person—to relate to persons in ways which were reciprocally both meaningful and helpful. "But," he remarked with deep feeling, "you can't love that way. You can't be a softie or you'll get smashed by society. Nobody gives a damn who you are or what you're like. People walk all over you, use you, give you a number and forget you. They couldn't care less about you, so why care about them? Why put out?"

I sensed the despair behind his seemingly callous words. "Not everyone's that way, Jim." Then I added, with a little less conviction, "*Most* people aren't."

"Oh, sure, Dad. You can say that, but you know it's not true. Church people are worse than anybody in their not caring. Don't tell me it's not true."

I searched my memory for examples of people who cared. I mentioned several, but it was obvious that no specifics could counteract his generalizations. His over-all impression was that society is heartless and impersonal, and exceptions to the rule were not going to change his mind about it all.

"I've been around, Dad. I've seen," he insisted. "You're not going to tell me anyone cares about the people who live in Hunters Point [a reference to one of San Francisco's more depressed areas, mostly populated by black people]. And what about our colleges—does anyone care who I am? You know they don't. People couldn't care less."

He gave example after example to illustrate his point, and I found it hard to refute his argument. So I changed the grounds of discussion. "But just because that's the way things are doesn't mean you have to be that way. In fact, to be that way yourself is only to perpetuate the problem. You have the choice of being different."

"Sure I do—like in the Haight. But you yourself have pointed out that that's a kind of escape—a running away. Why do you think they call them drop-outs?" he queried. I knew he was again touching the truth.

"They know how to love and care," he went on, "and I like to live like that. Hippies will share anything they've got with you. They'll spend hours talking over your problems. They'll take you into their pad. They'll accept you for what you are. They're human. They know how to love." His words were full of feeling and I was able to sense what his involvement in the psychedelic crowd meant to him. "But how many hippies are there?" His question revealed his distress.

We talked for several hours and Jim shared his experiences with me in greater depth than ever before. He talked about his acquaintances. He reflected on his feelings of inadequacy—and his fears—that kept him from entering into deeply meaningful relationships with people.

"All you do is set yourself up for the big fall," he asserted. "It just doesn't pay—it isn't worth it."

The conflict between his desires and his fears was obvious. He wanted to love—but he feared the consequences. Instead of expecting love in return, he expected a cold and uncaring response. What, by and large, he saw around him only confirmed his suspicion that "that's the way people are." As much as I might wish he could see things more positively, I knew he could not erase his reactions—sound or unsound—to his experiences. The most I could hope for was that something new could enter the scene now.

That conversation proved to be a major break-through. It paved the way for other times of candor in the months ahead, and being clued in so early in our time together as to the nature of his crisis gave considerable guidance to me in my responses to his words and actions and in my initiation of certain conversations and plans. What Jim outlined that night proved to be entirely consistent both with what I observed during the months that were ahead and with his psychiatrist's assessment after his death. It was also consistent with some happenings later—but to go into that now would be premature.

Ψ

Within a very short time we were both very much immersed in our studies. The concentration of planning, the perseverance and the direction of energy which had characterized those days of settling in, happily continued right into the school term. Jim began his work at Cambridgeshire College with an interest far beyond any he had shown for the past several years. Many factors no doubt contributed to this encouraging new attitude. Certainly the new scene itself inspired enthusiasm. Moreover, the liberal arts program at Cambridgeshire was planned in such a way as to provide for more individualized instruction than is to be found in most of our American colleges—even private ones. Classes were small and there was a weekly private tutorial session. There was a higher concentration on fewer subjects during a given term. In addition, his lack of involvement with psychedelic drugs and with his companions from the drop-out subculture meant that his attention could be focused more sharply on his academic endeavors.

Finally, an all-pervasive, important new element began to emerge which heightened the interest and joy of learning for both of us. We for the first time found ourselves students together. Not only were we both undertaking courses at institutions of higher learning—though at different levels and in different subject areas—but also we soon found we had in common an insatiable desire to know the truth, to find out facts and derive meaning from them.

Often, in the course of sharing something that had been said or a new insight which had dawned during the day, we would launch into a seminar of our own in the late afternoon or evening. These sessions were so fruitful in terms of my own intellectual growth, as well as beneficial for the deepening of our friendship, that I began to anticipate eagerly the sound of his approaching footsteps as he returned to the flat—almost always later than I, since he attended more classes—and the renewed conversation his arrival would bring.

We were both raising the same basic questions as we pursued our separate quests for meaning, but we approached them from quite different directions and thus found we had a great deal to learn from one another. I was busy re-examining (by a theological process for which I have since accepted the label of "reductionism") a quite elaborate system of belief to which as a Churchman I was presumably committed but in fewer and fewer items of which I was placing credence.* My approach now was to cast aside any theological concepts which seemed irrelevant to life, or which did not have a plausible basis in our human experience.†

* See my A *Time for Christian Candor* (New York: Harper & Row, 1964).

† For some of the results see *What Is This Treasure* and *If This Be Heresy* (Harper & Row, 1965 and 1967).

Jim, however, was starting from the other end. Having by the junior year of high school rejected conventional religion, even in the liberal form of which I was a spokesman, he was now—from the bottom up, as it were—searching for something in which he could believe. He saw no structure of meaning—or at least none that made sense to him—and he was seeking to build one. His mood was that of openness and expectancy, hoping that somewhere, somehow, meaning and relevance could be discovered.

We used one another as sounding boards, and neither would let the other get away with broad generalizations, platitudes, clichés or quick conclusions. We pressed for the truth, but we both felt the process to be of equal importance with the conclusion: we wanted the factual foundations to be convincing enough that the leap of faith would take along the whole man.

We began to discover the significance of an illuminating phrase we owe to one who was perhaps the greatest American preacher, Bishop Phillips Brooks: "truth mediated through personality." Each of us was discovering, by the process of sharing, discussing and reflecting together, something of what was *true* in the deep sense of that word—what could provide the ground of integration for the reality of our individual experiences.

Ψ

The kind of conversations we were having, touching as they did on the meaning of life, inevitably gave an opening for the opposite side of the coin—something that apparently had been in Jim's mind from time to time for years.

Death—but not only death. Suicide.

"It's no use." His expression was one of pain again. "I'm no good. I'll *never* be any good. Sometimes I hate myself so much I wish I were dead."

"I suppose we all feel that way from time to time, Jim. I know I have. Yet that's no solution either. That's the ultimate cop-out; the ultimate in escapism."

"Yeah, I know." He responded at the level I had hoped he would. "Sometimes when I feel really out of it—when I'm sure I'm no damn good and never will be—I seriously think about copping out. You know, why not just end it all now and get it over with. It would sure be simpler."

"But would it really?" I queried. "Suicide to me seems like *the* defeat. Our freedom lies in being able to change: to change our habits, our thoughts, our circumstances—indeed, to change our very selves, or to be changed. If we give up *that* freedom—if we admit we can't change—then that's really defeat . . ."

"Yeah, I guess so," Jim said with some lack of conviction.

"There can be a future for you, Jim, if you want there to be." My seriousness—and caring—must have been obvious, for he was listening intently. "I know you can grow in the areas which most concern you. We can find answers to the questions and doubts you have about yourself. You can begin to make changes. In fact, I think you already have since coming here. Don't you?" I looked directly at him.

"Yeah, I'm different in a lot of ways. It has been different. It's been great, Dad. It really has. I love you, Dad, and I like being here with you. But still . . ." He seemed to choke up.

I was choked up, too. It was not usual for Jim to express his affection. "I love you, too, Jim, and these weeks we have shared have meant more to me than I can say. Our relationship is important to me—very important," I said.

"In a way I suppose now I really would be stupid to cop

out. I suppose you're right about that, Dad. Maybe there is some hope."

"There is, Jim—I'm sure there is," I said with deep feeling.

Ψ

Within a couple of weeks after we arrived in England, Jim had used up the few marijuana cigarettes he had smuggled into the country with him. So for several weeks he had been completely off psychedelic drugs and, for the major part of that same period, also off pot. But as he became better acquainted with other students at Cambridgeshire College, he discovered that hashish, a more refined version of marijuana, was readily available.

Thus it was that before many weeks went by Jim frequently began getting high on hashish. And since the crowd that he began to run around with included "acid-heads," he was—before I was aware what had happened—also equipped with LSD.

I had taken great heart at his tremendous physical improvement during the first few weeks in England. He looked like a different person: alive, healthy, face full of color. The lethargic look had faded and the light had come back into his eyes. He was capable again of manifesting genuine interest, enthusiasm and excitement.

Then one evening I arrived home at 9:30 from a lecture on something like "New Frontiers of the Mind" to find Jim started on a trip. "Dad," he said, "I've just dropped acid. Will you sit with me and guide me through the trip?"

"Yes, of course I will," I said, quickly accepting his invitation. A deep concern—indeed dread—filled me at the realization that he was on drugs again. But of course I wanted to be with him, though I didn't know whether I could do much to help him. Right then wasn't the time to file a protest: we would have to see this through. Any usefulness on my part would have to rest on an affirmative feeling toward me on Jim's part, I knew; and his asking me to be his guide was an expression of confidence and trust, I was sure.

As I sat down in the living room Jim went over and arranged a stack of "way out" records on the stereo and started the player. Then he sat down and there was small talk during which I tried not to reveal my apprehensions as to what would be coming over him shortly. I sneaked glances at my watch. (A clock on one of the bookshelves was stopped at 12:15. It had been that way since we arrived. I made a mental note to wind and set it sometime—but not now.) 9:48 . . . it should start at about 10:15, I figured from what I'd heard. 9:57 . . . he still seemed unaffected. 10:06 . . . the same. Then, a minute or so later he seemed to be going into a trance. He was just sitting there, eyes open, looking toward the drapes. A glance showed that his pupils were dilated. I had never before been with anyone under LSD, but I had heard that that was normal—or, more correctly perhaps, an expected part of this abnormal state.

Ψ

I didn't know if I was to initiate conversation or just wait. But before I could decide that, Jim spoke. His enunciation was clear—quite unlike someone with too much to drink.

"It's a dark road, getting darker as I am along it. Shapes here and there [he gestured with both arms, fingers pointing] which I can't make out. They're *big*—I feel so small—can't cope. The sound is unearthly and from all directions. I—"

"A record's on, Jim," I interrupted, trying to introduce a

verifiable datum. "And the two instruments are being harshly played—they're discordant."

"*Two* instruments! There are *a dozen* different sounds," he said, looking distressed. Then I remembered that I had heard that acid—and pot for that matter—could break up a musical tone into its harmonics.

"Shall I turn it off, Jim?" I asked.

"*No!* It's part of the scene—the real scene." This comment raised epistemological questions, as well as psychological ones; but this was no time for a seminar. I just sat quietly.

"This leads," he resumed, "*no*where [still on the gloomy road, I gathered]—to nothing—*no* thing." He sort of laughed, but it was more macabre than cheering. "Nowhere, nothing, no thing." Then, with a very serious expression: "I'd better not go on—not even stay here!"

"Can you turn around and go back, Jim?" It had begun to seem real to me. Anyway it seemed best now to shift the dialogue to his frame of reference.

His? Just then he got up and walked to the kitchen and came back with a glass of water. That short journey was not on a dark path. Yet on sitting down again he went on talking about where he was in the dark and menacing scene. I guess it never left his mind though he went out of the room for a moment. *Which* was *Jim's* scene? Both, I guess. Then I remembered that the psychedelic experience was regarded as temporary schizophrenia. I shuddered.

Now answering my question ("Can you turn around and go back?"), he said, "I'm afraid that's no good, Dad. I'm too far along. I guess I go on."

A pause. Then, "But it's getting gruesome and blacker. There are big, gnarled trees. They're moving, *weaving*, REACHING OUT!"

I moved over and took hold of his hand. I tried to look him

in the eye. But his steadfast gaze was aimed just past the right side of my head.

"Let's try going back," I said—really feeling *we* would be trying it, if he were willing.

"All right, Dad."

I was relieved. But, more than that, I was strangely moved.

"Is it—lighter now?" I tentatively explored a terrain I wasn't seeing.

"No. I'm—we're [was I now in his scene with him—or was he being polite?]—moving fast—back, I mean. But I *said* it's too far. It's getting no lighter—the trees, moving, *reaching down!*—other things still—can't make them out."

Getting nowhere. Then an idea. I tried it out:

"Are there any crossroads, Jim? Have you seen any? Maybe we could cut across to another kind of road."

"No crossroads," he answered solemnly.

A pause. Then he went on.

"But I'm looking around. And it looks like there's another road—over there. Let's stop, Dad, and look."

"OK, let's do," I said. Now I was beginning to picture the situation.

"I think I see a little light—over there." He pointed toward the back wall.

"Can we cut across—the field?" I chanced (my picturing wasn't really *that* specific).

"I guess so," he said with doubt, "but [growing apprehension on his face] it's just as dark as we start across and I don't know what's underfoot—and, oh, those shapes!"

"But we don't have much choice," I suggested. "Anyway, it's *toward* the light. This road's toward the dark—either direction it seems. Let's take our chances, heading toward the light." I thought of the prayer Homer has Ajax utter in the midst of darkness: "ἐν δὲ φάει καὶ ὄλεσσον" (*Iliad* 17:647), which can be paraphrased "Let us have light whatever the cost."

That text had taken on a great deal of meaning for me during my attempt since 1960 to be intellectually honest, though a bishop. I told Jim about my recollection.

"That's beautiful," Jim said. Then: "Let's go."

Ψ

Silence . . . more silence . . . it seemed endless.

"Our footing's been safe and it's getting clearer—lighter! . . . It's all light—and there's the road . . . We've made it. Let's go this way [gesturing toward the hall]. No, let's stop and look. Oh, it's beautiful—the colors, the sounds [a more positive kind of selection happened to be playing on the stereo—I hadn't noticed that till just then]. The trees. These are alive, too; they're breathing. I see through their leaves. I see cells and veins."

He held up his hands and looked at them—"I see myself that way. I feel connected to the ground, yet I can move. I don't feel small now. And I feel one with everything around. I'm separate, yet I'm one. I'm One, The One. I'm God."

I knew this wasn't megalomania, or even arrogance. This was a reported experience of what millions of perfectly sane, modest Buddhists see as the shape of reality. Not pantheism (with which label we Western religionists have so often mistakenly dubbed—and dismissed—it), not believing that everything's all one blur or blob. But *panentheism:* everyone and everything is separate, yet continuous with the grounding of the All—which is the One, is God. Already I had raised seriously in my mind, and also in a long footnote* in a book which was even then being set in type, whether

* *What Is This Treasure,* note on pp. 45–47.

dualism (tied to the Creator/creature dichotomy—matching the matter/energy duality, now gone since all is seen as energy, and the soul/body distinction, now seriously modified by the insights of psychosomatic medicine) or panentheism was the more plausible world view.

And that he wasn't *feeling* arrogant was clear from the next comment: "Don't you feel it—your connectedness with it all—that you're God?"

"I get it." That seemed a safe comment since I hadn't yet decided the theological/philosophical question, but did *understand* what he was saying—and feeling.

There was now a long, long silence. But I could tell from Jim's expression that he continued on the lighted—light-filled—road and was drinking in the iridescent beauty of his visions.

By and by he rose and began to walk around, silently but serenely. Then he sat down and looked at me directly (the first time since he went into the trance a little after 10:00) and started to talk.

"The scene I've been in—am in still, I guess—fades out more than it floats in. This room and what's in it—including the two of us—seems more . . . more real now than the other. This was—is—a good trip, Dad. Was I able to give you some idea of it?"

"I should say!" I came right back. "*My!* . . ." I was finding it hard to speak about it. So I let some time—silent time—pass by before speaking. I had to sort it out.

Ψ

Psychedelic trips, like non-chemical mystical experiences, often take the form of a drama in two acts. I was now nearer, time-wise, to the second act, so my mind first turned to it, and to what it seemed to say theologically. I thought of what a distinguished Roman Catholic theologian had said to a friend of mine after an experimental LSD session under the auspices of a leading medical school's Department of Psychiatry: "As a Thomist, I'm a dualist. But I was a Buddhist for those eight hours. Not *relating* to God, but *being* God." I recalled the descriptions of Western mystics—Meister Eckhart, Lady Juliana of Norwich, St. Theresa of Avila, St. John of the Cross—reflecting non-dualistic experiences. Hence the Church's perennial nervousness about all this. "Mysticism = misty + schism" was a phrase I remembered from seminary days.

All this bore on Jim's—and my—pondering about the ultimate nature of things. He had been showing he could move with joy and health in the direction of the development of his conscious faculties. But ever hovering—and sometimes edging into our conversation—was the despair, the inactivity, the withdrawal from life—even the ultimate withdrawal. These negative feelings had become dominant during the summer when he was having session after session on drugs. They hadn't been apparent now for weeks; but here he was—starting on drugs again. However, this Trip I, New Series, itself reflected both sets of feelings, positive and negative. I had not wanted the trip to happen. But since it had, I was glad it took the shape it did, for with both acts of the play taken into account, a message which could speak to Jim's present crossroads situation was bound to emerge.

I then spoke. I said just that. I shared with Jim what came to my mind from my current study of the Dead Sea Scrolls and Christian origins—the doctrine of the Two Ways in the Manual of Discipline, in the Didache and in the Epistle of Barnabas. For example, from the latter: "There are two ways of teaching and power, that of Light and that of Darkness, and there is a great difference between the two ways. For on one are stationed light-giving angels of God, but on the other angels of Satan."*

I was glad something both applicable and illuminating could come to the fore from "offbeat" religious sources. Jim's religious attitude did not encourage quotations from Bible or Catechism. But he received the Essene material well, so that emboldened me to use a terse Biblical text much to the same point.

"There's something in Deuteronomy like that, Jim."

"Yes?" he responded.

"Here it is: 'I have set before you life and death, blessing and curse: therefore choose life.' "†

He paused. Then he repeated slowly, but firmly *Therefore choose life.* He repeated it several times in the next few minutes. He referred to it several times in the days to come. He even wrote about it to a friend in California, I learned later.

"I guess we'd better get some sleep, Jim." He nodded and we headed down the hall.

"Thanks, Dad." He smiled a little.

It was about seven in the morning.

* Barn. 18:1–2; trans. by Edgar J. Goodspeed, *The Apostolic Fathers* (New York: Harper & Bros., 1950), p. 42.

† Deut. 30:19.

3

To be forced by desire into an unwarrantable belief is a calamity.

—Professor I. A. Richards

. . . For I have learned
To look on nature, not as in the hour
Of thoughtless youth; but hearing oftentimes
The still, sad music of humanity,
Nor harsh nor grating, though of ample power
To chasten and subdue. And I have felt
A presence that disturbs me with the joy
Of elevated thoughts; a sense sublime
Of something far more deeply interfused,
Whose dwelling is the light of setting suns,
And the round ocean and the living air,
And the blue sky, and in the mind of man;
A motion and a spirit, that impels
All thinking things, all objects of all thought,
And rolls through all things.

—William Wordsworth

One evening Jim asked if he could bring a college friend, Peter, home for dinner. He would like to have me meet him, he said. I was delighted.

"Tomorrow night?" I asked. Jim said he would check.

The next evening when the two of them arrived we sat in the living room for a while chatting over coffee. His haircut and clothes halfway between Mod and conventional, our guest was both intelligent and articulate. He intended to go on the next year to pursue a degree in philosophy at a university in the Midlands. After dinner, in our by now familiar bachelor style, we all joined in cleaning up, while continuing what was for me—and seemingly for them—most interesting dialogue on the pros and cons of dualism and monism. As they started for the living room, I excused myself, saying I had some work to do (no white lie), and settled down at the dinette table with papers and typewriter. A couple of hours later his friend left and Jim opened the door close to where I was sitting. I looked up from my work.

"I think he's great," I began, "and he threw some interesting light on—"

"Then why did you cut out?" he interrupted. I could see from his expression that it mattered to him.

"Oh," I said disconcertedly, "I thought you two would be wanting to talk and play records, and I didn't want to be in the way."

"You wouldn't have been. It seemed you weren't really interested," he countered.

"I'm sorry. I *was* interested. Let's have him again."

We did. This time after supper and tidying up I followed

them into the living room and sat down with them. Then Jim said, "Well, Dad, I think we'll be running along."

Any parent gets used to such apparent arbitrariness, but actually more was involved. Jim's ambivalence regarding relationships and his role in them came up again and again. Through Peter, he had been drawn into a group of students, of both sexes, most of whom lived together in a big house not far from the college. A number of times he drove down there in the evening, and although he wasn't sharing very many particulars, I had the feeling he was sort of "in." I took this for a real plus in the total picture.

But one evening he had come home after being gone only an hour or so. He was quite silent and obviously depressed. I dropped what I was doing and sat down in the living room, hoping he would open up. He didn't as to precisely what had happened at the house, but what he did say revealed the tender, wistful side of his personality—in contrast to the "007" front he sometimes displayed.

"It's no use, Dad," he said as if in deep pain. "I'll never make it. I'm no good. I want to have friends. I want to be liked. But I just can't. Something's wrong with me—I can't," he said, almost in desperation.

"But you do have friends," I countered. "What do you mean you can't?"

"Yes, I have friends—or at least acquaintances," he replied.

"Take, for example, the group you have just been with. From what you have said from time to time I have certainly got the impression that you are 'in'—that you have been having a pretty good time with them, and they, I would imagine, with you too."

"That's not what's bothering me," he said. "I get along

fine with them as a group. It's just when I try, well, person-to-person . . ."

I verbalized what had been my fear when he came home. "Did something disappointing happen, Jim?"

"No, not really—not disappointing, that is. It was like it pretty much always is. I like people and they seem to like me. But when I start to really know somebody—I don't know, I just fall apart. I guess I get scared." He said the last word with deep feeling—but almost with a fear of the word itself. "I mean if I open myself up to somebody—really open up—who knows what will happen. I mean, a guy can really get hurt that way," he said.

"That's true, Jim. That's true," I agreed. "But it's also true that if you don't open yourself up you'll never know what it is to love and be loved. As the capacity to care—to love—increases, so does the capacity to get hurt." I was hoping he could receive my words without feeling they were platitudes. They weren't.

As if unable to respond, Jim turned, went down the hall to his room and went to bed.

Ψ

What I was seeing was growth in relatedness and in unrelatedness at the same time. He certainly was growing closer to me (and of course I to him). It was not long after the time I sat up with him all night that he looked me straight in the eye one day and said: "I know I really love you, Dad. I have come to know you really care, and I like being with you." Not too common among young people—even those less complex than Jim—is this kind of straightforward expression of filial love. And it wasn't just filial: the format of our lives in Cambridge was such as to nourish a genuinely adult relationship.

And it seemed that, as a result of our loving mutual trust, Jim had become able to relate readily to other adults as well. When colleagues of mine at the University came over, he not only greeted them with ease and even pleasure, but he almost always sat down and joined in the conversation. Also, I generally included him when I was invited out, and when he came along he not only fit in with no difficulty, but seemed to be interested and to enjoy himself.

Yet from time to time his response would be entirely the opposite. On some occasions which involved getting together with people close to my age, he would quite peremptorily opt out, giving as his explanation something like "They don't really want me," or "That's not my scene." It was as if he could blot out any positive experiences almost instantaneously.

There was one time especially that his distrust of adults and their world was not only surprising but embarrassing. In December, *Look* magazine sent a young but experienced senior editor, Christopher S. Wren, and a staff photographer, Bob Lerner, to Cambridge to do a story on some aspects of the current theological revolution, centering it on my quest. For nearly two weeks they were around, joining me in various things, including several meals. On some of these occasions Jim went along too. Our conversations were quite interesting—made not the less so by the presence of the charming Mrs. Wren, a graduate in Divinity from Oxford. Bob kept busy taking hundreds of candid shots. (He was so preoccupied with his art generally that he didn't participate in the "theology seminar." I will never forget once when we were discussing the "God Is Dead" theology. He suddenly alerted and said, raising up his camera by conditioned reflex, "How did I miss *that?*")

Midway during their stay, Chris and Bob asked if they could set a time for Jim and me to be photographed together in some informal out-of-doors scene. When I took it up with Jim, his instant response was, "I'm not going to pose for any pictures for any magazine."

"Why not?" I responded in surprise. "It won't take very long. All they want is a shot of the two of us walking along the bank of the Cam or on the campus of King's College, or something like that."

"How phony!" he said disparagingly.

"It's not," I said. "After all, we *have* walked together there and will again, I'm sure. Bob himself has a thing against *posed* pictures. It will be natural."

"No, to *schedule* it makes it fake and phony. I won't do it."

"Well, think about it" was how I left it. I felt sure his attitude must be the expression of a passing mood; so I gave some excuse to Chris and Bob. The trouble was they took the excuse at face value, and so they asked again the following day—and daily thereafter. My supply of white lies lasted until they forgot about it—or perhaps sensed the real point.

I couldn't think of any way to say that my son didn't want to be in a picture with me, particularly since I knew—more than I ever had before—that his predominant feelings toward me were positive. His unalterable decision was consistent to the point of woodenness—with his utter disdain for cant and artificiality. But it was more than that. It was a symbol of his distrust of and disgust for adult society as a whole. To cooperate with the mass media was to be a part of the general scene. So no shots of Jim and me were included in the article—though he played a very important part in the theological quest which was reported by *Look*.

Ψ

I remember vividly the night I went to the movies to see a film recommended by Professor Donald MacKinnon, whose lectures I was attending. I invited Jim to go with me and he had planned to, but at the last minute he changed his mind and stayed home. I got a seat in the front row of the balcony. Toward the end of the movie, I suddenly felt ill. A sharp pain in my left side gave me a feeling of nausea. The impact was directional—as if coming at me from the front left of the theater. (I later realized that was the direction of Carlton Court.)

My discomfort was great enough that I got up and walked out into the lobby for a couple of minutes. Since the movie was almost over, I did stay to the end; but the ominous feeling that something awful had happened didn't leave me.

When I arrived back at the apartment, I was almost afraid to go in for fear of what I might find there. I sensed that something dreadful had transpired. When I opened the front door, Jim heard the sound and right away came out of his bedroom with a look of horror on his face.

"Oh, Dad," he cried. "Thank God you're home!"

"What is it?" I said, with alarm.

"A bad trip," he said. "A really bad trip. It's been hell. I've been caught in a sea of monsters. They just won't go away."

We went into the living room and sat down. Jim talked out the trip with me. He agonized while struggling with the monsters. I tried to project more constructive images to him. Whether it was because of that effort or simply the passage of time or the psychedelic cycle, the scene grew more serene —though never really positive or joyous this time. He went on to bed about 2:00 A.M.

Soon after I got back around one the next afternoon, he roused. I fixed breakfast for him and lunch for me and we sat down together. I opened up the subject of drugs directly and frankly.

"Look, Jim," I said, trying to sound firm without the lecture tone or the sermonizing manner to which his instantaneous response was to stop hearing anything at all. "One of the reasons both you and I looked forward to this time together in England was that it would offer you a chance really to break out of the psychedelic scene. Now it would appear that we're back to 'square one' with—"

"Oh, come off it, Dad, don't start givin' me that stuff," he broke in. I remember the scene vividly, for it was the first of several occasions which confirmed for me an increase in the dichotomy in Jim's personality.

"No, sir," he went on, "the way I got it figured is this. You might as well do all your living fast while the gettin' is good. Might as well live now. There's sure as hell nuthin' to look forward to in the future. I say, just play it cool—stay uninvolved. Take what you can get when you can get it and forget it, man. That's the only way to live."

"What it does to you is not good," I insisted.

"I'm doing OK. It *is* OK if I'm doing what I want to do. And this is what I want to do," he rambled on. "I know other people don't think it's the thing to do, but I couldn't care less what people think. When you come right down to it, anyway, nobody cares what I do or think and—"

"*I* do," I interrupted.

"Yeah, I know, Dad, but I've got to do my thing, my own way," he countered.

"But there *are* other people, and there is a question of your being in shape to be of some value to other people," I went on.

"Other people?" he asked. "Why should I be thinking about them? Most of them aren't worth a damn. If any are, they can take care of themselves—and let them. Let them do their thing too. It's a dog-eat-dog world. You gotta be a dog-eat-dog kind of person to survive."

I grew a bit defensive. "I've survived, and I don't think I'm—"

"Don't be cut up personally by what I'm saying. I'm not saying it's bad to be that kind of person; in fact, I think it's good. And anybody who makes it that way, it's his *own* way. OK, your way's different, say. But anyway I can only speak for myself."

He was doing just that. Or for part of himself—or, to put it another way, for one of his selves.

Jim was leaning against the refrigerator in the kitchen while I was washing up some dishes. He slouched, ankles crossed and with cigarette hanging loose: he looked—as much as he *could* look that way—like a "hard guy," as his contemporaries would say.

I didn't like this at all. His talking was really a soliloquy, almost as though I weren't there. But I *was* there, and so I thought I ought to continue the conversation, trying a new tack.

"OK, let's say you're going to look at it as though you are all that counts. Even for your own benefit, for getting ahead, you ought to knock this stuff off."

"There you go like everybody else your age," he said, "wanting to impose your values on us. For people like you the idea is to become somebody important someday. I couldn't give a damn for that. You can't count on anything anyway because that would mean counting on people and they are not to be counted on. So you might as well do all the living you can as you go along. You might as well live it up right now, because you don't know what's coming up."

I tried still a third tack. "But even for now, really enjoying things involves other people and if you go on taking stuff you won't be fully up to it as far as relating to other people is concerned," I said.

He seemed to have an answer for that, too. "When other people fit in, fine; when they don't, OK too. Whatever is going for you, take it. And as far as wherever or whoever it came from, forget it, man. It's the only way to live. People can act nice and you run into a few who seem to care, but you might as well figure that nobody is gonna look out for Number One but Number One himself. People are mainly out for themselves anyway, so why let yourself in for a fall? Too many relationships are contests anyway. You gotta be tough—real tough. A softie doesn't have a chance."

"Now wait a minute," I tried to interrupt. "Wait just a minute. You can't possibly be serious about this. You can't live that way—without friends, without love, without people—"

"Like hell I can't. A cool cat doesn't communicate, he only hides and protects himself. And that's why drugs are really cool. I mean like you take off into a world all your own where nobody can intrude. I mean like that's *your* world, and it's really cool. You just take off . . . and float . . . and nuthin' can touch you—nuthin'. No sir, I'm nobody's fool. If you think I give a damn about anybody or anything, you got another long think comin'. No sir, it's Number One all the way—and if that's all the way on drugs, well . . ."

My attempts at protestations were going virtually unnoticed. It was almost as if Jim were in a trance. His "speech" sounded practically prerecorded. Even his language had changed.

His discourse completed, he turned and walked out without so much as a glance back to see my reaction—which was mainly one of disbelief. This was so unlike Jim—as I knew him, and especially during these latter months of closer friendship—that the forty-five minutes of guff I had just been given seemed like a bad dream. I couldn't just dismiss it, but it was obvious I couldn't deal with it, either.

Ψ

Fairly often I had speaking dates which involved taking the train to London or driving to various nearby parts of England, and the choice was always entirely Jim's as to whether to come along or stay in Cambridge. When he did accompany me we had a very good time together from start to finish, and he liked to share the driving.

On two occasions he also joined me on longer expeditions. Even before the plans for a sabbatical had developed I had accepted the invitation of the Chief of Chaplains of the United States Air Force to visit a number of bases in France, Germany and England in order to lead sessions for chaplains and to preach at base chapels. Jim could not accompany me on the whole journey because of his college schedule, but he was able to fly to Germany to join me for a long weekend.

The second trip, occasioned by the direction my studies on early Christianity had taken, made it appropriate for me to see the Dead Sea Scrolls in Jerusalem and confer with scholars there. I planned this visit to coincide with the Christmas holiday so Jim could go along. I had been to

Israel twice, but Jim had never been there, and he was happier on that journey than I had ever seen him, entering fully into everything we did.

Though armed with visas for the Hashemite Kingdom of Jordan and thus eligible to be in Bethlehem for Christmas, we decided to stay in Nazareth instead. I was finishing and mailing on December 24 the page proofs of *What Is This Treasure.* Therein I indicated that I regarded the Nativity narratives as pious midrashim; so it would have seemed hypocritical to couple Bethlehem and December 24 as the place and date the book had been finished when my study up to that time seemed to point to Nazareth as the appropriate place to associate with Jesus' birth. Jim very much liked the honesty of that and gave me a big smile when I showed him the last lines of the Preface, as revised:

✠ JAMES A. PIKE

Nazareth, Israel
Christmas Eve, 1965

I had been invited to participate in two services on Christmas Eve—hymns and prayers at the Anglican church (their Eucharist was to be the next morning), and also the opening Mass at the new-rite Catholic basilica. Partly because of being in Israel, with religious history so deeply rooted there; partly because of the haunting beauty, mysterious splendor and unusual music; and partly because of the ecumenical nature of both (in the Anglican service, as well as the Roman one, a Jesuit friend of mine from the United States acted as my chaplain), the two services were particularly meaningful for both Jim and me. In fact, Jim was so moved at the Eucharist at the basilica that for the first time in a long time he came forward to receive Communion. He had long been disenchanted with the Church, but something got to him in a deep way—as it did to me—and his spontaneous response was to come up.

It was my son's last Communion.

Ψ

It was late when we were about to go to bed. I was to preach (with the vicar as interpreter) at the 10:00 A.M. service in our Anglican church, and since Jim had been to two services (which were two more than he usually attended) I remarked, "Jim, there's no reason you shouldn't sleep in the morning if you want. You needn't come to Christ Church; it will be another Eucharist—in Arabic at that—and you have just been to church twice."

"No, Dad, I want to go," he insisted. "You remember that nice Arab girl I was visiting with at Christ Church? I introduced you to her." I indicated that I did remember and thought she was very attractive.

"Well, she will be at the service and I said I would join her."

"Fine." I was really quite pleased. "In that case I'll wake you. Why don't you invite her to come to the vicarage after the service? A few of the 'pillars' of the congregation have been invited to a reception for me. They'll be serving Turkish coffee."

"I don't like that stuff—it's too thick and sugary. But it might be fun to go there. I'll ask her," he said.

Just as we were about to go to sleep he said, "Dad, I hope tomorrow in your sermon you're going to tell it the way it is."

"What do you mean, Jim?" I asked.

"Well, I learned last night from Sayida—"

"Is that your friend?"

"Yeah. Well, anyway, she told me how disappointed the Christian Arabs feel who don't get in under the quota of four thousand allowed by Jordan to cross at the Mandelbaum gate for Easter and Christmas. Different ones get to go at different times. Her family, for example, didn't make it this time."

"I gather you aren't really too sorry about that," I said with a smile.

"I guess not. She's really nice." He seemed genuinely impressed.

"Anyway, you were starting to suggest something for my sermon," I went on.

"Yes. The people you will be preaching to really want to be in Bethlehem because they think that is where Jesus was born. Why don't you just up and tell 'em that they are actually in the right place."

"That's an idea, but I don't know how it would go over. Our Arab churches in the Middle East are quite evangelical, you know; they're near-fundamentalist."

"All the more reason to free them up. You've been trying to put truth first and expediency second. Why stop now? In the end that's really more loving anyway. Besides, it's a sign of growth to say it as it is—or at least that's what you've been telling me." This was the side of Jim I loved best and had come to know so well in these months together.

"OK, I will start my sermon that way and give out the brief explanation carefully."

"Good." Then there was silence until, evidently almost asleep, Jim said, almost in a mutter, "I see grain growing—wheat, growth in courage, growth in love."

Ψ

The next morning at Christ Church, after Matins and the Ante-Communion in Arabic, I began my sermon. I held up my passport, pointing to the visa from the Hashemite Kingdom of Jordan, and said that I could have been in Bethlehem—but that I was here with them because my studies had convinced me that I—and they—were in the right place for celebrating Jesus' birth. When this was interpreted to them by the vicar I noticed puzzled expressions on all faces but one—that of my son, who smiled supportively.

His expression took me back to the time I had preached at Webb School in Claremont when Jim was in the third year of high school. Knowing that I was to be the Sunday preacher had given him considerable apprehension, since preaching was in ill repute at his school (not so unusual these days) and he felt that he would be kidded about it if the sermon somehow didn't go over. The night before, just as in Nazareth, he talked with me about my sermon, going so far as to suggest that I eliminate what was going to be an opening bit of humor which his peer group might regard as corny and that I rearrange the order of ideas. The next day when I had finished my sermon and was coming down the center aisle at the end of the recessional, I saw Jim's face: his smile was one of relief and pride. That kind of response had meant a great deal to me then—as it did now.

I explained the point briefly but carefully and expressed my gratification that I could be with them this Christmas, and then went on to my sermon theme. I later learned that my point was not received too well, not so much because of fundamentalistic resistance to my point, but rather because the rare opportunities to go across into all-Arab Jordan presented more than devotional opportunities: a chance to see relatives, do a little direct barter, get funds into the hands of their less economically fortunate Jordanian relatives, etc.

Jim and Sayida left the service right after the sermon, but after a stroll came to the vicarage for the reception. When we were about to leave, Jim said what I felt was an almost wistful word of farewell to Sayida. Knowing how important relationships were to him, I was almost sorry we didn't have more time in Nazareth.

Jim and I were then on our way, driving east, descending sharply down to Tiberias on the Sea of Galilee, then north up the coast, rounding toward Capernaum. We stopped at a place on the north shore where it is claimed that Jesus appeared to his disciples, according to the Resurrection accounts in Matthew and Mark in which they were directed to go to Galilee to await his coming. Luke recounts, however, that they were told to remain in Jerusalem during the time he was still with them (Acts 1:3–4). As we left there to return to our car, we realized we were quite a long way from Jerusalem and the sun was already beginning to set. So we started out with no break in our travel, Jim driving at his usual safe but fast speed. It took us from sunset until 11:00 P.M. to reach our hotel in Jerusalem. As we were getting ready for bed there, we discussed what a long trip that was for the disciples to make on foot.

In Cambridge just before the arrival from New York of the galley proofs of *What Is This Treasure* I had read a new and careful analysis of the Resurrection narratives in the Gospels.* Of course I was aware, as is almost anyone who has been to theological school, that the accounts do not entirely line up, but I had hardly noticed what is a contradiction between the tradition which states the appearances were in Jerusalem (Luke 24:33–43) and that which locates them in Galilee (Matt. 28:16–18; Mark 14:28; 16:9, 14)—each being

* James McLeman, *Resurrection Then and Now* (London: Hodder & Stoughton, 1965; Philadelphia: Lippincott, 1967).

introduced by instructions from the Lord to wait at the given place (Matt. 28:7, 10; Mark 16:7; Acts 1:3–4).* In the text of *What Is This Treasure* I had referred to "the disciples' apprehension of our Lord's continuing life after death" as "corporate and multiple"; after reading this new book, I added a footnote introduced with the words: "And, it must be granted, inconsistent."

But then the matter had been fairly academic. Here Jim and I were experiencing the manifest difficulty of reconciling the traditions. It considerably shook my credence in any of the accounts and turned my mind again to the long gap between the time of the various reported events and the time they were committed to writing.

Jim and I talked a lot about the Resurrection accounts, for they had been an important basis for my continuing belief in life after death†—a belief Jim did not share. Now *I* had begun to doubt their historical basis. With no other evidence at hand from which to infer the ongoing nature of man's life, it was not very long before I felt that my reductionist method required me to admit, in all honesty, that I did not know of sufficient data upon which to base an affirmation of life after death. This was not going to be an easy stance to take. Nevertheless, when in January I gave a scheduled address at Ridley Hall, a theological college affiliated with Cambridge, I included it among the beliefs I could no longer affirm. (I made it clear that there was not sufficient data to deny it, either.)

Ψ

* John appears to have adopted both traditions. Cf. John 20:19–23, 26–29; 21:1ff.

† E.g., *A Time for Christian Candor*, p. 119; and *What Is This Treasure*, pp. 82–83.

The most memorable event of our time together in Israel—indeed each of us felt that it was the most impressive twenty-four hours ever experienced, and I would still say the same today—was our expedition to Masada, which had been strongly recommended by some of the scholars at whose feet I had sat. We drove down from Jerusalem one evening to the head of the Negev Desert and put in at Beersheba—the ancient place associated with Abraham.

Early the next morning we were taken in tow by a delightful and knowledgeable guide named Obadiah ("The name of the shortest book in the Bible," he snapped, "and I think I'm the shortest guide in Israel"). He took us first to the weekly market place where Arab Bedouins had come to sell and buy—a most unusual sight and rare experience. A Bedouin photographer there, equipped with a camel tended by a young Arab boy, urged us to have our pictures taken with the camel: he would give us a receipt, he promised, and mail the pictures out that afternoon. We had little confidence we would ever see the pictures, but the price wasn't high and the whole scene was an engaging one. Both Jim and I were diffident about ascending the camel, but were happy to have it as a backdrop. And sure enough, three days later in Herzliya, north of Tel Aviv on the Mediterranean, the snapshots came to our hotel in the mail—the only photographic record of our Israeli trip. They were very important to both of us; our vivid feelings about the rest of the day somehow became freighted onto the snapshots taken in Beersheba.

But the highlight of the day—and, indeed, the whole trip—was the climb to Masada, the diamond-shaped plateau rising sharply above the Dead Sea, on which the last 960 of the Israel resistance movement were finally defeated in A.D. 73 after a four-year siege by 10,000 Roman legionnaires camped in the desert below. Though the story was written up in detail in Josephus' *The Jewish War*, Masada was only discovered in recent times, and we were there the first year excavations had gotten far enough along for people to be allowed to climb it.

Standing at the top of the plateau and looking out over the vast, barren desert, I somehow felt caught up in the courage which must have enabled those 960 to stand till the very end against 10,000 Roman soldiers. So much so that I felt I too could almost believe—as they did to the end (as a recently discovered fragmentary farewell note shows)—that God *would* break into history, through the Son of Man and his angels, to bring victory to his people Israel if I would wait there long enough. I felt transported into a plane of hope where time is no longer significant and courage is the motivating force. It was a kind of psychedelic experience without drugs.

Jim felt that special spirit too, and as we followed the Snake Path (as Flavius Josephus called it) to the Dead Sea below we both sensed that a new dimension had been added to our already deep relationship—one which tied us to a heritage of courage and hope.

Ψ

From Israel I had to take two side trips to Africa while Jim stayed on in Herzliya. The first was to Rhodesia and the second to Malawi.

The Diocese of California was linked to the Diocese of Matabeleland (Western Rhodesia) through a special arrangement in the Anglican Communion called MRI (Mutual Responsibility and Interdependence). Before leaving for England, plans had been formulated for a diocesan excursion to Rhodesia as the means of acquainting us with the needs we might take responsibility for helping to meet. By December Rhodesia's prime minister, Mr. Ian Smith, had made his Unilateral Declaration of Independence in open defiance of Great Britain, and reports of the difficult political situation there were such that we canceled the group's plans.

A visit to England by the Rt. Rev. Kenneth Skelton, Bishop of the Matabeleland Diocese, however, convinced me—as well as our mutual friend, Bishop John Robinson, who kept urging me on—that in spite of the risks, it was important for me to carry through with the visit in order to be as supportive as possible to Bishop Skelton. He was taking a bold stand against racism and thus was being criticized within the Church there and also threatened by the Rhodesian "Gestapo Chief," euphemistically called the Minister of Law and Order.

So I flew off to Salisbury, leaving Jim in Herzliya. The next day he heard on the radio (on a station which broadcast in English) that I had been arrested. The report said little else, but Jim was able to supply a great deal out of his imagination, for he had read reports of the rising number of persons thrown into concentration camps (unrealistically called "detention centers") for indefinite periods without trial or even specification of offenses, and of the gross treatment of prisoners.

Early in the day I had tried to phone Jim from Nairobi, Kenya, where I had been granted political asylum (having been arrested and then deported from Rhodesia, possibly because of charges against me sent there by Fr. Frank Brunton, a priest of the Diocese of South Florida, who wrote directly to Ian Smith to tell him of my alleged communist connections, racial rabble-rousing tactics and heresy). But I had been unable to get through to Israel.

When after an all-night flight via Teheran, Iran, my feet were finally again on the soil of Israel, I immediately went to a phone booth and called the hotel. There was no answer in the room. Paging produced no results. Impatient to be back with Jim—and for him to know I was all right—I grabbed a cab for the trip to Herzliya. I walked to the south wing of the hotel and then up to the second-floor open-air ramp toward the rooms facing the Mediterranean, and opened the door to the room. No Jim.

I thought I would go down again and look at the outdoor tables in the sun, or out on the beach; but as I opened the door to go out on the ramp, there was Jim walking toward me just five feet away. A beautiful embrace it was, and particularly because for all he knew, by then I was off in some remote part of Rhodesia in one of the detention centers. But here I was. And here he was. All was encompassed within two warm and loving smiles.

Having been frustrated by State interference with Church in my attempt to see the conditions and needs in the Matabeleland Diocese, and having, fortunately, in my foreshortened stay in Rhodesia heard mention of the forthcoming Synod of the Province of Central Africa to be convened in Blantyre, Malawi, I arranged for an invitation there from the Archbishop (who was the Diocesan in Zambia). I flew there from Israel, and since there was a quite representative group of clergy and laymen (as well as Bishop Skelton, of course) from the Diocese of Matabeleland at the Synod, I was able by special meetings of the delegation and individual interviews (helpful toward candor in the case of black delegates) to gain a rather thorough grasp of the shape of things, and I was left with no doubt as to the urgent need of help—in a variety of ways—from our diocese. So I decided while in Blantyre early in January further to interrupt my sabbatical and make a quick round trip from England at the end of the month to our annual diocesan convention.

From Malawi I flew to Rome. Jim met me there and we returned together to London.

Ψ

Except for our warm and vivid memories of our experiences in Israel together, everything seemed just the same back in Cambridge. It was as though we had never left. Cambridge had come to be so much like home to us that when we returned there we automatically re-entered our newly discovered common life.

Our apartment at Carlton Court was filled with shared memories by now: memories of deep discussions, of evenings with visitors, of light banter and shared tasks. But it also held memories of trips, both good and bad, which we had shared —Jim on drugs, and I through empathetic concern.

No, nothing seemed to have changed, and unfortunately that meant my concern for Jim went unmitigated. There were indications that he was somewhat unbalanced, yet I did not fully grasp the extent of his troubled condition, in part because Jim attributed many of my reactions to his behavior to the "generation gap"—as reduced as I had hoped that had become. He spent long hours sitting on the floor in front of the stereo as if in a world all his own, with the music turned up so loud that it perforce drowned out whatever of the real world might have otherwise intruded. He used music as another kind of escape—different from psychedelics, but a trip of sorts, nevertheless. "When you really groove with music you just take off," I remember his saying.

He also put on the ceiling above his bed, using black friction tape, some designs which he called "concentration marks." He would spend hours lying on his bed staring up at their angular shapes. I would not have been bothered if I had felt this were a form of meditation, but instead I feared it was still another kind of escape.

And there were mysterious incidents which I didn't understand at the time and found it difficult to ask Jim about. For example, one evening I was going out to dinner and had invited Jim to come. He declined, saying he had invited some friends over for a party. I was glad he had, and I left in good spirits. "Have a good party," I urged as I went out the door.

Upon returning to the flat at about 11:30 P.M., however, I found no one in the living room—not even Jim. There were no signs of a party—no cigarette butts or dirty dishes or glasses. Moreover, the end tables (of which there were several) were all lined up in a row in the middle of the room. Though I studied the scene with genuine concentration for several minutes, I could make no sense out of any of it. Jim was in bed, seemingly asleep. It seemed obvious there had been no party. Had he even planned to have one? Was the party perhaps a fanciful one? Or had the guests failed to come? Whatever it was, I was disturbed and deeply concerned—though I was not quite sure about what.

Another day, after coming back from the University library in midafternoon, I was tidying up the apartment a bit. I saw an opened letter lying on the desk at which Jim centered his study. I was naturally interested—and indeed curious—and so when he arrived from college shortly, I said, "I see you've heard from Nazareth. I guess it's from Sayida."

"Oh, yeah," he said diffidently, as though one received letters from Israeli-Arab girls every day! "It came quite a while ago. Read it if you want to."

I did. It was the work of a bright girl whose form of expression in English was naïve and whose relatively simple mode of life showed through. It was direct, warm. It was wistful, too—not that it reflected the slightest hope of any face-to-face continuity of relationship, but it did display shyly the hope that she now would have an interesting pen pal.

"Isn't that nice, Jim," I said. "Have you answered her?"

"No," he answered flatly.

Now I joined in the wistfulness. "You will, of course, won't you?"

"No, there's no point to it."

And no point, I realized from experience, in my going on about it. He never mentioned the matter again. But the letter remained where it was on the desk.

Ψ

With Jim back at Cambridgeshire College and easily able to procure psychedelics, he was soon back on drugs fairly frequently. He knew of my negative reaction to that, so for the first time in our stay there he was less than candid about his intentions.

One day he went to his room at about 3:00 P.M., saying he was going to take a nap. I was just about to call him for supper about 7:00 P.M. when he came into the kitchen. I immediately noted his dilated pupils, but before I could say anything, suddenly he blurted out: "I've been seeing a column . . . a huge column . . . the column is all that is. I am being drawn slowly toward the column . . . now into the column . . . I have become the column . . . There is no difference between us . . . just me and the column . . . *just the column* . . . just me . . ."

His words were measured and halting. I could feel the intensity of them as if I were on the trip myself. He went on.

"I feel myself sinking now . . . falling through the column . . . Oh, God . . . everything is black, empty, hollow . . . God . . . I'm falling and there's nothing at the bottom . . . no bottom . . . I'm falling into nothingness . . . blackness . . . no way to grab hold, nothing to catch onto . . . save me, save me . . . what can save me . . . falling . . . nothingness . . ."

I listened to Jim's distress with more than empathy. I was experiencing vicariously his terror.

"Jim—Jim—I'm here, Jim." He seemed to hear me, but the power of the imagery held him transfixed. "Jim—" I tried again. "Jim, maybe if you took my hand it would help you re-establish contact with—" I was going to say "reality"; but I caught myself. I knew that one of the psychedelic dogmas was that my world was illusion and what was his now was reality. Anyway, I reached out, grasped his hand and led him into the living room. "Let's sit down, Jim," I urged.

For a long time he sat as if hypnotized by horror, staring glassy-eyed into space and occasionally shuddering or trembling with fear.

Then suddenly his expression changed. It was as if a shaft of light had been turned on his face as he lifted it up.

"My *God,*" he almost shouted. "There's *light* at the top. When I look up there's light, Dad—light."

I could almost see the light. I could see it reflecting as if on—or perhaps through—his face. "I'm glad, Jim, I'm so glad —I knew you could come through it."

"It's as if I'm being pulled up through the column by a magnetic force—through the column, yet I *am* the column—up, up, up toward the light—that's salvation, Dad—Dad, it's the—"

He stopped talking, and lettered out on a note pad: HINDU ESCAPE COLUMN. Then he resumed, "I don't want to forget it. Hindu Escape Column—that's what the light means. I'm safe—oh, thank *God*—I'm safe."

"Yes, thank God," I breathed.

Ψ

I suggested Jim might want to eat something. He did eat a little, and then we talked a while longer. Naturally, I was concerned about the fact that he'd taken another trip, but decided it was best not to talk until he was fully out of it and instead encouraged him to get to sleep at a normal hour. He did. In fact, next morning he went to classes. When he got home that afternoon, I brought up the subject of drugs again, but what I was saying sounded rather hollow. There was nothing I hadn't said before.

In fact, I had less to say than before. When once he had taken Romilar (in the form easily available in Britain from any chemist, i.e., pharmacist: twenty pills, rather than the syrup customary in the United States) I had been so concerned at the physical effects that I had gone to see the nearby physician we had chosen under the socialized medicine plan to ask whether there were special dangers in Romilar. He of course knew of the drug but had thought of it only in terms of one tablet at a time for an ordinary cough. He made several calls until he got in touch with one deemed to be an expert in psychedelic substances. The specialist told our doctor that the use of Romilar as a hallucinogenic had only recently been called to his attention, but the indications already were that there was more danger of short-term and long-term damage than with LSD. I had passed this on to Jim along with the details given me. Jim received it politely and thanked me. As an indication that he had thought about it, shortly thereafter he announced out of the blue, "Dad, I'm not going to take Romilar again."

"I'm glad," I had said.

"I thought you would be," he said nicely.

But he did take it again—one last time.

Ψ

As concerned as I was about Jim's use of drugs, there seemed to be nothing I could do about it. Talk about it though we had, the decision was always his in the end. Had I forbidden him to take trips in the flat, he would no doubt have gone out with friends when he wanted to drop acid; and then I would have accomplished nothing except alienation. If he were going to do it, I preferred he do it with me around, in case I could be useful talking with him—or acting, should things reach the point (a dreadful thought!) of needing to call a doctor. And obviously it was impossible to be with him every moment to see that he took nothing. He was, after all, twenty years old—no longer a child, by any means.

As time passed, I began to see that in spite of all the positive experiences Cambridge—and Israel—had brought into Jim's life, nothing had basically changed. He was back into the same patterns which had prompted me to bring him to England. He himself seemed to sense the sameness of it all—the seeming lack of effect which the events of the past few months had had. For he wrote:

> The days move
> like identical sliding doors
> That get heavier day by day
> Solely [slowly?] pushing them past
> is not pushing at all
> but nothing doing
> That's why they're heavy

I must confess that I was genuinely discouraged. True, there had been a great letup as far as the frequency of his drug use went, but there was no way of being assured about the future even in that regard, let alone to hope that he would drop the practice entirely. Yes, I was troubled and not the less so, certainly, in the light of the fact that Jim now really had to make up his mind on a matter which all along had been troublesome.

Ψ

That I had decided to fly back to San Francisco for our diocesan convention in order to share what I had learned about the situation in Rhodesia and get across the urgency of immediate and sustained support of the Diocese of Matabeleland meant I would be returning to the States for three days just about the time Jim would need to go back if he was to begin the second semester at San Francisco State.

"I don't know what to do," I remember Jim saying. "I don't mind staying here in Cambridge while you go home, but if I do it will mean staying on after your sabbatical is over, too. And that will be a long time—almost three months."

"That's true, Jim, but since you like your work here, maybe it's worth it," I commented. "If you go home to San Francisco State now you'll get no credit for what you've done here; if you stay, then you would have credit for a full year's study."

"Yeah, but that means taking those national exams. I don't know if I can make it," he said, his voice betraying his uneasiness at the thought. "I mean, what a ridiculous system! Imagine not giving any marks throughout three terms and then letting the entire year's work be graded on how you do on the final exams."

"It's a double-or-nothing game, I admit; but I'm sure you can pass," I said, trying to be reassuring—and really believing he could pass.

"How could I possibly know? I haven't any idea how I've been doing—no idea at all." A note of anxiety had crept into his words.

"Well, you've been studying a lot more than you did last year, and you certainly *seem* to be learning, if my evaluation is worth anything," I affirmed. "Besides, your tutor should be able to give you some idea how you're doing."

"Yeah, he says I'm doing OK, but I don't know," he shook his head slowly, "I just don't know. I mean, if I flunk the finals I will've blown the whole year."

"Well, you're certainly free to return home and start the second semester at San Francisco State," I reminded him.

"Yeah, but then I miss the last month and a half with you. And besides, I don't want to go home. It's been good to be away. Where would I live, for example?"

"Well, you can always live at home—at least for a starter."

"No—I'm not going to. I need to be out on my own. A guy's gotta have some independence—some freedom." I felt that same mood that had prompted his first move to Haight-Ashbury begin to emerge again—a feeling-tone which had been completely absent during the months in Cambridge.

"Well, I'm sure you can find someone to live with. I hope it won't be back in the Haight-Ashbury scene, though." Even as I expressed my sentiment in that regard, I knew that that *would* be the kind of scene he would return to—or at least I feared so. It wasn't easy to advise Jim in the decision he had to make. I wasn't anxious for him to return to San Francisco, for I was sure he would fall back into his same patterns and habits of living. Yet I didn't feel his staying in England would solve anything, for he was on drugs there, too. And I was very uneasy about leaving him alone. Frankly, I didn't see any solution to his dilemma—and neither did he.

Ψ

After much discussion about the alternatives, Jim finally decided to return to the United States when I went to the convention, and to enroll again at San Francisco State for the second semester. He planned, however, to stop off in New York for a few days, since I had to leave on Wednesday, February 2, and he didn't have to be in San Francisco until Saturday, February 5, the final day for registration.

He was very eager to see some friends he had made at a party I had been invited to in New York, where he and I had stayed a couple of days on the way to England because of television programs which I had been scheduled for and some counseling I had agreed to do. At the party were several persons I knew quite well; so of course I introduced Jim around.

The following day when I had to fly to Toronto to do a television program there, Jim decided to tarry in New York in order to accept an invitation to go out for an evening in Greenwich Village with three people who had been at the party: Nan Lanier, a friend of hers named Billie and a good friend of mine from California, Michael Murphy (head of the Esalen Institute at Big Sur). He'd had such a good time that he had mentioned several times in Cambridge that when he went home he'd like to stop by and see Nan and Billie, with whom, incidentally, he corresponded a few times.

So it was that Jim and I both had reservations to leave from the London airport on February 2, 1966, to fly to the United States—I via the polar route to San Francisco, and he to New York City.

When we arrived for check-in, Jim discovered he had inadvertently left his passport in Cambridge. The plan had been that I would see him off and then leave an hour later myself. Now the plans had to be changed. The ticket agent told us Jim could go down to the American Consulate-General in London and get a substitute passport; he wouldn't have to go back to Cambridge. Then he could catch a plane to New York leaving about three hours later.

There was little else to do; so I gave Jim money for a taxi into London and back. We embraced and said goodbye. I went up to the second level to pass through immigration and buy some gifts duty-free. As I reached the head of stairs, I remember looking down to the lobby below just as Jim happened to look up. We both waved and smiled, but I suddenly shivered. I feared his going to New York. In a way it was a free-floating anxiety; in a way it was grounded in the problem of drugs.

Ψ

I was immediately caught up in a round of meetings when I reached San Francisco, preparing for the Convention. I had written out my address on the flight home, feeling it to be especially important since it outlined a five-pronged project for the Diocese of Matabeleland and supplied fully the background—gained in Africa—out of which my sense of urgency about the plan had emerged. On Friday, I presented the matter to a joint meeting of the Diocesan Council and its Division of Mutual Responsibility and Interdependence. That afternoon I addressed the clergy on the significant decline of our Mother Church of England and the warnings it seemed to provide for us. Then to the Bishop's House for a reception for about four hundred clergy, clergy wives and diocesan officials. After a quick bite to eat, down to the Cathedral for the opening service of the Convention and my address.

Though I was busy those two days, I was not so preoccupied that I didn't notice that Jim had not called as he had promised me he would, to let me know what hotel he was in and the time he planned to arrive in San Francisco. As Friday wore on, I became even more concerned, for he should have been arriving in San Francisco that night if he was to get registered the next day at the college. Still, I thought, young people his age are not conspicuous for their recognition of the fact that parents worry about their whereabouts.

Before entering the Cathedral for the service that night, I checked with Esther and confirmed my fear that no word had come yet from Jim. She indicated she would leave immediately after my address to go home and wait for his call. "Maybe he'll just come, without phoning ahead," I said, trying not to reveal the deepening uneasiness I felt.

Everything seemed to go according to plan until, during the hymn after Evensong, I was led by the crozier in the hand of my chaplain, the Rev. David Barr, from the cathedra to the pulpit for my address. Though I was not unaccustomed to the presence of television cameras, photographers and newsmen in the Cathedral, and to their movements in the course of sermons, at that point there seemed to be an undue amount of commotion. Reporters were rushing in and out, talking with each other; I even saw Canon Howard Freeman, the diocesan communications officer, moving about in the north aisle and transept and in conversation a couple of times —something I had never seen him do before. I found this distracting and puzzling.

I got through the address, however, and felt it had gone well. As I turned to leave the pulpit and reassume cope and miter over my rochet before proceeding back to the cathedra during the anthem, I noticed that Canon Trevor Hoy was standing there with my pastoral staff. Such a change had not only not been scheduled but it is, strictly speaking, inappropriate for one with the rank of canon to act as chaplain.

"Oh!" my voice registered surprise. "What happened to David?"

"He was called out," Trevor replied, and at once turned and led me toward my stall. But at the same time the Suffragan Bishop, the Rt. Rev. Richard Millard, had arisen from his seat and was moving to join me. Then Trevor turned right toward an exit to the ambulatory and simultaneously Dick followed, taking my arm and starting to turn me, too. This seemed a most extraordinary bit of ceremonial and certainly not one provided for in our Cathedral Customary. "What's this about?" I insisted.

"You're needed outside right now."

Then I saw David standing in the ambulatory without his vestments and with his suit coat on.

"What's up?" I said, now sensing something very strange.

"There's something I have to tell you," David replied. "Let's go over to Diocesan House." He guided me out into the parking lot. I remember that my mind was completely devoid of any speculation as to what news could be important enough to require calling me out of the service. It was like being suspended momentarily in a vacuum—without thought or feeling.

"It's Jim . . ." David opened.

"Jim?"

"He's—dead," David said with effort.

I barely heard the words. I looked at David in disbelief.

" . . . in a hotel room . . . New York . . . he took his own life . . . shot himself."

"That can't be true," I said feebly, not having fully taken in what David had said. "Are they sure? Do they know it was Jim?"

David had been moving me steadily toward Diocesan House. "Come on inside," he said quietly. "Howard's waiting for us and will have the full report for you."

Blindly I followed David into Trevor's office. Howard was there and embraced me, with tears in his eyes, as I now saw were also in David's.

"Jim," he said, quietly. "I've kept this from breaking in the press up till now since no good would have come from not having you give the address on something which mattered so much to you—and to Jim, too, I gather. After all, there was nothing you could have done by knowing a little bit sooner."

"I see. But is it verified?" I asked again.

"Yes, I've checked it all out thoroughly. I called New York directly and talked to the sergeant myself. There's no doubt."

"In a hotel room?" I hardly knew what I was asking.

"Yes. In a hotel on Thirty-first Street. It was clearly suicide. He used a rifle," Howard went on.

"How long have you known?" I asked numbly, not really caring about that. "When did it happen?" which mattered more to me.

"They think it happened in the early hours of the morning, New York time, but no one heard the shot and he was not found until sometime in the afternoon. It took some time to check it out—his passport wasn't found—and to trace the gun purchase through a receipt found in the room to a nearby sporting goods store. We got word about 7:00 P.M. I had a hard time getting the press to agree to hold up; but they've been very kind and cooperative."

I took Howard's words in, but their meaning had not yet

struck me. "What about Esther?" I suddenly remembered. "Has anyone told Esther?"

"No," David replied. "Someone saw her leave the Cathedral as soon as you finished speaking."

"Yes, of course," I nodded slowly, "she went back to wait for Jim's call. Phil," I turned to my long-time friend, Phil Adams, Chancellor of the diocese, who had quietly joined us. "Will you call and tell Esther not to answer the phone till I get there? I'll go right home," I said. I didn't want her to hear it from the press.

During the interchange I had, without even thinking, removed my vestments. David had my suit coat and topcoat ready, and we quickly got into his car and left.

Ψ

Esther was waiting for me at the door. Phil's phone call had, as I would have anticipated if I'd been able to think more clearly, alerted her that something was wrong; and, since she hadn't heard from Jim, she was already fearing the worst.

"It's Jim," she said, her eyes searching mine for confirmation of her fears—or the quelling of them.

"Yes," I said quietly as I led her to the sofa in the living room.

"I knew it," she said, dropping her head into her hands. "I just knew it."

"He took his own life in a New York hotel room." Even as I said the words I didn't really believe them yet. "He shot himself." My own words rang in my ears. Like me, she couldn't cry—not yet. Only later when the reality struck her with full force did she break down. I tried to be of some comfort.

Unobtrusively, others began to join us. One by one the

children came and Esther and I together broke the news to them. Then some priests of the diocese who were especially close friends quietly took over, keeping the children company and being of whatever assistance they could. Some clergy wives manned the phone for us so we didn't have to be bothered with calls. A few close friends came by to offer their condolences. Esther and I talked with people, telling them what little we knew about the tragedy.

In the Cathedral the service had been closed by the Suffragan Bishop with prayers for the deceased and for the bereaved family.

It was not until much later that night that I made my way upstairs for a moment of solitude. As I walked into the bedroom, I was greeted by Jim's warm smile, and for the first time I broke down and cried. I turned the photograph face down on the mantel, unable to look at it, and sank down on the bed, tears flowing in recognition of the reality that Jim was gone—dead. The grief pressed in on me.

Ψ

The next few days were made easier by the presence of three or four of Jim's contemporaries who had been close friends since his days at Town School down the street, who were there to run errands and do whatever was of help—twenty-four hours a day. Clergy wives continued to answer the phone, make coffee, etc., and the diocesan and Cathedral staffs and other friends, both priests and laymen, quietly handled details that needed tending to. Family began to arrive from various parts of the country.

Esther and I talked by phone to New York several times. An old friend, Carl Newton, an attorney, handled the arrangements that needed to be made with the police and the medical officer, and an old friend, the Rev. John M. Krumm, identified the body, since he had been at that party in Greenwich Village in the fall of 1965 and therefore had seen Jim within the required time limit. I was thus spared the necessity of flying to New York and performing this painful duty myself.

During those days I was unable to offer comfort to the family on the basis of a belief in life after death. Elemental honesty ruled out offering solace on the basis of what I felt then was an insufficiently supportable ground of hope. Of course, I was able to relate a great deal of the joy of the months Jim and I had shared in Cambridge. I could also join in common reminiscences and affirm with the rest of the family all that Jim had brought to us. But I could not say to myself or to anyone else that I believed that Jim lived on—nor, of course, did I have a basis for believing that he didn't; so I didn't say that either.

In any case, decisions about the here and now were called for, so we assembled in the library for a family conference. My views on conventional American funeral and burial practices were on the record—through TV and in Jessica Mitford's *The American Way of Death:* cremation as soon as possible, a memorial service without casket, some simple disposition of the ashes and asking would-be donors of flowers to contribute to a worth-while cause meaningful to the deceased. These were the unanimous family views as well, but we needed to make some practical decisions under the agreed-upon principles.

Cremation would be in New York, with John Krumm taking the brief committal service. There would be a memorial service in the Cathedral—the Burial Office (that is, Matins for the Dead) and Requiem Eucharist—with close family friends among the clergy participating, including the Very

Rev. John Coburn, Dean of the Episcopal Theological School in Cambridge, Mass., and Rabbi Alvin Fine of San Francisco. In the service too would be the four friends of Jim's age—two of them Roman Catholics—who had been around night and day to help: one to read the epistle, the others as crucifer and torchbearers. Then Jim's ashes would be simply scattered at a place he loved (we all did)—where the waters of the Golden Gate meet those of the Pacific. And to far-off Rhodesia would go the "in lieu of flowers" gifts as financial help for college students like Jim—but disadvantaged because black.

Ψ

The Cathedral was full. The service helped so much, meant so much. The congregational participation in responses, chants and hymns was very moving. People from many traditions—and none—came. The readings appointed by the Prayer Book, the hymns selected and the whole tone were such that it was like an Easter service.

That was Monday. On Wednesday we drove to San Rafael, in Marin County, north of San Francisco, and boarded a comfortable boat with an enclosed cabin. Jack Riley, then Rector of St. Paul's, San Rafael, a close friend since my coming to the diocese, had made this arrangement with kind, boat-owning parishioners and went along. We proceeded out from shore into the Bay, south past barren Angel Island and then due west.

Just beyond the Golden Gate Bridge, on the ocean side where the tides flow out to sea, we scattered Jim's ashes onto the water. As the wind carried them out over the rippling surface of the sea, I felt the deep sorrow of having lost not only a son, but also my closest friend.

4

I am unaware of anything that has a right to the title of an impossibility, except a contradiction in terms.

—*T. H. Huxley*

Scientific caution and humility are not enough. A certain boldness also is required, a readiness to grasp *a vast range of converging evidence,* each item of which, standing alone, can lead us nowhere.

—*Prof. William McDougall*

As is the case in any scientific exploration, it is important to distinguish two steps in the process: (a) determination of the factuality of reported phenomena, and (b) the evaluation of hypotheses of explanation—and, if a given hypothesis is sufficiently plausible, its affirmation. Failure to keep this distinction in mind . . . has caused many arbitrarily to deny verifiable data in order to avoid being forced to accept a conclusion against which they already have a mind-set—a process which is the unrecognized partner of an over-eagerness to accept any reported psychic happenings in order to maximize support for the desire to believe in eternal life.

—*J.A.P.* in *Jubilee*

My return to England was of course delayed by the unexpected tragic events of that early February morning. When I began to feel my period of principal usefulness to the family in their bereavement—and theirs to me in this regard—was past, however, I did make reservations to return to England.

My chaplain, David Barr, had gone on ahead according to the earlier plans I had outlined in my address to the opening session of the Convention. It had been my thought then that David could help me collate all the necessary information for the Matabeleland project (which the Convention accepted), work out a complete and accurate summary of all the particular pieces of work in the Diocese of Matabeleland and, with me, propose correlations for each of these with churches, schools and institutions of the Diocese of California. Communications with Bishop Skelton were spotty, for the government frequently opened mail and, in fact, confiscated some of it; so we were fortunate that there was in London a Central African mission office, which was a storehouse of information. After Jim's death, it was felt that it was even more important that David not only go, but be there ahead of me so as to be there when I arrived.

Meanwhile, David had made arrangements for Mrs. Maren Bergrud to join him. Mrs. Bergrud was from the Diocese of California and had, on occasion, helped me as an editorial assistant when I was trying to meet deadlines on manuscripts. She had for some time been recuperating from a very serious operation and was as yet unable to take full-time employment. Having relatives in Norway, Maren had taken advantage of her months of convalescence to make an extended voyage by freighter to Europe and the Scandinavian countries, and was still abroad when Jim's death occurred. David was able to get in touch with her, and she met him in Cambridge in order to help him with various tasks designed to make things easier for me upon my return.

Jim had left quite a few things I'd agreed to ship home in my trunk. These were gone through: some things thrown out, some given to the British equivalent of the Good Will Industries, some put in a closet for later packing, some neatly folded in drawers to ask me about—but not right away. Then Maren and David cleaned the apartment thoroughly and laid in supplies. Third, on another level, they rescheduled speaking dates and consultations with scholars which I was missing due to my unanticipated late return, answered as much mail as they could, and sketched out (for consideration on my arrival) plans for developing the Matabeleland project.

Ψ

I arrived back in London on Tuesday morning, February 15, nearly a fortnight after my son's death. David and Maren met me at the airport. It was a joy and a comfort to have the company of these two colleagues and friends, each of whom was warm and supportive in what was, of course, a difficult time for me. As soon as I joined them, past immigration and customs, I sensed that I was glad to be back in England and glad to be with them. They drove me to the airport motel where they had spent the night and, after we had breakfast, they checked out and we headed for Cambridge.

I would be less than honest if I did not admit that it was with some apprehension that I faced the prospect of returning to the flat which my son and I had shared for those several months. I feared somehow that it would be depressing to re-enter the rooms which had so recently provided the setting for the period of my most intimate association with Jim. So I sought to delay the return with touristic excursions en route, the ostensible purpose of which was to introduce my chaplain, who was making his first trip abroad, to sample edifices of the Mother Church. So, en route from the airport to Cambridge (bypassing London), we inspected carefully the Cathedral of the Diocese of St. Albans and its Close and various parish churches—large, middle-size and small—almost enough to make Quakers out of my colleagues!

The three of us talked at length, of course, of Jim's death and of our speculations about it.

We raised the questions which had already been asked in San Francisco, and which were to come up over and over again in the months ahead: What more could have been done to help him? Why really had he taken his life? Was it a mistake to let him return to the United States alone? Or, how could I have prevented him—at twenty—from doing so? Where had I, as his father, failed him? I felt sure he had been on psychedelic drugs (the Chief Medical Officer's reports supported that) and the incoherence of some of the poems he had written indicated that he must have really lost touch with reality. But details were not known. Whatever had happened, drugs certainly contributed substantially to the outcome, I was sure. If he had had a psychotic break, was it perhaps better this way? What could have happened during those days in New York? Had he premeditated his death?

When we finally arrived at the Cambridge flat, I entered first and surveyed the familiar scene. Surprisingly enough, instead of the sense of depression I had anticipated I was immediately flooded with a warm rush of happy memories.

In spite of the threatening periods when Jim was on drugs, we certainly had shared some deep and happy experiences there. We had grown close and learned to love and appreciate one another as never before. I felt grateful for the time we had had at Carlton Court. It was good to be back.

And so, with a sense of relief—and with considerable eagerness, actually—I turned to the tasks at hand. That was good, as "grief therapy," *and*, even with two ready helpers, there was lots to do; March 15—the end of my sabbatical—was just a month away. Nor did I feel any disloyalty to Jim in getting with it—the major agenda were things he had been very eager for me to make headway with. For example:

The day after my return from the Synod in Malawi, I had —with Jim in the same room—called a scholar at the University of Manchester, Mr. John Allegro, to whom Professor Yadin had directed me. After I reached him at his home near Manchester, we had been talking almost an hour (although it seemed but a few minutes) when Jim called out, "Dad, there's no point in going on and on on the phone. Why don't you make a date and we'll drive up and see him?" I did. And I liked the "we'll."

Well, that date arrived the Friday after my return, and we set out—a "we" which did not include Jim.

At Mr. Allegro's home, which is on a lake near a village south of Manchester, we went right on from the telephone conversation, discussing his studies of the Dead Sea Scrolls. My mentor was apparently enjoying it, for he gave us till 10:00 that night—with tea and dinner thrown in, courtesy of Mrs. Allegro. Then we drove on to Manchester and checked into a hotel, to be at hand to see the Dead Sea Scrolls from the Kingdom of Jordan which were on display that week at the John Rylands Library. Next we headed across country to Lincoln via Sheffield, whose Cathedral we hit just in time for the impressive installation by the Lord Bishop of the new Provost.

Having put into an old inn just before dinner, I spent the evening working with Maren Bergrud on *You and the New Morality*, while David Barr used the time to go through new materials which had arrived from our Rhodesian companion diocese.

The next morning we went up the hill to Lincoln Cathedral for Matins and the Eucharist (a beautiful choir—and about the same number in the congregation!). Then, after mid-day dinner, we drove home to Cambridge, via King's Lynn and Ely. We entered the flat about 9:00 P.M.

Ψ

The cleaning lady had still been there at work when we left on Friday, so she would have been the last one out. It was upon our return that we discovered the two postcards on the floor between the beds in my room, lying so as to form a 140° angle with their outer edges.

Since the three of us each disclaimed any knowledge of the postcards, we naturally assumed—odd as that would have been—that they must have been dropped by the cleaning lady. We questioned her, however, and she too knew nothing about them. I knew her to be both honest and reliable—as well as exceptionally thorough in her work—so we had no reason to doubt her word. There seemed to be no explanation as to where they came from or how they had been dropped in that particular place, since the cleaning woman always locked the doors as she left—even though that had not been our habit.

Thus it was that we brushed the incident aside as strange, but relatively insignificant. And, though it made us *think* of

Jim—who had been the one who bought postcards in every new locale—it never occurred to us that he might in any way be related to their appearance. We did, however, decide that from then on we would lock the apartment, which had never before seemed necessary, to prevent anyone entering during our absence. And of course the cleaning woman continued to do the same.

On Tuesday morning, February 22, another strange thing happened—even more inexplicable. David and I were already having breakfast when Maren emerged. David immediately greeted her with, "What happened to your hair?"

"What do you mean?" Maren answered.

I saw what David was getting at. "Part of your bangs is burned off," I explained.

David and I examined closely what we had immediately observed: one section of Maren's hair, which fell over her forehead, had been burned off in a straight line, leaving black ends (she was a blonde) but no sign of a burn on her forehead.

Maren went to look in a mirror and returned completely puzzled as to what could have happened.

We talked for some time about that, speculating. It appeared plainly to have been burned; yet the result had almost the precision of a scissor cut. We could not fathom how it could have been done. Feeling somewhat uncomfortable as one does when confronted with an unexplainable phenomenon close at hand, we turned with some effort to other conversation, hoping some light would eventually be thrown on the matter.

The next morning, much to our discomfort, the same phenomenon repeated itself. Another third of Maren's bangs had strangely disappeared, seemingly burned off in a straight line. We were extremely puzzled—even disturbed. Yet we had no explanation. After much discussion Maren said—trying to make light of the whole matter—"Well, some people didn't like my hair in bangs anyway, so maybe it's better this way."

Her words jarred, for I recalled Jim having commented to me in San Francisco, after dropping off some work at her place for me one time, that he didn't like Maren's bangs and that he had told her (in his "say it the way it is" spirit!) he thought she should cut them off.

Ψ

The next day (Thursday morning, February 24) we were due in London for separate midday activities which we had deliberately coordinated. I woke first, got up early, put on the coffee, woke David and started toward Maren's room to wake her. Just as I raised my hand to knock on the door, I heard her cry out as if in pain. Opening the door slightly, so as not to intrude, I said tentatively, "Maren?" There was no answer, so I stuck my head in. She was sitting up in bed, staring out the window as if in a trance. Apparently in response to my presence, she uttered some unintelligible references to "them out there" and "the archdeacons."

By this time David, having heard Maren's cry, had joined me, and we stood side by side, not quite knowing what to say or do. The expression on Maren's face was clearly one of horror and fear.

"Maren," we called almost simultaneously. She moaned quietly, as if hearing us in a deep sleep and trying to rouse herself.

"Maren, what is it?"

As she began to wake up she grasped her right hand with her left, groaning as if in pain.

"My fingernails," she moaned. We examined her nails and

found that the third and fourth fingernails were injured. It appeared that a sharp instrument—such as a needle—had been pressed under them. One of the nails was actually broken and later fell off. The other was not broken, but the flesh beneath it was surely wounded.

"We've got to get you right to a doctor," I said, feeling the urgency of doing something. David and I were both quite shaken. Everything seemed strange these days.

"No, I'll be all right," Maren said, but not very convincingly.

David was wandering around the room in a state of confusion. "We can't do that," he said bluntly. "We'll all three miss our appointments."

I knew David was right, but I felt his reaction reflected more our inability to cope with the situation than it did his concern about our several tasks in London. I felt we ought to do something for Maren, and asked: "Do we have any medicine around?" though I was the one who should have known.

"I'll look." It was Maren herself who responded, starting out the door.

"Let's see what we can find around here, David," I said. "There must be some sharp instrument that went through the skin under Maren's nails."

The two of us began looking in drawers, under the bed, in the bedclothes, all over the floor and in the closet—but to no avail. We could find nothing out of the ordinary: no needles, pins or any other sharp objects.

Maren came back in with a Band-Aid over the nail which was split. "My God, Maren!" David almost shouted. "The rest of your bangs are gone!" The two of us almost ran to where Maren was standing in order to examine this continuation of what was becoming a most upsetting series of events.

"What*ever* is going on around here?" I asked, knowing full well that no one had the answer. Not knowing what else to do, David and I began to query Maren as to her "dream" about the "archdeacons." She remembered almost nothing, and the most I could contribute was a reminder to David (it was news to Maren) of the in-group nickname for archdeacons—*archdemons*. Such was the traditional negative reaction to those diocesan administrators and trouble shooters that since medieval times they have been called *oculi episcopi* ("the bishop's eyes"), and among the familiar topics for formal public disputations in medieval universities was "Can an Archdeacon Be Saved?"

None of our speculations really served to alleviate the disturbing feeling that we were caught up in an unfathomable mystery. The pressure of time was such that we had to get our trip under way if we were to arrive in London on time. So each of us got organized as quickly as possible, put down a scanty breakfast and headed for the car in the garage behind the flats. We were less than composed, however; I remember that my own breakfast did not settle very well.

Ψ

David and I kept talking at an incredible rate, as if sheer quantity of words could make up for lack of understanding. Having explored every possible avenue of explanation—or so we thought—we determined jointly to begin to record the events (starting with the postcards), giving the date, describing the phenomenon, and indicating who first discovered it. Nothing, we decided, would be recorded unless we had all three witnessed it and had eliminated all possible "normal" explanations. Maren began making notes (she later typed them on a sheet which we left in one of the typewriters in order to keep a sequential listing of phenomena) and we all helped fill in the details. From that day on, events were reported as they happened. That list has been invaluable in the writing of this book. Finally we tried to divert ourselves by talking about the events which awaited us in London. After considerable time had passed, I became aware that Maren had said nothing since we got into the car.

"What's the matter, Maren?" I asked her. "Are your fingers bothering you? You haven't said a word since we left Cambridge."

"They do hurt some," she responded, "but that wouldn't be so bad. It's the whole thing. I'm not sure I can stand much more."

"I know," I said sympathetically. "This has really been something. I'm sorry you've had to go through this. I just wish we could understand what's going on."

"Well, I guess I could stand almost anything as long as I could trust—and respect—the two of you; but after that speech you gave me last night, frankly, I've had it as far as you're concerned."

"What do you mean?" I asked in genuine innocence.

"You know," she went on, "what you said after you went into your room last night."

"I don't know what you mean," I declared. "I went right off to sleep." I had gone to bed somewhat earlier than David and Maren the night before, wanting to get a good night's sleep before our trip the next day.

"Well, I had assumed that you did. I listened at your door, and since everything was silent, I went in as quietly as I could in order to get a book David and I needed, which was lying on the top of your dresser," Maren explained. "But then you sat straight up in bed and started in."

"I *what?*" I interrupted.

"Well, I assumed that my footsteps woke you up," Maren went on in a higher pitch, the words pouring out. "What you said was not only revealing, but *most* disillusioning. I was glad to come and help this time, like I did back home, not just for the sake of earning some money while I'm recuping, but also because I had respected what you seemed to be and what you stood for—or at least so I thought."

"Thanks a lot," I said sarcastically. I know we have been under a lot of strain, I thought to myself, but this is really too much! "You *had* respect . . ."

"Yes, *had*," she retorted. Then, duplicating my thought, she said, "I know you have been through a lot, and I am glad you felt you could come out with how you feel. But no one would represent himself as being like that if he really weren't."

"Like *what?*" I broke in. My utterly perplexed expression finally registered with her.

"You mean you really don't remember what you said? If you were a drinker I would think you had had a 'blackout.' "

"I don't remember your coming in, or my sitting up, or talking at all," I said in real confusion.

She looked me straight in the eye for a moment. David interrupted, "Obviously, Maren, he *doesn't* know what you are talking about. Go ahead and tell what you heard, because I may want to share something, too."

So she began to spell it out. As she recalled it, my conversation (or "speech") had gone something like this: "Caring about people is a great mistake . . . You can't count on anybody and I certainly don't want anybody counting on me. In fact, they can't . . . The only thing that matters is getting what one wants for oneself. If that involves 'using' people, letting them down, getting them out of the way, OK. I'd just as soon not, but sometimes it's the only way to have things work out the way you want them to . . . It's better to be hard than to be soft; you can't get hurt that way. Principles should serve pragmatics . . . Look out for Number One; that's the only policy . . ."

Maren said frankly that what had upset her was that the words seemed to reflect a callousness and harshness she had not before found characteristic of me. She felt she had somehow been deceived into thinking I was a caring, sensitive person when actually—underneath—I was quite the opposite. In fact, she said, because of her own disillusionment she had not reported my words to David, deciding he "need not know" what I was "really" like.

Opened up by Maren's account, David shared his nocturnal experience. He had gone to our bedroom quite late. I was sound asleep by then; but he had real difficulty getting to sleep in spite of the hour. He reported that after finally drifting off, he had awakened around 2:30 A.M. with a terrible feeling of anxiety, stemming from what seemed to be a fear that he would never be able to *be* anyone in this world. He reported an overwhelming sense of self-deprecation, feeling himself to be weak, unattractive and ineffectual. He said he felt completely hopeless, as though his future were entirely black.

In order to break the mood, David said he got out of bed and went back into the living room to work for a while. The nightmarish experience had not been easy to shake, however; he still remembered it vividly as he reported it to us. He had intended to tell us about it; but the strange events of the morning had made him forget his own experience temporarily. Now Maren's account had reminded him.

As David talked I felt a growing uneasiness, for I was beginning to feel that somehow all the phenomena of the night before and the morning had something to do with Jim. I didn't like to think so, yet certainly they were inexplicable by any ordinary causes. I wondered if it were possible that somehow some of the more negative, depressive and irrational aspects of Jim were left "in the air," so to speak, and were in some way causing these bizarre events. The good could also be in the air: I had a flashback to the surprisingly warm, good feeling which surrounded me as I returned to the apartment from San Francisco. I had the feeling, though I knew of no evidence to support it, that energy fields could have been affected—and left unsettled, or in a state of imbalance—by the events leading up to Jim's death, and by the death itself. And though I knew of no theory at all which would explain such a phenomenon, it seemed possible to me that we were in some strange way picking up and reflecting undirected energies.

I didn't voice this suspicion—for two reasons: I felt the theory itself was quite "way out"; but more important, I didn't really *want* it to be true that any of this should be associated with Jim or with anyone's memories of him—even my own. Such a thought was most unattractive to me and went unexpressed for the time being. More than that, it was unaccepted.

It turned out that the other two were now speculating also, but were keeping their thoughts to themselves. Neither of them had a sufficient basis for connecting particular happenings to particular facets of Jim's living personality. But I learned later that they had talked about it that day, wondering about the apparent interlocking of the various inexplicable happenings, and a possibility had begun to suggest itself to them: *what if Jim himself . . .*

Ψ

We did arrive in London in time for our appointments that day, and the next day we wended our way back to Cambridge. The strange—and obviously still unexplained—happenings of the several days before were by now temporarily forgotten and our thoughts were again focused on the tasks we had before us.

But on arrival back at the flat, we were confronted with such an array of strange phenomena—in spite of our care in having locked the doors—that a bolder hypothesis began to take form in our minds.

On the floor between the twin beds in my room were two paperback books, lying in precisely the same position as the postcards had been, and in the very same spot in front of the nightstand. I had not taken those particular books to bed for reading, and neither had David. In fact, one had never been read at all, but had remained on the shelves in the living room ever since its purchase. Prior to leaving for London, there had been two books on the floor in that place: the Bible and *Suicide and the Soul* (by James Hillman). Both had been picked up, however. One was left on the dresser and the other taken on the trip.

In one of the paperbacks now found on the floor, *Armageddon* (by Leon Uris), was stuck (as if glued) a postcard of Peterborough Cathedral which had previously been on the top of the dresser together with three other such cards. The touch of mucilaginous substance which held it in place did not seem to be glue; yet it was not clear what it could be—or where it came from. The other book, *To Bed at Noon,* was placed so as to form the 140° angle.

The three of us were standing in the bedroom pondering how*ever* the books and the postcard could have gotten where they were and how the card could have gotten stuck to the page, when Maren interrupted.

"Where did the camel pictures go?" she said, pointing to the mirror. The two photos which the Bedouin in Beersheba had taken for us were missing. When Jim and I were unpacking on our return from Israel (early just the month before! I suddenly thought), I had tucked them in the side of the frame of the mirror in my bedroom. They hadn't been moved since, and David and Maren had both seen them there, of course. In fact, the marks left by the cleaning lady when she dusted around them could still clearly be seen on the mirror.

"The Masada pictures are gone," Maren added, unnecessarily.

"Not Masada, *Beersheba*," I corrected—to no end. The petty accuracy was a reflection of my edginess.

David said nothing, but almost immediately whirled around to his right and went directly to the foot of the left side of the inside of the closet, reached under some clothes inexplicably piled up on the floor *and pulled out the pictures.*

"Why did you go there, David?" I asked in high confusion.

"I don't know!" he said—almost in distress at the mystery of his success. "I just felt pulled in that direction."

Astounded by the whole scene, we nevertheless gathered our wits enough to examine further the closet in which David found the snapshots. On the floor on the one side the clothing was in complete disarray. It was as if everything had been pulled down onto the floor and churned around together. Under the mess we found some blank stationery (which none of us had ever seen) and some postcards. The latter were not those previously found between the beds, but none of the three of *us* had purchased them—or even seen them.

We slid both doors over to the left side of the closet in order to see what the conditions were on the right side. Much to our surprise, everything was not only orderly, but unusually so: suits and heavy winter shirts hung up neatly and at even intervals, shoes and slippers lined up on the floor with precision. It struck me as I surveyed the situation that I never was so neat as this side of the closet, nor so messy as the other side.

Ψ

I had heard of "poltergeists," but I didn't have a precise idea of what the word connoted. My memory of what I had heard (or read?) was that it had seemed on occasion that the spirit of a dead person was causing some kind of disturbance in the house where the person had resided before dying. I felt forced to consider whether what we had observed could be the result of a poltergeist. And then for the first time I faced the real possibility that the source of all that had been happening *could* be my son—dead, but still living.

While I stood caught up in my thoughts, Maren and David left the room. David, as he later reported, had felt moved—though not with the same "drive" as in the closet incident—to search the living room. Very soon he noticed that Jim's alarm clock, which had been sitting on a bookshelf, read 8:19. He thought he recalled that the clock had been stopped at 12:15 ever since his arrival from America, so he called out: "Hey, *Jim!*" I came promptly into the front room, and hearing David's urgent tone, Maren stepped in from the kitchen. Having covered the face of the clock with his hand, David inquired, "Tell me what time this clock says, Jim."

"Well, let's see," I paused. "The clock is stopped. The hands are somewhere around—I think I'd say twelve or so—twelve-thirty at the latest." I was thinking back to the morning of February 22 when I had been counseling a young English seminarian and his fiancée in the living room. David and I were due to depart for London, and since I was more or less facing the bookshelves, I had occasionally glanced at the clock, fully aware that we had to leave by 12:30. Being absorbed in the conversation, I completely forgot (though I had known it) that the clock had not been running, and was oblivious to the fact that the time was the same each time I had looked up. David finally felt he just had to interrupt and inform me that it was 1:15 P.M. and it would be difficult to make it to London on time for our appointments.

"That's what you thought before," David said, still holding his hand over the face. He then referred to the cause of our late start to London that day—which I had also been thinking about.

"OK," said I, turning away. "What's the complaint? You knew I was sincerely misled—and you drive so darn fast you got us to our appointments on time anyway."

"Oh, forget that," David retorted. "Take a look at this." I did, only to discover that the hands were now set at 8:19. The clock was still stopped, but now the hands formed a 140° angle.

"That's funny," I observed. "Isn't that pattern the same one which was formed by the two postcards and the two books which we found between the twin beds?"

"Don't be obvious," Maren declared impatiently. "The real question is: what could it possibly mean?" We speculated at some length about the significance of such a symmetrical pattern, but it was not until long into the conversation that it occurred to me that there might be a connection between the time thus represented on the clock and the wee hours of the morning assigned as the time of my son's death by the coroner in New York City (around 3:00 A.M., New York time). By calculating the difference in time between London and New York City we decided that 8:19 could very well be the corresponding London hour for the time Jim took his life. We began to live with that assumption and that particular time became quite significant to us.

It also occurred to us, however, that the symmetry could well represent Jim's persistent interest in the balancing of patterns and lines and objects. He often spent time drawing symmetrical patterns on papers or arranging objects in some balanced shape. I remembered particularly the cold, gray Sunday afternoon in mid-January when I had arrived home from Norwich, where I had driven to do "telly" for the East Anglia station, to discover Jim napping, his door closed, and all four of the identical coffee tables in the living room arranged in a row out from the fireplace as if for some particular aesthetic effect—just as I had found them the night I came home when Jim's "party" looked like a non-event.

Ψ

Whatever the meaning of the 8:19 pattern, we were all three now rather sure that in some mysterious way Jim was causing these things to happen. It seemed too much of a coincidence that so many odd events could occur within such a few days, most of which in some way or another recalled Jim: his preoccupation with the purchase of postcards, his displeasure with Maren's bangs, the "007" side of his personality, his interest in symmetrical patterns, his own insecurities about his ability to succeed, etc. What was the unifying explanation for these events? I was slow to accept the possibility that it was Jim, since I had not believed that he lived on. And neither did Maren and David believe in life after death. Yet we could think of *no* other explanation—a result, I now realize, of our naïveté and our lack of sophistication with regard to the whole field of psychic phenomena.

However, once we had really become convinced of the possibility that Jim was somehow present in the apartment and able to cause the phenomena to occur, we began noticing every strange thing, seeking eagerly to explain it—then and there—by some "natural" cause *or* to attribute it to Jim. David, for example, walked back into the bedroom and noticed that the Venetian blinds had been closed contrary to the way both he and I were accustomed to closing them. It was, of course, possible that the cleaning lady (who had been there that day) had pulled the cord in the opposite direction upon finishing her tasks, but we did not recall her having done so before—nor did she—so we chalked it up as another unexplained phenomenon. Then Maren observed that a small picture of Connie, my younger daughter, was gone. Jim had tucked it in the edge of a light fixture close to the door in the living room in order to have it conspicuously in view, since he liked the photo—and its subject—very much. After much searching we gave up; but the next morning it turned up when, while getting dressed, I pulled out the top drawer of my dresser. There it was, in the same place I had put the cards found in the first episode.

Finally, looking through the glass panel of the front door from the inside, David noticed scrawled on the outside some yellow crayon marks which none of us had ever noted before. We could not make out any letters very clearly, but it seemed possible that either GO or CO were two of the marks in the upper right-hand corner, and just below them the letters AY could be made out. There seemed to be four letters, followed by another letter and the AY, but we could not read the others. So at length we all walked down to each of the apartments below to see whether there were similar marks on the outsides of their doors. The glass was unmarked on the ground floor. On the door of the apartment on the second landing we did find some illegible marks in white chalk. We thought that maybe the yellow and the white notations were of the same category, made either as shipping instructions or by pranksters. Nevertheless, the fact that we had never noticed the letters before made us feel somehow uncomfortable about them, and that added considerably to our feeling that something mysterious was indeed going on here.

It was only with a great deal of effort that we finally settled down enough that night to do some work before turning in. We felt we had to use the time to the best possible advantage. Yet it was hard to concentrate in the light of such extraordinary experiences, the likes of which were foreign to all of our past personal histories. Moreover, we somehow had the feeling that we ought to be able to make sense out of it all. We later mutually confessed that we had even begun to suspect one another and had begun to watch each other to be sure no one was playing jokes—and a strange game that would have been indeed! And if indeed *Jim* was somehow causing these things to happen, I, at least, felt a responsibility for discovering the meaning of it all. Eventually, however, we did manage to get some work done before going to bed.

Ψ

The next morning (which was cold and drizzly) David, in fixing himself breakfast, poured some milk over his cornflakes from a half-filled bottle in the refrigerator. One taste told him the milk was sour. He opened the other bottle in the refrigerator and sniffed it. It smelled somewhat bad—so he poured a very little out into a spoon and tasted: it was spoiled. He then opened the door between the kitchen and the balcony to retrieve the milk stored there. (I always left extra milk out on the porch when there was not room in the refrigerator, for the weather was cold enough that storing it there was just about as effective as keeping it inside in the icebox.) Anyway, David picked up the fourth bottle from the door, in order to use the older milk first. He poured some milk from this bottle over a fresh bowl of cereal. This turned out to be sour too! The next bottle he had a sip from first—sour. So, putting cereal in a fresh bowl (the flat was equipped with only four), he poured milk over it out of the new bottle delivered that very morning and impatiently dug at it with a soup spoon and—

"Jim! Maren!" he cried out.

The speculations, temporarily discontinued the night before, began anew. I recalled having read once an account of "witchcraft" wherein it was reported that the mere presence of a presumed witch made cows run dry and milk curdle. Such an association made me shiver, but it did seem to me that here we were dealing with phenomena which fell *somewhere* in that realm. How all the sour milk could be explained was difficult to perceive, yet the *fact* of the quite physical occurence could not be denied by any of us.

Before finishing breakfast we uncovered another loose piece in the dismantled puzzle: a garbage bag was found to be attached to the disposal device on the wall by the sink. None of us had done this; in fact several times I had said—as recently as the evening before—that one of us ought to put a bag up. Of course the cleaning lady could have done it—but the last three times, since Jim's death, she had used a garbage bag to line a wastebasket rather than putting it on the fixture. It immediately struck me that one of Jim's responsibilities around the flat had been to remove the garbage bag when full, drop it down the chute on the balcony and attach a clean one. It had been his habit to fasten it in an insecure way, which was how we found it now.

At 6:00 that evening I had a long-standing engagement to preach at Evensong at the chapel of Clare College. I suggested that Maren and David come along, feeling that this would provide them an opportunity to get out of the flat. So many strange occurrences made that a happy prospect.

I had been invited to stay after the service for dinner in the college refectory. My colleagues went on to dinner at the Blue Boar Hotel nearby, where they were to wait for me. During coffee with the fellows after dinner, though absorbed in conversation, I suddenly had a great awareness that the hour was important, and almost without thinking I turned and looked up at a large clock. *8:19!* The configuration of the hands hit me with an almost physical impact: 8:19 had become practically a symbol of Jim's living presence. I turned back to the conversation in which I was engaged, but the tone of the evening had changed and emerging was the conviction that my son was somehow making his presence felt in every way possible. I soon excused myself, although I had told David and Maren not to expect me before 8:45 or 9:00, and walked through the courtyard, out the great gate into an ancient lane, then down narrow Trinity Street to the Blue Boar.

Ψ

By now we had developed almost a ritual to be enacted upon each return to the flat. We carefully unlocked and opened the door as if we expected to see someone standing there—yet not really believing that that would be possible; we carefully surveyed each room to see whether anything had been moved or changed since our departure; and we reported and discussed each incident of unexplained phenomena whenever such was discovered.

On that particular Sunday evening, February 27, we entered the flat to find the rooms very warm—much warmer than would have been our preference had we been present. I had had a counseling appointment with a young priest of the Diocese of Ely just before we left for Clare College, and I knew I would have turned the thermostat down had the room been that warm during the interview. In any case, as the one who had been in England the longest and therefore most accustomed to lower room temperatures, I remembered checking the thermostat to see that it was down a bit while we were gone. By this time we had become quite impressionable and I could not help but remember that from time to time Jim had turned the temperature extremely high—so much so that it was a point of minor irritation.

We all searched the flat and found nothing until we entered my bedroom. There we found the Bible, which I had placed on the dresser after using it, on the floor between the twin beds by the night table—in the same place where the postcards and the books had been found. Further search turned up the Church of England Yearbook propped against the wall on the floor behind the electric heater. I remembered having used the directory in the living room that afternoon, for I was hoping by chance to find in it the phone number of the office of the Presiding Bishop of our American Church. When I was unable to find it I put down the Yearbook on the counter under the bookshelves and went into the bedroom to dial "Overseas" in order to reach him. I distinctly remembered that I had not taken the volume into the bedroom with me, let alone placed it in so bizarre a location. Moreover, there would have been no occasion upon which anyone would have placed the Yearbook on top—least of all behind—the heater.

These experiences were enough to convince me that something had to be done, so I organized a "Council of Advice." We sat down in the living room to make some decisions. I recalled and told them about a conversation I had had the previous spring.

When I went to England in May of 1965 to lecture to the five hundred priests ensconced in a Butlin's Holiday Camp at Clacton-on-Sea, Bishop Stockwood invited me to go to dinner in town one evening, together with Canon John Pearce-Higgins, Vice-Provost of Southwark Cathedral. We had a leisurely five-course meal at a good French restaurant and talked of many things—among which, quite memorably, were psychic phenomena. Since I had told the two of them about my forthcoming sabbatical, and of my plans to take this opportunity to rethink reflectively doctrinal questions, using the *facts + faith* method, they suggested that it would be a good idea for me to spend some time in London, where both the Churches' Fellowship and the Society for Psychical Research had extensive files, learning more about verified psychic phenomena as a basis for the affirmation of life after death.

Canon Pearce-Higgins, who spends many of his hours in this field, had offered to guide me in examining available data. As the subject-matter was not of predominant interest to me, however, and as I became so quickly engrossed in my study of Christian origins, I had not gotten around to contacting either the Lord Bishop or the Vice-Provost. I had, from time to time, noted that the press gave news coverage to reports of "hauntings," poltergeists or exorcisms (one by a brother Anglican bishop); and I gained the general impression that people were much more open to the possibility of not only survival but also communication with the dead in England than they were in the United States.

Ψ

We jointly made the decision to get in touch with John Pearce-Higgins to see whether he could be of any help. On the morning of February 28 I reached him by phone, and explained with some embarrassment that I regretted not having been in touch with him sooner. "But I am calling now not out of academic interest, John, but rather because I need—uh, professional help."

I then summarized for him the numerous odd events of the past eight days, and expressed to him our reluctantly arrived at conclusion that all of this somehow related to my son, who had recently taken his life in New York.

"Oh, yes, forgive me for not having expressed my condolences. I do recall a notice in the paper," Canon Pearce-Higgins responded. "Just how long ago was it that your son passed on?"

"It was in the early morning on February 4," I recalled, "so that would be about twenty-four days ago."

"And these phenomena began to occur when?" Pearce-Higgins asked.

"On February 20," I told him.

"Yes, of course . . ." he remarked. "In the case of a violent death—however caused—the spirit is left bewildered and is usually not able to manifest himself until a period of two weeks or so has gone by," was his explanation.

"I see," I replied—though I didn't exactly. "But what would be the point of such things?"

"In such cases there is usually one of two things going on," the Canon answered. "Either the entity is feeling hostility toward someone who is inhabiting the place which recently was his domicile, or the phenomena are attention-getting devices."

"Well, I can't imagine that it would be hostility about my staying on in the flat," I commented, "and if he is trying to get my attention—well, he's got it. What shall we do now? Do you think I should see a medium? I remember your mentioning—who? . . ."

"Mrs. Ena Twigg, yes. But it may well be a very simple message that your son is trying to give you," the Canon observed, "in which case it would not be necessary to see a medium at all. I would suggest that you sit down with another person, take an inverted wineglass and place it on a smooth surface, cut out pieces of paper with one letter of the alphabet on each and place them in a semicircle around the edge of the table; include slips with the words 'yes' and 'no' as well, and then the two of you place your fingertips lightly on opposite edges of the glass and see what happens."

I was not very enthusiastic about the idea. It sounded for all the world like a homemade ouija board, and ouija boards had always connoted dimly lit rooms and gypsy fortune-tellers. Nevertheless, something had to be done and I knew John Pearce-Higgins was not a fool, nor would he at a time like this be playing games. So we undertook the experiment. With the wineglass, the YES, the NO and the letters before us on a waxed coffee table, Maren and I sat attentively with our fingers poised on either side of the glass. Relatively quickly, the glass moved toward the letter M. Then after we returned the glass to the center of the semicircle, it much more slowly began to move toward the letter F.

Time passed, and nothing more seemed to happen, so David and Maren changed places. At one point the glass began to move again—after what seemed hours to me—and in order to test myself (and David) I gave it a little push to the left. Apparently now off course, it adjusted its direction and headed precisely the way it had been moving: to the letter B.

That was surprising, as was the fact of the moving of the wineglass at all. Nevertheless, I gave up. The whole process was too slow and ineffectual for me. And no amount of pondering produced a message out of MFB. MB = Maren Bergrud, maybe; but the F? I had no intention of spending hours sitting by a coffee table waiting for a wineglass to move around. I had too much to do before returning to the United

States to be playing parlor games. It seemed a waste of valuable time.

So I called Canon Pearce-Higgins again, reporting what I thought was the ineffectiveness of his suggested procedure, and asked again if he did not perhaps think it would be wise to call Mrs. Twigg.

"Well," Pearce-Higgins remarked somewhat hesitatingly, "I can try to get an appointment with her. She is the best sensitive I know, but I know that she is very busy and has very few appointment hours open. The best I can do is to try. I will call you back as soon as I have some word."

He did call back later that afternoon and informed me that the appointment had been arranged for two days hence, March 2, at 3:00 in the afternoon.

Ψ

So with a sense of relief, the day was spent working industriously on our several projects. Just before retiring that evening we noticed that there had been no phenomena all day. I commented, lightly, "Isn't it strange that there have been no episodes today. Maybe Jim is not going to come around any more. I've rather missed him." The episodes had been harmless for several days and we had become accustomed to the feeling that Jim was somehow present there. I did miss him, and didn't mind saying so.

"I hope we didn't wait too long to do something about all those phenomena," I added. "This is all so new to me that I took a long time to think of seeing a medium. I hope our slow response didn't discourage Jim."

As if on my invitation, an impressive series of events followed my remark that I "missed" Jim around. The next morning, March 1, we found books which had been moved, windows opened which had been closed, safety pins lying open in several places, clothes misplaced, and a broken Marlboro cigarette (Jim's brand, not smoked by any of the three of us) in front of the nightstand between the twin beds. The culmination of that day came in two episodes.

As we were examining a number of clothing items in Maren's bedroom which seemed to have been moved without our doing, we witnessed the first and only object in motion. Maren had reached into the closet for something when one of the four tissue-wrapped pieces of a silver dresser set bought in Wells, a little cathedral city in the southeast of England well known for its silver shops, began to move toward the edge of the shelf above the pole. As we watched in disbelief, the silver piece slowly slid off the shelf. Maren reacted just in time to catch the object before it hit the floor. Unwrapping it, we discovered it to be the hand mirror—the only one in the flat. We checked the other pieces of the set, only to find them securely placed at the very back of the shelf—which, if it slanted at all, slanted inward and down toward the back. Again I was reminded of the stories I had read of demons and witches. Mirrors often served as omens —usually ill omens. We were puzzled, yet certain that Jim was again making his presence felt.

"Let's try to get back to work," I urged, and we all returned to the living room. David went back to the table where he had been working with our diocesan journal and directory, but it was nowhere to be found. After a cursory look around by all three, Maren suddenly felt "led" (or "pushed"?) to my Samsonite attaché case in the bedroom.

As she started for the bedroom, with David and me trailing behind, I was saying reassuringly, "I'm sure it has to be here in the flat somewhere, because none of us has ever taken it anywhere else. Unless," I said smartly, "it has been moved somewhere like the C. of E. Yearbook."

And there it was in my attaché case, on top of the pamphlets and books I had taken with me on our last trip—a few days back.

As I look back on it now, I feel that perhaps we were overly credulous in attributing these various things to Jim. Yet the whole mood had developed to the point where we had really stopped searching for a different hypothesis. We now quite readily credited all otherwise inexplicable phenomena to Jim. We felt sure he was somehow responsible for it all. It was not until much, much later—far into my studies in the broad field of psychic phenomena—that another possible (but not simple) hypothesis was brought to my attention.

Ψ

Friday morning we rose in anticipation of finding out what the sitting with Ena Twigg might bring. Canon Pearce-Higgins was to go with us to take notes, and he suggested it would be better if only two strangers went along, due to the space limitation of her small "sitting room." (I gathered that this phrase was used in a special, not the general, sense.) Since David was eager to return to San Francisco within a few days and still had a great deal of work to do, he offered to be the one not to go.

In the hours prior to our departure we observed three more startling phenomena. First, a lock of blond, singed hair was found in the "usual" place by the nightstand between the twin beds. It was clearly Maren's hair, but a full week had passed since those episodes when her bangs had been burned off one section at a time. We had never been able to find even a trace of the burned-off portions. Yet here was a lock. Moreover, there was no sign of burning on Maren's hair that particular morning, nor had her bangs yet grown back noticeably.

Second, two open safety pins appeared on the ledge in the bathroom. We took note of them, but left them lying as found, at some distance from each other. Later, one of us discovered the pins rearranged. We all took note of the fact that the two pins were now in the same symmetrical position as the hands of the clock when they read 8:19, forming a 140° angle.

Finally, *Armageddon* was again found near the night table, somewhat under the left bed. In it was the postcard from Peterborough which still carried the small, torn piece of paper from the last time it had been "stuck" to a page. This time it was also attached with a mucilaginous substance which was smeared in such a way that a partial thumbprint could be seen.

"A thumbprint!" I exclaimed. "How can that possibly be?"

I looked (eyes narrowing a bit, I'm sure) at David and Maren. "Let's compare this with your—" then I added hastily to avoid revealing a suspicion—"and my fingerprints to see if there's any connection." We didn't have professional thumbprinting equipment but we all joined in the comparing and perceived no similarities.

How indeed could this—or any of these things—be? Later events and lengthy reflection helped me to provide two alternate answers to that question, but for the time being the assumption was that it could only be because Jim was somehow making it so.

5

Professor Bergson . . . urged that statements about life on the other side, properly studied, like travellers' tales, might ultimately furnish proof more logically cogent than was possible from mere access to earth-memories. . . . I am inclined to think that the time is getting ripe now for the production and discussion of material of this technically unverifiable kind; to be *scrutinised and tested by internal consistency and inherent probability,* in the same sort of way as travellers' tales have to be scrutinised and tested. . . .

—*Sir Oliver Lodge*

One of the arguments customarily used for life after death (and also as a partial answer to the age-old problem of evil) is that the obvious injustices and inequities men enjoy or suffer in this life can be put to rights in another one. But there is no empirical basis for this argument. It assumes more knowledge as to the nature and ways of God than we know or have any way of finding out. Similarly it assumes more knowledge of the arrangements after death than we have any factual or inferable way of knowing.

The consideration is not an irrelevant one: it falls in the same category as the comfort that belief in survival affords in bereavement and the answer it provides to the fear of death. As we saw, if one believes in ongoing life, these values indubitably exist; but the fact that the belief has these values neither proves it nor adds data to that from which the affirmation can plausibly be made. When it is used as an attempt at proof, it deserves the unbeliever's retort, "Wishful thinking!" So with the argument that if God is, He would raise all or some from the dead in order to even all scores.

Within the terms of the *data* + *faith* method, personal survival as natural—not supernatural—has been affirmed by the author and it would have been whether or not, using the same method, belief in God—which we are now considering—can be affirmed.

—*J.A.P.* in IF THIS BE HERESY

The home we approached in East Acton looked like a hundred others in the same vicinity: modest, with small, pleasant rooms, furniture of no particular period and a distinct air of "homeliness." Mrs. Ena Twigg, a woman in her forties, met us at the door. She was dressed in a becoming dress and looked very much like my image of a proper middle-class English housewife.

Mrs. Twigg had an engaging smile and a pleasant manner—halfway between talkative and garrulous. She invited us from the narrow stair hall into her living room, and, as we sat down, I couldn't help thinking how ironical it was that we should have come into such a common scene for what was for me a completely uncommon experience. Though as yet I had seen but little of the house, already I was sure that therein there were no dark rooms, red lights, incense pots or heavy curtains. This was obviously her home—in the most usual sense of the word.

Canon Pearce-Higgins had warned me as we drove in his car all the way from Southwark Cathedral, near that end of London Bridge which most sight-seers don't see, to East Acton in West London not to give away any information about myself, my family and least of all about Jim. "Then anything which might come through will be more evidentiary," he explained.

Had our hostess known literally nothing about me it would have been surprising, if not even a little insulting. She is a member of our Church, and, over the years, I had preached at St. Paul's Cathedral, Canterbury Cathedral, at York Minster and at various parish churches; on British

TV I had done several one-night stands and also a series. Further, English dailies and Church weeklies had carried stories about various heresy charges against me. And there had been pictures from time to time, including a large one of the Duke of Edinburgh and me in conversation. In any case, she at least knew my name, for John Pearce-Higgins had given her that when he phoned to set up the appointment.

The preliminary get-acquainted talk somehow turned to the state of the Church. Mrs. Twigg approached the subject with knowledge and candor. She seemed very much aware of the state of decline in the Church of England and spoke freely about it. Though she was not surprised to learn that the Episcopal Church still appeared to be relatively healthy, she had been enough of a thoughtful observer of the downward trend in England to predict that *our time would come.* Of course it *has,* as all now know except the most blithe optimists and parochially minded myopics in places which are still exceptions.

Still another psi manifestation? Precognition? Hardly. It did not take a "sensitive" to see that the Church of England was in serious decline because it had failed to meet adequately the challenge of the times. Having reached that conclusion myself, I had, in San Francisco on February 4 (the date of Jim's death), addressed a special conference of our clergy about the dangers ahead in the United States for our churches, which had fallen short of the mark in many respects already. I spoke with the urgency of a Paul Revere and with the solemnity of the handwriting on the wall at Belshazzar's banquet. The gist of the message: "Let's renew the Church while there are still people around to renew it with!"

But the fact that my prediction that we would decline if we didn't begin a rapid program of renewal is proving to have been correct doesn't mean that I am gifted with precognitive powers. The most widely available book—the Bible—challenges us all to read the signs of the times. Nor did Mrs. Twigg's astute comment, which is proving to be increasingly true so far, necessarily prove that she has psychic powers.

"She'll want to spend some time just getting acquainted," our canonical escort Pearce-Higgins had told us, "chatting about matters which have nothing to do with the purpose of your visit while she gets a feeling for you and your 'vibrations.' Then we will go upstairs to a small sitting room."

Ψ

When I sensed we had talked long enough, I asked to be excused to use her w.c. Frankly, the anticipation had made me a little nervous and uneasy. She directed me upstairs. I was again struck with what an ordinary house this was—like *anybody's* home.

Away from the others, I suddenly felt rather ridiculous for having been swept by a series of events into such a new situation without too much thought. The burden of work had been enormous. There had been deadlines for each segment hanging over the scene like swords of Damocles and an overarching ultimate deadline: the end of this marvelous, tragic, illuminating, somber, joyous sabbatical. In the midst of it all, I had had too little time for reflection. I now wished that, in regard to this matter, I had been less precipitous in my responses.

Then, as I put my hand on the doorknob to re-enter the hallway, I had a distinct awareness that my son was there; at that moment it would not have surprised me if as I came out I had met him in the hall—smiling at me. That was the life-sized picture which flashed through my mind as I opened the door. Not replacing this image, but sort of superimposed on it like a gloss, was a flashback to that other beautiful moment of meeting back in early January in Herzliya, Israel, when I opened a door, he smiled like that and then we embraced in joy.

Actually in the hall I saw nothing, and my conscious attention turned to the fact that I heard the others coming up the stairs and all together we were starting in to the small sitting room at the front of the house. Nevertheless, as I entered and took a chair, the intuition I had had that Jim was there remained as a quite warm feeling, beyond the momentary flashback to the reunion in Herzliya and the obvious recognition that neither Jim nor anyone else was visible as I re-entered the hall.

Ψ

The sitting room was quite small and was modestly furnished. But I was not unhappy about that. My fear had been of the opposite—heavy drapes, fringed silk lampshades, exotic ornaments, cluttered semidarkness. What unexamined assumptions we make about the unfamiliar! The furnishings were in fact so undistinguished that I cannot recall them. I do remember that the light was simply that which came through a window—flat and silver-gray, appropriate to a London afternoon in February.

"Do you happen to have something of your son's?" Mrs. Twigg asked me quietly as we all sat down. She smiled, with tenderness, as she waited for the answer—which was simply my reaching into a jacket pocket for Jim's passport, the original one he had left in Cambridge. I had brought it along because of Canon Pearce-Higgins' suggestion. But it was clear from the way she asked the question that having something of my son's was not essential. Her comment when I showed it to her was, "It will help."

We all fell silent. Though the idea was not suggested as appropriate, I felt prayerful; my head bowed some. The feeling—or *sensing*—was like what a Roman Catholic or Anglican generally feels when sitting or kneeling in a chapel where the Sacrament is reserved in a tabernacle or aumbry. He doesn't grasp the how of what is called "the Real Presence"; further, God is obviously present *everywhere*; yet . . .

Now Mrs. Twigg began to show some signs of discomfort and distress. "He's here," she said. "He's working hard to get through." She did not close her eyes nor did her posture or countenance change in any radical way. It was almost as if she were continuing our conversation of a few moments before.

"He was normally a boisterous and happy boy," she commented. Then she seemed to be speaking as if for another. "I failed the test, I can't face you, can't face life. I'm confused. Very sudden passing—have had to do this—couldn't find anyone. God, I didn't know what I was doing. But when I got here I found I wasn't such a failure as I thought. My nervous system failed."

Again—or should I say still—I sensed Jim's presence. In fact, I had a direct impression that he was standing behind and to the right of Mrs. Twigg, though I could see nothing. I listened intensely, sensing something of the suffering which seemed to be expressed. Mrs. Twigg went on, as if reporting someone else's words.

"I am not in purgatory—but something like hell, here," Jim seemed to say. "Yet nobody blames me here."

I puzzled over the words. What could this mean? Suffering, but not being blamed . . .

Then, "I hope nobody blames me *there.*"

"I've met my grandmother," was the next remark. That's not right, I thought to myself. (Both of his grandmothers were—and are—alive.) But I said nothing.

"You were under pressure at the same time. I was worried about you, Dad, because they were kicking you around."

Jim had called me "Dad"—that was characteristic—and we had, indeed, both been under pressure. Just how much I was under I was not fully able to tell then—or until nearly two and a half years later when the time of troubles I had actually gone through seemed finally to have passed.

"I came to your room, I moved books, I knocked on the door—came to your bedside—you dreamt about me and spoke to me," Mrs. Twigg's voice went on rapidly—speaking, it would seem, for Jim. The words rang true to our experience of the past two weeks even if the exact items did not match. I had not, for example, heard any knocks on the door. Yet the essence of our experience was certainly being articulated.

"I love you very much," the medium's voice went on. "So much love and no means of giving it." How true, I thought, how true. True in one sense now, true in another sense before he died. He was a loving person, yet he seemed incapable of breaking free to express his love. He had come to be able to express his love for me in words now and again during the last three or four months. But still I had the feeling he was blocked—generally not able to tell anyone freely what he really felt.

Mrs. Twigg went on, still quoting in the first person. "I'm tied to my regrets. Yet they are showing me the way out, and we must make progress together. I have to live my way and you yours."

Ψ

Then, after a pause, Mrs. Twigg shifted to the third person, speaking to me. "Send his love to the family—two girls, one boy," she directed. "He is saying something about a gate—golden . . . a golden gate. He says he's glad about that. Does that mean anything to you?" Mrs. Twigg asked.

Of course it did. My mind flashed back to the sadness/beauty of the day we scattered Jim's ashes on the blue, windblown water just beyond the Golden Gate.

Then back to the first person: "There are no clouds where I am—no confusion in the land of light." That sounds a little overdrawn, I thought to myself, in light of what seemed to be his earlier confusion.

"This is the way to freedom: to come back and try to explain," Mrs. Twigg's voice continued. She spoke haltingly now. "It wasn't intentional—everything snapped—too many pills."

I remembered Jim's desire to buy Romilar pills before leaving for New York—in direct contradiction to his earlier expression of intention not to take any more. I had discouraged him from buying any, but feared he might have anyway. This reference seemed a direct hit.

He then went on (if indeed it was Jim communicating) to mention Maren's August birthday and then the last name of a couple who are old family friends from the States, who will not here be identified as the material which follows is not entirely complimentary. There was reference to having seen them and then the words, "But they don't talk our language."

They had called Cambridge one evening in January from

London and it so happened that the next afternoon I was going down to London by train for an appointment, and Jim had decided to go along (under his standing invitation for all such trips). I suggested they come to our hotel, the Cumberland at Marble Arch, at six. My meeting ran late and I had difficulty in getting a cab in the rush-hour traffic and when I did the going was slow. So when I arrived they had come and gone since they had to make a plane for Copenhagen that evening.

I was sorry—but not too sorry—to miss them, but I found Jim quite irritated as a result of his visit with them alone. They had, he felt, given him quite a going over as to his studies, knowing of his former lack of motivation, and as to his future plans, still entirely uncertain—even the immediate future.

My response to his reaction was an obvious one. "Why, Jim, they were really interested—and wanted to show their interest."

"They weren't interested in *me*," he retorted. "They were nosy and prying and . . ."

"But . . ." I interrupted.

"It's not like *our* talking about things like that," Jim went on. "They're a whole generation away from us and I don't like them."

I remembered appreciating his sense of identification with me (though I felt he was probably a bit hard on his companions of the hour before) and the implied compliment (the couple are, I think, a little younger than I). My memory of this episode was quite clear because it had been another of those exceptions to his increasing ease in relating to adults —of various ages and make-ups—and an expression of that more negative side of his own personality during that period:

"They're not interested in *me* . . . I don't like them . . . I felt like splitting."

They don't talk our language./They're a whole generation away from us.

Ψ

"I'm breaking down the last enemy—death—so I suppose I have overcome."

Mrs. Twigg now spoke in the third person, looking directly at me with a kind of knowing smile, and said, "He had an eloquent tongue—big vocabulary—wanted to write—can help you with your writing."

"I'm not being blamed," she reported Jim as saying. "I've been met with compassion and understanding . . . *so* sorry it happened . . . so much to live for. Give my love to my sisters and to my buddies."

"He says to send love to Hillsborough—would they forgive him?" Mrs. Twigg commented. "He says he didn't mean to hurt." I wondered what that had reference to. I didn't recall anything he had done in Hillsborough that had hurt anyone. I would have to inquire about that, I thought.

"I've been so unhappy because I didn't have a voice and had to find a way to tell you. I can't believe in God as a person, but I do believe now in eternity," Jim seemed to comment. "*I thought there was a way out; I wanted out; I've found there is no way out. I wish I'd stayed to work out my problems in more familiar surroundings.*"

There flashed into my mind a page from a notebook of Jim's. There were some words—whenever written in it—which were not unrelated to what I was now hearing. When I got back to San Francisco I looked it up among his papers. It read:

The hospital is asleep. The bed squeaks; into a corridor. Dim even neon lighting casts no shadows anywhere; no corner crevices to hide. The layout is unknown: hall into hall and doors into rooms and doors into corridors. Sameness and dismal clean. Some instinct showing the way through to the one and main entrance from the dark cool night. Walk as if free but silent. The group breath is felt from all the walls, Faster. A double door metal green with horizontal bar; slow push aah. No, same door walled long hall. Good for cushion soles. To the left, laughter wheeling; follow it softly. There, there at the beginning, far down—the way. A black head and hands in bright white, leaning and reading and guarding. Walk on; Understand man understand. A grim nod no. Walk on, tensing, gathering growing and Now! Through into out. Run! Where? Run!

These words actually represented a more positive attitude —or at least a more active one. Only a short time before that Jim had described just such a hospital, saying he would have liked to "blow his mind" so he would be put in such a place for the rest of his life and just be taken care of. He had not chosen that way—but running had been to no avail either.

Mrs. Twigg's voice went on: "I know I can't die. But I couldn't be a Christian. I'm going to work very hard. Finals this year—perhaps I can take them over here? I think I'd have made it."

The words were coming so quickly I was glad that John Pearce-Higgins was getting much of it down in notes. I would certainly want to read his "minutes of the meeting" and think about it. But for now it seemed quite remarkable enough that I was here, and that I had such a persistent feeling that Jim was there and that somehow we were in touch.

Ψ

I had been, up to this point, silent—just listening. There was a hushed, nearly worshipful atmosphere in the room. I felt almost shy about addressing myself to Mrs. Twigg—or to Jim, if he were really in the scene *and* if he were addressable. But now I ventured to say, "Tell Jim I am flying to Chicago in a few days for a meeting and—" (I was intending to go on to say I'd call his mother from there to tell her about this session.)

"—and go on with the battle," the interrupting voice began. "Don't pull your punches."

The *Look* article had come out right after Jim's death. The churchly complaints from those who felt it exposed me as a heretic had sufficiently barraged our Presiding Bishop, the Most Rev. John E. Hines, that when he called me from the San Francisco airport (en route to the South Pacific) to express condolences, he also told me of his concern about these charges and suggested that I should meet with him and the eight bishops who were presidents of the provinces (regional groupings of dioceses) soon after my return to the United States at the end of the sabbatical.

I readily assented. In fact I told him that in preparation for the confab I would send to each a copy of *What Is This Treasure,* due off the presses any day. I was glad that the timing was such that I had not been able to alter the text of *Treasure* to reflect the decision I had reached by January that there was not sufficient data to affirm an afterlife, for through my own experiences I had come again to an affirmation which made the charge that I did not believe in the Resurrection of Jesus a false one. My own experiences made me more sympathetic with the difficulties the writers of the Gospels must have had when trying to record, so many years after their occurrence, events which would be hard to believe under any circumstances. Nevertheless, the inconsistency of the accounts in itself was not sufficient reason for questioning the events. That some kind of communication took place between Jesus and his disciples following his death would seem apparent from the fact that he alone, among many Messiah-pretenders, was elevated by a considerable number of his contemporaries to the status of "the one who will come again in glory" after his apparent defeat on the cross. So I was eager to meet with my brother bishops and to discuss all this and other doctrinal matters with them.

I was surprised indeed, however, to receive in Cambridge a cable from New York signed "John Hines" with the flat announcement that the meeting was all set for a Thursday in late February, three weeks before I was due to return. An overseas call to his office revealed that Bishop Hines was somewhere across the Pacific. His secretary had sent the wire after clearing the date with the other bishops. It was, she said, one of three dates suggested to her by the Presiding Bishop before he talked to me.

I felt this began to smell of inquisition—or, to change the figure, I felt as if I was being called on the carpet. And, on a lower level of disturbance, I chafed somewhat at the inconvience of making the extra trip so short a time before I was to return to the States for good. On the other hand, I really looked forward to the session. I had been urging—with no results—ever since the St. Louis convention of 1964 that the bishops have theological dialogue. Now here it was to be—or at least so I then thought.

It seemed that Jim, through Mrs. Twigg, had immediately grasped the main present import of "Chicago" and I appreciated his supportive if brief comment.

"*Thanks*, Jim," I replied. "But what I was starting to say is that while there I'll be calling your mother to tell her about what's going on here now."

"Good," was the response. "I want her to know—to know I really love her—that I'm alive."

"She believes that, Jim," I responded reassuringly. "*She* did all along. By the way, about things in your new situation: are you . . . alone, or—"

"I have masses of people around me, and hands lifting me up, as it were," came through—and, after a pause, "I was so unhappy until I could make you know."

Then, unmistakably, Mrs. Twigg spoke for herself. "Someone with a foreign accent—German, I think—is speaking. Wait . . . *Paul*, there is a Paul here. He says, 'Don't worry about the boy. He's in safekeeping. He is surrounded by our love.' And he says to tell you, Bishop, to be a rebel with a cause, for a rebel without a cause is ineffective. He says he's still working—that nothing destroys his faith. He sends you his love, and shares a common bond. He says, 'Thank you for dedicating your new book to me.'"

I was taken aback—and deeply moved. There was indeed a deceased friend with a German accent to whom (along with Bishop John Robinson) I dedicated my *What Is This Treasure*. The dedicatory page of that book read:

TO
PAUL TILLICH
PRINCIPAL MENTOR AND
DEAR FRIEND MUCH MISSED
AND
✠ JOHN A. T. ROBINSON
GOOD FRIEND AND
COMPANION-SPIRIT ALONG
THE WAY

Dr. Tillich, who had died the previous winter, had been a guest in both the Deanery in New York and the Bishop's

House in San Francisco. Jim and he knew each other but it seemed unlikely that Mrs. Twigg could have known that. Neither did it seem likely she could have known about my book or the dedication. At the time I spoke to her Harper & Row back in the States just barely had *What Is This Treasure* off the presses.

Unfortunately, at that time I was too new to the whole process to react quickly enough to ask any questions which might have further pointed to his identity. It was much later that I began to develop some sophistication as to how identity can be checked during a séance. Never having given thought to such matters, I simply received what was said more or less "straight."

Paul Tillich seemed to go on. "The boy was a visionary, born out of due time. He found a society distressing in which sensitivity is classified as weakness." That rang true enough to what I knew of Jim's problems.

Jim seemed to interrupt. "I want to thank the scribe [Canon Pearce-Higgins] for acting as an intermediary and helping me to find the path."

Ψ

I then made bold to address Jim directly, feeling somewhat strange in doing so since he was of course nowhere to be seen. "Did you know that was going to happen when you left me at the airport?"

He seemed to reply, "I had a fear of it—because I dreaded your leaving me this last time."

Paul Tillich seemed to break in again—it was almost as if the two of them were competing for the privilege of speaking—"Fight for freedom. Why fear to rush in when the angels are already there? It is—"

"Now, Paul," Ena Twigg interrupted with a gentle, chiding tone and expression suggesting both irritation and amusement, "one of you will have to speak at a time, and this man's son has been trying to say something."

Apparently so. The next words were: "Have I betrayed your trust?"

"No, of course not," I answered. Then, wanting clearly to be reassuring, I reported, "David Barr and I are working here on a detailed plan of linking the churches, schools and other institutions of our diocese to needs in the Diocese of Matabeleland. You'll remember the very difficult problem of education for young Africans there. Also, remember we discussed how they couldn't have a regular vote unless they had property or education and—"

"—the whites saw to it few could have either," came as an interruption, but one relevant—and correct.

"Right," I continued. "Well, we knew you wouldn't want a lot of money spent on flowers at the service for you; so we said, in effect, don't send flowers—"

"I know—the two bouquets in the sanctuary were quite enough," was the response.

Strangely enough—or maybe not so strangely—by now I was feeling quite at ease in what seemed like relaxed conversing with Jim. And so I went on.

"Well, instead we spread the word—that was easy: the diocesan Convention was on all the next day—that people could give to a college scholarship fund for black Rhodesian students. And *lots* of people did—close to five thousand dollars to help with. And the news about [I hesitated] . . . you at that point added to the impetus of the appeal I had made for purchase of grade school scholarship tickets—you know the idea we thought up—"

"The price of a fifth of Scotch will educate a kid for a year," came as interrupting words, "—that?"

"Yeah," I went on. "Well, three hundred plus were 'sold' right away. So you will have helped a lot of people here, as well as your—should I say, 'program' there."

"I am working here," was the response, "in order to learn to utilize any gift I have to serve the world. Better communication is one thing; but meanwhile my book of poems—you have it—will you keep it?—it's yours—can you get it published?"

Jim had had at 9 Carlton Court a ruled pad in which he wrote poems—sort of prose poems. He always left it on the top of the small desk near the window in the living room. He added poems as the spirit moved him. Sometimes he would show me one he had finished. I would always read slowly and thoughtfully—for three reasons: because it was supportive, because I could thereby know my son better, and because, generally, I liked the poem. Not always—a couple, I remember, had been written while he was on a trip. Interesting, had I not been his father; but disturbing since I was. The handwriting was always clear—but not the import.

He took the pad with him to New York. When I next saw it in San Francisco, where it had been mailed by the New York City police, there were quite a few more poems in it. These he had written in his hotel room. Handwriting clear. Meaning? Total nonsense.

All this quickly flashed through my mind. It was a winnowing process: I was left with a focus on the Cambridge poems written when he was himself. I answered in terms of these.

"Some of them, Jim, maybe could be published," I said quietly. "I'll look at them when I'm—[how to put it?]—a little further along."

"When *I'm* further along," he seemed to say, "when I get more experienced I will try to use words again and help you in your future thought and writing. In fact, I already have helped you. Remember our discussions about life after death? *Well, I guess we settled that one.*"

I did indeed remember—and it did seem to be settled. And although since that time I have examined and re-examined the events which led me to become convinced that Jim lived on—and therefore, that we all do—and although I am aware of some alternate explanations for most of the whole body of phenomena I myself experienced, nevertheless, these same events and phenomena led me into a vast field of study which has enabled me to affirm, on a basis of quite independent, well-established and scientifically assessed data, that men—even now before death—do indeed transcend the time-space continuum, and that this conclusion, plus much reliable psychic phenomena, makes plausible the inference that it is of the nature of man to survive death. Yes, if this was indeed Jim, he had most certainly headed me toward a great deal of evidence to help me settle (with care, learned counsel and some intelligence) a concern which is a fundamental element in my structure of faith.*

Ψ

Paul Tillich then seemed to break in again. "I did not know that this was possible." The reference seemed to be to communication through a medium. And then three terse sentences: "Which way will the Episcopal Church go? It's good that there should be lots of disturbance. Don't go hat in hand."

* See the chapter on "Life after Death" in my *If This Be Heresy* (New York: Harper & Row, 1967), pp. 112–62.

Taken without any contextual background these comments seemed both disconnected and irrelevant. But they really weren't—as was particularly evident to me as I sat in London that afternoon. I had mixed feelings about that round trip I would soon be making to Chicago.

In the silence which followed, a warm, indeed tender, feeling about Paul Tillich came over me. *Which way will the Episcopal Church go?* recalled his ambivalence about Anglicanism. He was attracted by the philosophical, sacramental and mythological aspects of its heritage; but he was put off by its pretensions, its stuffiness and its staidness. *It's good that there should be lots of disturbance.* Paul had been a resource for some of the disturbance manifest already. Several images arose. First, I remembered his surprise—combined with a modest amount of pleasure—when I told him during a two-day visit one summer at his East Hampton home that as of that time it appeared that he and Martin Buber were the most significant contemporary influences on thinking in the Episcopal Church. Next, there flashed through my mind the Theological Reformers window we had put in one of the newly constructed bays of Grace Cathedral, in which he and Dr. Buber appeared along with Father Karl Rahner, S.J., as representing the bold edge of theological reconstruction. Finally, I thought of one of his best-known books, *The Courage to Be,* as a token reflection of his own witness to courage and the disdaining of compromise. *Don't go hat in hand.*

These words did me good. But quite apart from their being supportive as to what lay ahead of me, I was struck with how much in character they were with their purported source.

Ψ

I was not sure at this point whether Canon Pearce-Higgins had made a connection with Paul Tillich in his mind; but it seemed that he sensed that a significant and thoughtful person had "come through," for he appeared to ask for advice on the pursuit of what had been his principal intellectual and pastoral interest.

"Is it a good thing," was his question, "to spread knowledge of survival and communication?"

An answer seemed to come from Dr. Tillich: "A prairie fire can cause chaos if it's left uncontrolled. *Work carefully.* But keep in mind the familiar words, 'Ye shall know the truth, and the truth shall make you free.' "

"That reminds me . . ."

"Yes, Jim," Mrs. Twigg interposed.

". . . that nothing I've seen over here makes me any more inclined to believe in God."

"Are you trying to say something, Paul?" Mrs. Twigg asked. Then, directing her words to me, "That German accent again."

"Well, he hasn't been here very long," the voice continued. "*I* still hold the belief, but I now conceive of it somewhat differently—"

"Give my love to Mom." This seemed to be Jim, interrupting—as though he sensed that the channel of communication would not long be open. I also seemed to be sensing that right then: it was sort of like a battery running down. But there were a few more scattered comments: "We've all got to grow. Be kind, gentle. Tell her I've been back. Give her a kiss from me. I'll be with you in June. We are beyond grief—we've defeated the last enemy. And, by the way, Dad, there'll be no more disturbances now, no more movements."

And indeed there weren't—for a long time.

6

I believe it is foolish not to recognise that psychical research may have much to teach us about our mysterious selves. We should not rule out the possibility that the next great advance in our knowledge will come in this part of the field. Eminent philosophers are now aware of the need to take account of the phenomena and their interpretation; it seems that theologians cannot long remain indifferent. . . .

The case for telepathy is so strong that one is tempted to say that the only way to retain disbelief in it is by steadily ignoring the evidence.

—*The Very Rev. W. S. Matthews*

Telepathy is something which ought not to happen at all, if the materialistic theory were true. But it does happen. So there must be something seriously wrong with the materialistic theory, however numerous and imposing the *normal* facts which support it may be . . . I would again like to address myself to the people . . . who agree that psychical research has succeeded in establishing various queer facts about the human mind, but think that these facts are mere curiosities and oddities, of no particular importance. Certainly card-guessing does appear at first sight to be a rather trivial occupation. And if a few dreams turn out to be telepathic visions, why should anyone make such a fuss about it? On the contrary, these queer facts are not at all trivial, and it is right to make the greatest possible fuss about them. Their very queerness is just what makes them so significant. We call them "queer" just because they will not fit in with orthodox scientific ideas about the universe and man's place in it. If they show, as I think they do, that the materialistic conception of human personality is untenable, and if they throw quite new light on the age-old conflict between the scientific and the religious outlooks, we shall have to conclude that psychical research is one of the most important branches of investigation which the human mind has ever undertaken.

—*Prof. H. H. Price*

The next twelve days passed all too quickly since there was a great amount of work to do. My attention turned, after the sitting, almost entirely to my various projects—including some remaining speaking engagements and a day-long conference with a Dead Sea Scrolls scholar. With the time short, and no phenomena to distract, persistence—even pressure—characterized my mood.

This regimen carried over to the time on the plane to Chicago and back. Along went my attaché case, in which there is room for my battery dictaphone. The contents of this small piece of luggage fully occupied me until I was drowsy enough to lapse into a few hours' sleep before arrival. Before resuming work after getting settled in my room at the O'Hare Inn (day rate, since I was due to take the plane back to London at about 6:00), I called Esther in San Francisco. Of course I would have anyway; but I also remember vividly what, at Mrs. Twigg's, had seemed to be a request from Jim that I give her his love.

I hadn't wanted to carry out this assignment by letter, for one not directly participating in what I would be reporting would find it hard to believe. I wanted to spell out all the preceding happenings in the flat at Cambridge as well as to report on the séance, and to do so (as the length of the present book up to this point would suggest) would have taken a very long letter. Because *before* I had been with Ena Twigg I had known that the Chicago trip was upcoming, I had decided to wait these few remaining days and carry through from Chicago—from which the toll rate for a phone call would be considerably cheaper.

In this long call I spelled out everything from the appearance of the two postcards between the twin beds on through the content of the hour with Mrs. Twigg. Esther's response was one with which I have since become quite familiar. Since she was the first one to whom I had told the story I was quite relieved to find that she neither denied nor minimized the data. She expressed not so much as an inference that I was deluded or that I had made it up—for example, to try to provide additional comfort to her, or to me, or for any other reason. Further, as has already been mentioned, she believed in personal survival after death—a belief which of course encompassed our son.

However, she was quite hesitant to accept the reality or possibility of actual communication from the dead to the living. Thus, while not dismissing out of hand the psychic communication hypothesis, she felt sure that there must be some other explanation (or, to be more precise, some combination of explanations) for what she was willing to accept as actual happenings.

Ψ

This whole field not having been of particular interest to me, I had not read a single book or essay by anyone—scholar or otherwise—on any aspect of the subject. Hence, I wasn't particularly familiar with what I later learned were well-recognized alternative categories of explanation for various types of phenomena. So I wasn't in a position to appreciate the implications of the possibilities Esther presented then and later—from what was a quite "lay" background in this regard on her own part.

However, neither did Esther's reaction disturb me. I felt a kind of obligation to pass on what had happened. The earthly connection with and memories about the loved one to whom it all related were our shared possession, and it would have been difficult to ignore what had seemed to be an explicit request from him. But I felt no evangelistic drive to make a convert—of Esther or of anyone else—to belief in the reality of psychic communication. Nor did I feel a pastoral responsibility to seek to convince her. She believed in ongoing life—even when, at the time of Jim's death, I had not; so all along she had had the comfort which that firm conviction brought her.

The more obvious counterexplanations, I had, of course, thought of. As has already been pointed out, though I had no particular reason to mistrust either David or Maren—in general, or in this particular regard—I had become quite watchful of them, as indeed each of them later indicated that they had become of me, and of each other. Also I had wondered a little about myself. But Maren's and David's sharing in the observation of the poltergeist phenomena, the presence of Canon Pearce-Higgins and Maren at Mrs. Twigg's, and especially the "minutes of the meeting" the Canon had promptly supplied had eliminated from my mind the possibility of some kind of wish-fulfilling self-delusion.

I don't quite recall what Esther suggested as the alternative hypothesis for the Cambridge happenings. But as to the somewhat surprising content of the London sitting, she proposed that what came out could well be explained by a combination of things: previous knowledge of the medium, extrasensory perception of items consciously present in my mind, a telepathic drawing on items in my unconscious mind (a kind of "depth ESP") and, as to the items left over, "memory traces" somehow remaining extant after Jim's physical death.

My response to the mention of these categories was a

mixed one. As to previous knowledge of the medium, I had no reason to believe that she had much. As for conscious-level ESP, I readily enough granted the part this could have played. (Since this comes up fairly often as a proffered alternative explanation, it has interested me to note how the increased attention focused on psychic phenomena has brought forth, as a by-product, a positive affirmation as to the reality of ESP on the part of many persons—I am not here including Esther—who had not believed in it before, but who will readily support telepathy when confronted with inescapable facts which would otherwise seem to suggest communication from the dead.)

As for unconscious-level ESP, this was a category I had not thought about before and as to which I had heard of no laboratory experimentation. This was in contrast to my awareness of experiments in which conscious attempts are made to "send" symbols, words and pictures—a process which I had understood required a high degree of mental concentration. And, finally, I knew of no verified data pointing to the existence of disembodied *and* depersonalized segments of what had been human memory. Superficially perhaps, it occurred to me that unless there were some significant data which could be subsumed under the category of memory traces, belief in this explanation would require as much faith (perhaps more) as belief in the possibility of communication from surviving conscious personalities.

Ψ

This spelling out of possible hypotheses for explaining various items without use of the survival and spirit-communication hypothesis was indeed a useful guide to analysis. However, there is something which the "sitter" may sense which a person to whom the experience is retold does not—or at least to the same degree—which somehow transcends all such categories. It is this. In the forty-five minutes (plus or minus) of such a dialogue, a person present can be impressed with a seeming unity about the whole thing. The experience is somewhat similar to talking over the phone for a comparable length of time with an acquaintance. As far as actual proof goes, five or six different persons could be spelling one another on the other end of the telephone line. But an inference is made that it is only *one* person—both because of the continuity of thought and because of a subjective-intuitive sensing of the "style" of communication.

A related point occurred to me—one not quite so subjective. It is easy to grant that a medium would at the least be sensitive to what is in the conscious mind of the sitter (in fact, a synonym for medium is "sensitive," used as a noun). Somewhat less easy to assume is that a given medium (or any medium for that matter) is sensitive to what is in the unconscious mind of the sitter and to "memory traces" (if there be such). But let's assume for the moment that a given medium has this wide-ranging ability of reception. There are quite a few items in one's conscious mind at any given time, and there are many, many more items stored away in the unconscious—some near the surface, some deep down in the vault. And, to complete the picture, if the memory-trace hypothesis reflects reality, there must be vast numbers of such traces floating around. Yet in the séance with Mrs. Twigg the *scope* of communication was relatively limited. There was a "lead" who had practically all the lines, with one other taking what could be called a "bit part." So this question occurred to me: what would account for the severely delimiting selection process which was apparently at work?

I had no doubt that it would take faith to attribute what had happened to an entity or entities on "the other side." The phenomena which occurred—even if such were multiplied many times over through séance after séance—did not absolutely *require* the affirmation of survival and communication. Or, to reverse the statement and put it in the framework of contemporary semantic analysis, the survival-communication conclusion is not *entailed* in the data.

Yet it seemed that the more complex alternative would certainly require no less faith. To break it down, requisites would be

faith that sensitives have the capacity to pull facts and images out of another's unconscious mind;

faith that memory traces of the past are objectively real in the present;

faith that these can be "read" by a sensitive;

faith in some hypothesis (what it might be did not then occur to me) about a selector or constellator able to provide a relatively focused interview.

Then, in addition to all this, one would need a plausible hypothesis (again, apart from that of the activity of a deceased entity) for the many external happenings in the Cambridge flat. As to those, by then nothing had occurred to me as an alternative to have faith in. But quite apart from this last category, it seemed that the more complex hypothesis called for more faith than my initial response to what, granted, were most unusual happenings.

This called to mind two respectable norms of selection which, though somewhat different in genesis and in forms of statement, come down to about the same thing when applied to the present field. The first is what has been commonly (though erroneously) called *Occam's razor:* categories of explanation are not to be multiplied beyond need. The second is *the principle of parsimony:* the more is in vain when the less will serve (to account for the facts to be explained).*

Some of these thoughts which flooded my mind, with the conversation with Esther as a catalyst, I expressed in words —tentatively, not evangelistically; some I did not. My relatively detached reaction to the possible alternative explanations was natural, for I had no particular intention of carrying through with this field as a major area of study, experimentation and analysis. The conversation moved on to catching up with the other children and some speculation on my part as to what might be coming up at the forthcoming session that day.

Ψ

Before long it was time to look for my fellow bishops, whom I was to meet at lunch. Small talk of the ecclesiastical genre was as far as we got—and were supposed to get—at the meal. But as we rose the Presiding Bishop suggested that I go to my room and that he would call me when they were ready for me. This I did—and I was glad that I had along a new book on Jewish sects at the time of Jesus. As I read and underlined passages (I always try to follow the injunction of our Collect for the Second Sunday in Advent: "Read, *mark,* learn and inwardly digest."), competing somewhat with that work was reflection on some of the categories mentioned by Esther. And in competition with both activities,

* See more fully the author's *If This Be Heresy* (New York: Harper & Row, 1967), p. 154, esp. notes 58 and 59.

increasingly, was concern as to what I would be hearing from my brother bishops closeted in another part of the motel. As time went on I reassured myself that I was certain to hear the phone ring before it was time to take the mini-bus from the Inn over to the airport. But I became less and less sure that there would be adequate time left for full and careful dialogue on all the points which the *Look* article could possibly have raised hackles about.

But my fears were groundless. When the call came and I had joined the others down the hall it was almost immediately evident that, whatever had been discussed behind my back, the approach agreed on was not one of substantive discussion of the truth, falsity or permissibility of various expressions of belief. Apart from a somewhat complex debate (which scarcely related to the Kingdom of God) sparked by two diverse and groundless charges by a fellow lawyer-bishop of violation of a provision of canon law and a Prayer Book rubric, the rest of the discussion fell more into the category of public relations than of theology.

The outcome was a ready agreement on my part to write a letter to *Look:* correction, in regard to a couple of points; clarification, in regard to several others; fuller explanation and apologetic, with regard to the remaining points in question. I frankly expressed my serious doubt, having had considerable experience with popular magazines, that a letter of this type would be run—and especially in this case, for three reasons: they were already about to run a letter covering the only serious error, which I deliberately limited to this one point so that it would be of sufficient brevity to be published; there would be quite a span between the publication of the article and the arrival of the letter; and the type of statement which would accomplish what my brethren in the purple had in mind would have to be far longer than any letter which, I'm sure, had appeared in the thirty or so years of the magazine's publication.

Bishop Hines reassured me that this didn't matter: that the main thing was to be able to get out copies of it right away to the Church's hundred and ninety bishops—both for their own edification and to enable them better to answer challenges coming to them from the priests and lay people of their dioceses.

Ψ

As our jet took off on my return trip to London late that afternoon I thought again of the words "Don't go hat in hand," and I had a quiet sense of satisfaction that, in spite of the post-luncheon agenda, which had provided a very appropriate format for such an attitude on my part, I had at no point slipped into a suppliant or defensive role. (Not atypical was my response to Bishop Hines' opening gambit: "Jim, have you ever thought of the little people?": "John, I find the little people are getting bigger all the time.") My thoughts about what seemed to relate to this subject in the session with Mrs. Twigg went on from there for a little while. Whatever the source of the sentiments, I thought, they had been supportive. Of the two possible reactions at O'Hare —accommodation for the sake of peace and safety, or saying it the way it is and keeping one's cool—the latter is the way I hope I would have chosen in any case.

But the temptation to choose the former is, in such situations, always there and, though I dislike admitting it, I know what it is to choose it. Suppose, I thought, a case seemed to be 50/50 as to the wisest approach in regard to this or any other pair of possibilities in a situation. And suppose, further, the counsel was known for sure to be from a deceased relative or friend—one most certainly benevolent, not malevolent. Then, I asked myself, should one regard such instructions as though they came from an oracle, as though they were infallible?

I drew what for me seemed the only possible analogy within the limits of earth-bound thought. It so happened that I had received advice from Jim and from Paul Tillich while each was in this earthly plane. And on reflection I realized that in each case I had taken such advice seriously: both were certainly benevolent toward me and knew me well enough to be able to advise me. Paul did not know me as well as my son Jim, particularly after our coming to Cambridge, but he knew me quite well and, in addition to being a very wise man, had experienced a lot of living.

Yet, on reflection, it was quite clear that at no point had I regarded either of them as infallible. In fact it was not with too much difficulty that I recalled an instance or two, with respect to each, when I had not followed proffered advice—and, it would appear, for good and sufficient reason. Therefore it seemed to me that a person continuing on after death would not simply by virtue of that fact become automatically infinite in knowledge and insight and infallible in decision and judgment. Whatever else might be true about all this, I concluded that the oracle idea was out.

But I did not find such a conclusion disappointing. Rather, it was a warming thought—particularly with reference to the instance which started these reflections: I could think of my dear son Jim and of a good friend of long standing like Paul Tillich as real persons, limited but loving.

Ψ

With a six-hour time change it was morning when I landed in London. My chaplain drove down from Cambridge the night before, put up at an airport motel and met my plane. Naturally he wanted to know what went on, and the narration was a good springboard for talking out—while we bypassed Greater London and drove directly northeast toward Cambridge—the lengthy letter to *Look* which I would have to get written right away—after a little sleep.

If this expenditure of time were to have its expected value, it was important that the work be completed as soon as possible. So, with all else there was to do—principally the completion of the Matabeleland project—I put everything aside and concentrated on a statement which, hopefully, would put to rest various misunderstandings and at the same time avoid any compromise or yielding of ground on positions thoughtfully taken.

After several revisions, the final version of the document was completed and copies were ready for mailing, with covering letters to the appropriate person at *Look* and to the Presiding Bishop. The effort took much more time than I had anticipated, and since I was determined to let nothing get in the way of doing my part to clarify the issues raised by my brother bishops, several important matters went unattended to. Among the latter was a letter to Esther.

Before heading down to the post office with the two rather bulky missives (seeing them off in person and finding the method of sending them with the utmost dispatch seemed to be of high priority), I decided to push myself further to the borders of my remaining energy and cover the points about some important family matters in an Express (the British for Special Delivery) letter to Esther. I rolled a blue "air letter" into the typewriter and proceeded automatically to type the well-known addresses without the need of concentration. In fact, I was talking to David about our forthcoming photo-finish mailing expedition. Then I reversed the sheet and typed the letter. As soon as this sheet was sealed, we drove down to the center of Cambridge and fulfilled our intention of getting everything off before the main post office closed.

But it turned out that I needn't have been in such a hurry! Both the longer and the shorter compositions had frustrating fates. I learned late in the debate of a resolution to censure me at the House of Bishops' meeting in Wheeling the next fall that, much to my surprise, the essay I had prepared for the bishops had not in fact been mailed to them. It was only after the censure was voted, and when thereafter I reminded him again, that the Presiding Bishop mailed the copies out—*eight months* after he had received my letter. A clear case of "locking the barn door after the horse was stolen."

As for the letter to Esther, I found to my surprise in a telephone conversation from Washington, on my way home from Cambridge, that it had never reached her. In fact, when after three days of Lenten preaching I was able finally to get to San Francisco, the letter still was not there.

Several days after I had gotten back to the office routine I received a letter from my only surviving aunt, Mrs. Walter F. Larkey, who lives in Campbellsville, Kentucky. She enclosed, unopened, the letter I had mailed to Esther. We do not frequently correspond. In fact, the last letter from my Aunt Ethyl came to Cambridge in the early fall and I put it, after reading it, in a pile (which grew increasingly higher) on a corner of the long counter in the kitchen-dinette, which was the locale for letters I planned to answer, or reports I hoped to read, when and if there should be time. I had not seen the letter since then. Nor did I know her address by memory.

Yet on that March afternoon it was the Larkey address I used when, my mind not at all on it, I was filling out the part of the air letter form for the addressee. The factor in common was "Jackson Street." The Bishop's house was—is—at 2510 Jackson Street, San Francisco. The address for my aunt and uncle was 508 Jackson Street, Campbellsville, Ky. 42718. But, as we shall see, before I learned of the actual misaddressing of the letter, I had been given a clue as to why such a thing might have happened.

Ψ

The very evening the important mailings got off, I bore down with my companions on the revision of the long Matabeleland report. Two days later all loose ends had been tied up and it was in final form with covering memo, and ready for David to take back with him to San Francisco for stenciling and mimeographing. So he and Maren were able to pack their bags and get under way.

The remaining days I spent getting ready for my final departure. I sorted, threw things away, packed the quite considerable library to which the few books I had brought had expanded during the six months and began to divide books, papers and clothing into the categories of sea freight, air freight and luggage for the plane. I also took the various steps required to detach myself as a British resident, some contact being necessary with each of the public agencies (there are more such under a socialist state) and private companies I had become involved with in settling in. In the midst of all this I had final interviews with several of the scholars with whom I had worked most closely in my major fields of interest—theological method and Christian origins.

The last thing I did was to resell (as per previous arrangement) my automobile to the dealer. Then I left by train for London.

I thought of Jim often during those last few days, for it was really like a motion picture being run backward: going through in reverse—and alone this time—the process that he and I had shared with such joy only six months before as we settled in as Cantabrigians.

Ψ

It had occurred to me that should I ever have occasion to want to be in touch with Jim in the United States, I wouldn't have the vaguest idea how to go about it. So, although there had been no additional "signals," and my schedule was tight, I decided it was appropriate to see Mrs. Twigg once more before leaving—not knowing then when I would be getting back to London. I had made an appointment to see her at 10:00 o'clock the morning of March 14, four hours before I was scheduled to fly to Washington, D.C.

Unfortunately, I have misplaced the notes of that occasion, and at two years' distance with so many intervening events, it would be foolish even to attempt to reconstruct the full or exact content of that sitting. There are, however, certain unforgettable items which are worth mentioning even though I have no notes to substantiate them.

Mrs. Twigg went into a trance on this second occasion. I had never experienced trance mediumship before, and I found it even more perplexing than the clairaudient approach. She closed her eyes and seemed to go to sleep (though I have since learned a trance is not really that). When she began to speak, my son Jim seemed to come through entirely in the first person in contrast to the third-person form of a number of the statements the previous time. It seemed throughout that I was in direct conversation with him.

It came through that I was going to continue a life of scholarship and Jim wanted to be of help to me. In fact, as I recall it, these words were used: "You will soon be leaving your post in order to continue your studies." I demurred, since I had not at that time thought of resigning as a diocesan. This evoked, "You will. I'll be with you come August." This entirely puzzled me; but I didn't forget it.

Then I turned to something seemingly more realistic: "Should I want to be in touch, how would I go about it? I don't know anyone in the States who is a medium."

"Just a minute," Jim seemed to reply. There was a pause, as if someone were being consulted. Then not a sentence, but four phrases. "Spiritual Frontiers—a Father Rauscher—priest of the Church—in New Jersey."

There followed some words of caution—or I should say, instruction, since they were not really negative or prohibitory. They had to do with the possible effects—on me—of being involved often in mediumistic sittings.

"You mean I shouldn't do this very often?" I asked. My reaction was one of curiosity, not one of disappointment.

"No, I don't mean that," was the reply. "It's just that it can have an 'opening up' effect, I gather. There may be less screening out. The effects can be surprising, I've been told. But surprising is not the same as 'bad'!"

I understood, both in theory and from having gone through analysis, that most of what is in the unconscious mind is blocked from conscious perception most of the time. All the more was this true of items in what the late Dr. Carl G. Jung of Zurich called the "collective unconscious."

I also recalled that LSD and other psychedelic drugs work as they do, not by themselves providing the various images and experiences, but by numbing, as it were, the portion of the brain that serves as a filter, thus allowing material to float up from the unconscious. I learned later that the same result can occur non-chemically. Religious experiences reported by Western mystics often took place after periods of fasting which resulted in dietary deficiencies. (St. Jerome's vivid "trip" in the desert is an obvious example, and it is certainly possible that what are reported as Jesus' "temptations" in the desert fell into that category.) And soon after my return to San Francisco I learned of research at the Langley-Porter Clinic at the University of California Medical School in which experiments intended to determine whether subjects could learn to discriminate and then control states of electrical activity of the brain resulted in the occurrence of states resembling those induced by meditation.

(Selected for these latter experiments, Mike Murphy dropped over one evening after a session at the clinic and gave a very fresh account of what had happened. He had been invited to participate in the experiments because of his years of practicing meditation. He said he had been placed in a small, totally dark room where he was to sit, eyes closed, with his head connected to an electroencephalograph. He was then given two main tasks to perform: that of turning on a sound, or tone, or that of turning the tone off. In a surprisingly short length of time, Mike said he was able to be successful at the task. The tone sounded when the alpha-wave appeared on the encephalograph and was silent when the alpha-wave disappeared. The occurrence of the alpha-wave is common in meditation states, for the emptying of the mind facilitates it. In the course of the experiments when he had begun to be successful at controlling the electrical activity of his brain, Mike had a series of experiences. The imagery of one corresponded very closely to the trip Jim told me about in Cambridge in which the words HINDU ESCAPE COLUMN came to him: Mike also felt and saw a column which he was able to "enter" and "ascend." At the time I had been amazed at the similarity of the two experiences.)

I also recalled, while sitting at Mrs. Twigg's that afternoon, having learned in 1965 from Eugene Exman, at that time religious editor of Harper & Row, and "Bill W.," founder of Alcoholics Anonymous, about the accidental discovery that schizophrenia can result from the corruption of bodily adrenaline into adrenaluten, which has the same effect chemically as mescaline (the synthetic equivalent of peyote): it releases the inhibiting "screen" in the brain. The biochemical result is that the sufferer is kept on a continuous trip, with images flooding his mind. Fortunately it had been discovered that the result of adrenaluten in the system can be counteracted by massive doses of vitamin B_3 (nicotinic acid) and that recovery can be nourished along through participation in a new type of group, Schizophrenia Anonymous, of which Bill was also recently the founder.

So, by a combination of facts, intuition and analogy, I readily got the point that Jim seemed to be making. If by these other causes an individual's guard could be lowered, there was no reason why in the profound process—whatever precisely it is—which is operative in psychic communication, something of the same sort could not well occur. It was this concept which I later felt might explain my mystifying mistyping of Esther's address. Perhaps all the phenomena in the apartment and the London séance had somehow reduced the effectiveness of my selective screen and I had "picked up," by some process of ESP combined with the association of the word "Jackson," my aunt's address instead.

As for séances, I saw no real danger of my susceptibility

to the "lowered guard" thesis. It did not seem likely I would overindulge when I had never before had any particular interest in such activities. There had been a distinct reason for each of the two sittings I had experienced: the earlier one because of the many physical phenomena, and the second because I was departing from England with no idea of when I might be returning. In any case (and that's the way it turned out) the circumstances of my life kept me so occupied with pressing matters that there simply was no time to become preoccupied with psychic activities, even if I would have tended that way under less-pressured circumstances—which I doubt.

The events in Cambridge had been surprising enough, however, that I had no reason to foreclose the possibility of phenomena—seemingly notice-giving, or otherwise—in the future; hence I had raised the question about the United States and mediums. So, in responding to the words about possible effects I also expressed thanks for the lead in case I should need it since I was now going back to the United States.

"I know you are," then came through. "In fact you are going to Virginia."

"No," I corrected. But it occurred to me that the geographical reference might be to the fact that sometimes in going to Washington for preaching or speaking there had been time for me to go to Annandale, Virginia, in Fairfax County across the Potomac River, where Jim's aunt and uncle, the Stephen Haycocks, lived, or to the part of suburban Washington which is in Virginia for an address or sermon. So I went on, "This time, Jim, in addition to the noonday sermons at the Church of the Epiphany downtown, I am doing an evening series at a Presbyterian church in a Maryland suburb. With all this, plus late-afternoon engagements, I won't be able to get out to see Aunt Ruth, Uncle Steve and the children or do anything else across the river."

"But you *are* going to Virginia." The words were repeated.

I saw no point in going on with the matter. The fact that this seemed clearly in error did not serve as a negative in evaluating the process. It occurred to me that "it's the hits that count." Also, I recalled again my reflections on the fallibility and finiteness of persons, in whatever setting.

Ψ

I remember, too, that gratification was expressed because I had not compromised nor "yielded ground" at the O'Hare Inn session. Also, an indication was made that what I had said in the letter was good, but that "the time of troubles" with the bishops would not come to an end for some time.* I was advised—with Paul referred to as supporting the conviction—to keep on preaching, speaking and lecturing along the lines of theological reconstruction and not to hesitate to let my thinking continue to evolve.

This brought my mind back to the brief theological comments expressed the first time I had been with Mrs. Twigg, and I spoke up: "How about yours? Any new insight?"

"Yes," was the answer. "Now I feel there is *Something*. It's beginning to make sense to assume that Someone is making things hang together and develop." Just as I was about to say, "Good," more words rushed out as though what

* This whole unedifying bit of ecclesiastical history, including *ante* and *post* "wheeling dealing," is covered in the thorough and carefully documented "Who Done It" by William Stringfellow and Anthony Towne, *The Bishop Pike Affair: Scandals of Conscience and Heresy, Relevance and Solemnity in the Contemporary Church* (New York: Harper & Row, 1967). See also: The Rev. Lester Kinsolving, "The Bishop's Not for Burning," *Ramparts*, January 1967. As to the final outcome of the matter, see chapters 7, 8 and 10 below.

I was going to say was sensed: "—but since I've been here I haven't heard *anything* about a Jesus."

Then it was indicated that, nevertheless, there was a great deal more to be learned and there were a number of people helping. And then the words: "I'm beginning to feel somewhat more at home—more at peace."

The reference to "people around"—and it wasn't the first—was an affirmative one and carried the impression that there was appreciation of relationships. This was good to hear, in the light of how things seemed to be before Jim passed on. "Apparently you are aware of individuals," I went on.

I was reassured that he was, indeed. And the desire was expressed to know more people and to know them better.

"Do you think of people there as male and female?" I continued. "Is there something like—like intimate expression?"

The terms of the answer seemed almost to express amusement at my delicacy of expression: it was very much like Jim. Without a pause: "Sex? Yes, there is sex. But it is not like it is there. It is not physical, of course, but actually there is less limitation. It is more obviously like what sex really means. Here you actually can enter the whole person. It is like you are in fact merging—becoming one."

Ψ

I know that much more came through in the session, but without notes I am not certain of more—except I do recall that several times in the sitting there were the words, "I am beginning to learn." I do remember, though, how it ended. It just sort of "ran down," and Mrs. Twigg lapsed into silence. She was breathing heavily and was showing no signs of coming to consciousness. I began to be somewhat concerned but I was in doubt as to what, if anything, should be done. Not being experienced with persons in trance states I instinctively responded in terms of my years of pastoral calls on the sick: I reached in my pocket for my "oil stock" (a small silver container for olive oil which is traditionally used in the sacrament of healing—as provided in our Prayer Book), laid my hands firmly on her head and anointed her forehead with the sign of the cross. Mrs. Twigg immediately "revived," saying, "What—what did you do?"

"I used Holy Unction. I hope that was all right to do. I got concerned that you didn't seem to be coming out of it," I explained.

"You did just the right thing," she said, smiling. As soon as she was fully alert, knowing that I had to leave for the airport shortly, I called a cab. While waiting I tried to get a clarification of one of the answers which had come through —the one which pointed to a possible entree in the future should that seem needful or appropriate.

"Could you tell me more about the group that was mentioned—'Spiritual Frontiers' I think it was." She looked blank. I pressed a little, "Don't you recall?"

"You just mentioned my not seeming to come out of the trance. Well, when I've been that way I have no way of knowing what may have come through for you."

I was embarrassed by my naïveté and hence overlooked asking the question differently: namely, did she in fact know anything about an American organization called Spiritual Frontiers and/or a Father Rauscher. Instead, I simply said, "Of course," and expressed my gratitude for her time and effort, promising to keep in touch. The cab came promptly and I was on my way to the airport.

Ψ

As we winged over southwestern England, southern Wales and out over the Irish Sea I simply let myself *feel* . . . a jumble of feelings. Negative ones: I had flown this route the other way last September with Jim and I was returning without him. As for the purpose of the sabbatical leave, so much not accomplished, so much more to pursue—especially on Christian origins. Some dread of the pile-up of things awaiting my attention in the diocese. A marked sense of aloneness. Positive feelings: A warm recognition that "this realm, this England" was the place where I had come to know my son deeply. And how many windows of thought opened during the time in Cambridge! Anticipation of being back with family and colleagues, so many of whom were supportive —and would be in the things I cared about.

By the time we had left sight of Eire I had brought such rumination to an end, not allowing myself to decide whether I was more sad than happy, by plunging assiduously into the contents of a large attaché case—an accumulation of papers I was unable to sort out before my departure. I read, threw away, clipped, wrote notes—not even interrupting the work when dinner was served. With the five-hour time change it was still light outside when my attention was arrested by the last word of a routine announcement: "Please fasten your seat belts. We are beginning our descent to the Dulles International Airport—in Virginia."

Virginia! When I had been told that I would be going to Virginia my mind only reacted in terms of the city to which I was going—Washington—not thinking of the airport at which I would be landing. So I had simply "washed out" the comment—whatever its actual source. I was struck with astonishment when the word came again through the loudspeaker in the plane's cabin.

Ψ

The few days in Washington were filled to overflowing. For years I had preached at Epiphany Church downtown in the capital city at the Wednesday late afternoon service and noondays on Thursday and Friday. But that year I also preached at evening services in a suburban Presbyterian church, Chevy Chase, and in addition there were the usual television and radio appearances, visits with friends, interviews, etc. On Saturday I flew on to California and immediately plunged into the full range of my diocesan duties.

During Holy Week I returned to the East to preach noondays at St. Thomas Episcopal Church on Fifth Avenue, another long-standing yearly tradition for me and one which I particularly cherished after moving to California, since it gave me an opportunity to keep in touch with friends in New York where I had served for many years. But more than that, there was a continuity to these occasions—both in the possibility of really developing a theme for five consecutive half hours, and in the fact that many of the people came for all of them, since I had over the years developed a kind of "following" in Manhattan.

Because of the new insights gained during my sabbatical it was with particular enthusiasm that I launched my sermon series that particular Monday, challenging for the first time from a pulpit the credibility of the conventional *omni*-affirmations about God.* The response of the parishioners at the door matched my own enthusiasm.

After I had greeted a few people, one of the curates, the Rev. J. Lawrence ("Larry") Williams, stepped up to speak to me a moment. Pointing to an older man, about my height with a rather ruddy face, standing near the tract rack, he said,

* The thoughts there expressed have been more fully developed in *If This Be Heresy*, pp. 195–97.

"There is a minister with whom I am having lunch who would like to speak to you for a moment."

I told him that I was due at a luncheon with the editorial staff of *Time* magazine, but that I would be glad to visit with him briefly, and I smiled over at the clergyman in question. When finally I had finished the greetings in the narthex I went over to the gentleman.

"I'm glad to meet you," I said, not having caught his name.

He explained that he had arrived a little early for his engagement with the Rev. Mr. Williams, saw there was a service going on and slipped into a back pew.

"I wanted to tell you," he continued, "that while you were talking there were two figures standing behind you. One was a tall young man—the name 'Jim' was coming through—your son, I presume; the other was a patriarchal figure, quite a bit shorter—the name 'Elias' kept coming through, which I believe is the form in the Greek Old Testament and in the Latin Vulgate for the name of the prophet Elijah."

I was somewhat astounded by this outpouring. Who was this man? How did he know that my son's maternal grandfather was named Elias?

"I seemed to see grain—growing wheat," he went on. " 'Courage!' seemed to be the word to you, and I just thought you should know."

I thought of Jim's reference to grain growing as we went to sleep after the Christmas Eve Midnight Mass in Nazareth when he had urged me to preach candidly at our church at the service on Christmas Day.

I was really quite amazed, yet I was conscious of the luncheon appointments each of us had, so I decided not to pursue the subject no matter how interesting a conversation with him about the whole matter might prove to be. However, not to be abrupt, I said, rather vaguely, I'm afraid: "Yes . . . well, thank you. What church do you serve?"

"Well, I'm actually not at a church. I am connected with a group called Spiritual Frontiers Fellowship."

That rang a bell, of course. Then, testing what had come through Mrs. Twigg, I asked, "Where is that?"

"It's all over," he replied.

That got me nowhere. I tried again. "Does it have anything special in New Jersey?"

"Well, our president, a Father Rauscher—of your Church—is in New Jersey. Perhaps that's what you're thinking of."

"Yes . . . yes, of course." There it was: the confirmation of the information which had come through in the trance séance. This was impressive indeed. Things were so busy on my return I hadn't even so much as thought about that part of the sitting in the intervening weeks.

We parted.

It wasn't until a year and a half later—in Toronto—that I learned the name of the man who spoke to me that day in New York City. He was the noted American medium, the Rev. Arthur Ford, a Disciples of Christ minister.

Ψ

Back in the diocese I soon felt like the canary bird caught in the badminton game. After six months of relief from administrative duties—with freedom to pursue my academic interests and time for reading, study, thought and writing—I found it difficult indeed simultaneously to maintain my role as a diocesan corporation president and to continue my work as scholar and communicator. It didn't take me long to decide that I did not want to go on trying to be both administrator and theologian-teacher. I became convinced that one or the other role had to be chosen, and I decided for the latter.

As to how best to implement the decision, in late April I sought the advice of one whom I had always much admired and in whose judgment I had great confidence, Dr. Robert M. Hutchins, President of the Center for the Study of Democratic Institutions in Santa Barbara. I liked one of his suggestions especially—and ended up on the staff of the Center. I could imagine nothing more suitable: a kind of graduate faculty without students. I knew I would have the freedom to write and speak while being nourished by, as well as contributing to, the common life of the Center staff by means of the daily seminar sessions. In May I made my decision to resign as Bishop of California.

The effecting of such a dramatic change was not exactly uncomplicated. Pursuant to canon law, first my resignation had to be submitted to the diocesan Standing Committee. Its members were kind enough not to be enthusiastic, but after a couple of hours talking it out, they concurred and I decided to make my resignation effective September 15, 1966, going on vacation and terminal leave July 15.

Then I needed the consent of a majority of my brother bishops on the basis of a letter of explanation from me to the Presiding Bishop. Somehow the word leaked to the press well before this process was completed; but fortunately the consent was granted. The deluge of events which automatically followed the announcement of my resignation was almost overwhelming: farewell visits to each of seven deaneries of the diocese, letters, memos, radio and television shows, and planning with the Standing Committee for the election of a new bishop—such as the selection of a representative nominating committee and the initiation of their work. In addition, there was the ongoing flow of daily responsibilities.

Getting my things packed and ready to move seemed relatively minor in relation to the host of arrangements that had to be made just to make the physical move possible. My eighty-two-year-old mother had to be taken into account. For the previous several years (since the death of her third husband—the third she outlived), she had been living in a retirement home in San Francisco. As her only offspring, I could not responsibly leave her there, however. It seemed the best thing I could do was take her with me to Santa Barbara. Since I would be living alone (the family was staying in San Francisco), we determined to get a rather large apartment (two bedrooms and two baths) and move in together. Also, this arrangement made it more feasible to see the family fairly frequently.

Then somehow I knew I needed to make provision for help with my work once in Santa Barbara. The Center would engage a full-time secretary at my recommendation, so mustering all of my persuasive powers (knowing she had served for twenty years as secretary to the bishops in the Diocese of California), I invited—indeed urged—Miss Myrtle Goodwin to continue with me and move to Santa Barbara to serve as my secretary at the Center. After due deliberation she agreed to go, and that gave me a genuine feeling of reassurance: I knew she would be of inestimable help since, in addition to being an excellent secretary—and person—she was interested in my scholarly pursuits, was familiar with all ecclesiastical aspects of my life and most of the persons connected therewith, and would help provide an important link of continuity.

I was also trying to finish the book I had begun in England. I didn't see how I could finish it for the November deadline when beginning a new job unless I had help on it, too. It was natural that I should think of Maren Bergrud, who had put in some time with me on the book in Cambridge. Inquiry in Maren's direction also bore fruit: she was still in convalescence and had not yet taken on full-time work, though she had been back from Europe for some time; she was ready for a change, having already spent quite a bit of time with each of her three stepchildren; and she was happy to pitch in and help on the wrap-up of the book. It was agreed that she would come to Santa Barbara to finish her convalescence, working part time to help me finish *You and the New Morality: 74 Cases* (published by Harper & Row in February of 1967). Although that project was a short-term one and I could only speculate whether I would need—and could afford—further help in other projects following its completion, she, like Myrtle, agreed to make the change.

Then finally, adjustments had to be made in my fall schedule to accommodate the change of residence. I had already agreed to teach a course at the Law School of the University of California in collaboration with the Graduate Theological Union, in Berkeley, on "Law & Ethics in State and Church: Conflicts between, and Reconciliation of, Structure and Conscience." I scheduled it for Friday afternoons to allow me time to fly up for them each weekend, so that as one of the non-stipendiary clergy of the diocese (a category I had encouraged—and was now joining as the fifty-eighth "worker-priest") I could more conveniently take confirmation services in the diocese on weekends. Such episcopal assistance was needed for that fall on a more frequent basis than was necessary once my successor had been elected, confirmed by the majority of the standing committees and bishops of the other dioceses, and then (already being a bishop) installed.

My closing three weeks in San Francisco were full indeed. By long-standing previous arrangement I was teaching two summer session courses in Berkeley at the Pacific School of Religion under the titles of "The New Theology" and "The New Morality," winding up all arrangements for moving, finishing—or delegating—chores still on deck and working out my mother's move. Finally, the evening of July 15, I winged my way to Santa Barbara—and a new life.

7

Human experience, which is constantly contradicting theory, is the great test of truth.

—*Dr. Samuel Johnson*

. . . There can be no doubt that the events described happened and were correctly reported; that the odds against chance-coincidence piled up to billions to one; and that the nature of the events, which involved both telepathy and precognition, conflicts with one or more of the basic limiting principles. . . .

It seems to me fairly plain that the establishment of paranormal precognition required a radical change in our conception of time, and probably a correlated change in our conception of causation.

—*Prof. C. D. Broad*

If only one percent of the money spent upon the physical and biological sciences could be spent upon investigations of religious experience and psychical research, it might not be long before a new age of faith dawned upon the world.

—*Sir Alister Hardy*

Memory has somehow conflated the events of my first weeks in Santa Barbara into a blur of impressions without fixed sequential order in time. Getting settled into an apartment with my mother was no small trick. Confusion reigned, with furniture, books and papers, clothes and box after box of miscellaneous items, unsorted, which neither of us knew quite why we had but could not readily determine to throw away. I arranged to have bookshelves built and the process of unpacking and sorting went on.

At the same time I made a few forays up to the Center for the Study of Democratic Institutions, where I was to begin work on August 1, checking my new office, arranging for essential supplies, getting acquainted with some of my new colleagues, sitting in on a seminar or two. My mood was one of eager anticipation; I knew that I would be very happy there.

And in the middle of it all there arrived from Texas some good friends, in bereavement from the loss of their baby girl whom I had baptized in Houston just a few weeks before. Along with our talks, I put them to work helping me unpack and sort my library of about five thousand volumes into piles of books to go up to my study at the Center, books to shelve in the apartment and books to store; took them with me to the Center for a seminar and luncheon one day; and somehow caught up with their news in the midst of the disorder surrounding us.

It is perhaps surprising, then, that anything could really capture my attention (even momentarily) during those days, but not unusual that I should have failed to make detailed notes of the order of events. The occurrences themselves are clear enough in my memory for me to be able at least to point to their significance, however.

It was my intention, in addition to my general responsibilities at the Center, to pursue two principal special areas of study: Christian origins and the relationship of the institutional Church in its time of troubles to the health of other institutions and values in transition in our society. I had begun my work on the former, as already mentioned, while on sabbatical in England and had kept up with it as best I could in the months following my return. It was much on my mind, especially as I more and more began to see connections between factors in the formative period of the Church and its current problems and tensions—especially in regard to today's issues in society. Interest in the latter was sparked by recently published studies by sociologists which had revealed disturbing inverse correlations between frequency of church attendance and the number of doctrines believed on the one hand, and wholesome socioethical attitudes and behavior, on the other. I felt that it was important to delve further into the significance of such data and its roots in the Christian tradition.

Gaining an understanding today of the origin of Christianity is like putting together a huge jigsaw puzzle. Both because it would take far more space than would be appropriate to use in this book and because it will form the subject of two forthcoming books of mine, I will limit myself to a brief description of one small part of that puzzle which is connected with a most peculiar phenomenon which occurred in the newly occupied apartment before two weeks of our residence had passed.

It has been conventionally assumed that the Last Supper, i.e., the Passover Seder celebrated by Jesus and his disciples before Jesus' crucifixion, took place on Thursday night, "the night before He was betrayed." This, however, presents an almost impossible time-squeeze for the actual occurrence of all the events recorded. Required to be fitted in are the Seder itself, the walk to the Mount of Olives, the period of prayer in the Garden of Gethsemane, the hearing before Annas, the trial before Caiaphas, the trial before Pilate, the scourging, the Via Dolorosa, the crucifixion, the period of Jesus' dying on the cross and his being taken down from the cross—all from "Maundy Thursday" evening through Friday at sunset, when the Sabbath would begin.

There had been called to my attention a study by a French Roman Catholic scholar, Mlle. Annie Jaubert, on this question,* in which she discusses the difference between the official Jewish calendar in use in Jesus' day and the earlier calendar still used by the members of the Essene movement (among whose literature are the Qumrân, or Dead Sea, Scrolls). Calculating according to the latter, the Seder in question would have been celebrated on Tuesday night. Needless to say, this date makes all the rest much more plausible. And the observance of this feature of Essene life by Jesus and his followers and/or the writers of the Synoptic Gospels and/or the Christian Jewish communities in the milieu in which they wrote would not be intrinsically impossible—in fact would be quite plausible—in the light of the many other connections which were becoming more and more apparent to me in the course of my studies.

It was in this context that one day during the period of settling in—if I remember correctly, the last before I was actually to begin at the Center—I happened to think about this particular point and wondered how this theory would fit with the account in the Fourth Gospel in which it would seem that the supper was not in fact the Seder, but rather was celebrated on the *eve* of the Passover. I must see if Mlle.

* *The Date of the Last Supper* (New York: Alba House, 1965).

Jaubert talks about this question, I thought; or if she doesn't, maybe with some digging around I can figure it out myself.

The question was interesting to me, but not a matter of the greatest moment, and soon my thoughts were interrupted by a sudden realization that I was up against a deadline on a response I had agreed to write for *Playboy* magazine to an article published in their August 1966 issue, "The Death of God" by Dr. William Hamilton.

This recall occurring late in the day, I had phoned to ask Maren Bergrud if she could join my mother and me for dinner and then stay on to help me get the piece out. Close to dinnertime the evening paper arrived and I sat down on the couch to take a few minutes before Maren's arrival to catch up on the day's news.

My attention was drawn to a book on the coffee table which I had not seen there before. It was *The Date of the Last Supper*! Naturally I picked it up and started to open it. It could not help but open at the place where there was a postcard inserted. The card was one of the Beersheba camel pictures, which I didn't remember unpacking. Further, it was lightly stuck to the page with one little spot of mucilaginous substance something like that which had appeared in similar situations in England. I immediately thought of the Cambridge flat and had a rather "here we go again" feeling. Then I noticed that the place in the book (page 95) where I found the card was the beginning of a small chapter entitled "Solution of the Conflict Between John and the Synoptics"!

Just at this point Maren arrived and the three of us sat down to dinner; after clearing the table, Maren and I immediately settled down to work there on the piece for *Playboy*. I was dictating directly to the typewriter, moving right along on the writing, when it occurred to me it would be helpful to have the first of the UNESCO volumes on the history of civilization for material by which I could make somewhat more precise a point I had in mind. I told Maren how helpful that book would be, but added that all my books were in such a mess there was no point holding up the completion of the article to look for it.

The rather extensive "Letter to the Editor" (prearranged by request of the editor, with "equal time" allotted to Professor Hamilton) completed, Maren left, taking the envelope to mail as she went. I eventually went to bed to do a little reading before falling asleep. I reached down to get the Jaubert book, which I had put on the shelf of the nightstand —after telling my mother and Maren what had happened —just before dinner. I was anxious to read the chapter which had so surprisingly come to my attention. In groping for the book, I dropped it; and to retrieve it I couldn't avoid noticing a sizable volume there on the floor: the first volume of the UNESCO series on the history of civilization!

Could this be Jim again, I wondered. Then something from that second sitting with Mrs. Twigg—the day I left England —flashed through my mind: *I'll be in touch come August.* And then I remembered that that had been said after the advice—and the prediction—about changing my position. Perhaps, indeed, he wanted to be in touch. Tomorrow morning was August 1 and tomorrow morning I was beginning in the new situation. Tonight? As an Episcopal clergyman I was liturgically acclimated for it to fall in place: tonight was as significant as tomorrow. Tonight was the eve of the feast day!

Ψ

The next morning, driving up from the apartment house on Coast Village Road to Eucalyptus Hill and the Center, I had a feeling that I should be following up soon on the two happenings—perhaps meant as attention-getting. I of course remembered (it having been mentioned twice now—in the sitting room at Ena Twigg's and in the narthex of St. Thomas' Church) Spiritual Frontiers. So I wondered whether anyone connected with that group was to be found in the Santa Barbara area.

I went directly to my new office with this question still hovering subliminally. In a matter of minutes one of my new colleagues, Mr. Irving Laucks, came into my office to return a journal I had lent him several days before, one of the times I had gone up before arriving officially. "This isn't the kind of thing I meant," he explained.

Mr. Laucks had approached me the day I took the Maco Stewarts to a seminar at the Center to ask if I was interested in a scientific approach to religion. Thinking immediately of the statistical correlations and analyses being done by sociologists and psychologists on religion, I reported that I had recently learned of—and, at its invitation, joined—an association called the Society for the Scientific Study of Religion, which publishes a journal on that very subject. I offered to lend him the only copy I had of the journal, suggesting that when he looked it over he might decide he would be interested in reading the subsequent issues, which I would be glad to share with him as they came along. I took it up to him the next day or so. He was now returning it.

"What I really had in mind," he explained, "was the study of ESP, psychic phenomena and the like in relation to religion."

"Oh, I see!" I was genuinely surprised to find someone at the Center who was interested in such things.

"Have you explored those fields at all?" he inquired.

"Well, as a matter of fact, I just had some experiences last night that I think tie into that very area," I replied with some hesitation—I hadn't yet begun to speak about any of this except to the family. I very briefly indicated, in summary form, the variety of experiences I had had which had caused me to take an active interest in the whole psi field, suggesting that we could talk further about it all sometime. As we walked out into the colonnade which surrounds the central open court I commented that I had a feeling I should be seeing someone if indeed my son was trying to contact me again. "But I don't know anyone here," I remarked.

Mr. Laucks shook his head slowly. "No," he said, "I don't either."

Just then I looked up and saw coming toward me a tall, blue-eyed fellow with gray hair. "John McConnell!" I called out, extending my hand.

"Bishop Pike! I knew you were coming to the Center, of course, but I didn't know whether you would be here yet. I'm so glad I caught you," he responded.

"Come on in." I motioned to my office. "What brings you to Santa Barbara?"

"We've been having some meetings for persons interested in Minute for Peace," he explained. John heads a movement which urges radio stations across the country to set aside a minute for peace, providing tape-recordings for the brief interlude. (After the sounding of the United Nations Peace Bell, a public figure says a word about peace, which is followed by a short meditation period. The idea is to offer people of all creeds an opportunity to unite, each in his own way, in thoughts or prayers for world peace.) I had first met John in San Francisco when he had come to my office in Diocesan House to explain his program to me, to ask for my support and to see if I could suggest other persons for him to contact.

"Well, how's it going?" I asked with genuine interest. John was now seated across my desk from me.

"Very well; getting off the ground. I'd certainly be pleased if you would agree to record a message for us," he said.

I said I'd be happy to and suggested that shortly we could go down to the seminar room and do the brief recording. In the meantime I inquired how the meeting he attended in Santa Barbara had been.

"Good group?" I asked.

"Yes. Incidentally, there was a very interesting minister at the meeting Friday night, the Rev. George Daisley."

"Oh? What church is he with?" I asked—mainly to show polite interest.

"Well, it's not exactly a church," he answered. "He's affiliated with Spiritual Frontiers."

"*Spiritual Frontiers*," I repeated. Then: "What's his name again?"

"George Daisley," John reported, and I quickly jotted down a note. "A quite remarkable man," he observed.

"He's probably a medium," I commented, not knowing how much John knew about the subject.

"Yes, he is. In fact, I arranged for a sitting with him," he remarked matter-of-factly. "It was my first experience with a medium. I wish you could meet him."

"I'd like to," I said instantly. "I *will.*"

"You'll remember," John continued, "I promised to get you the names and addresses of those who I told you had those experiences the night of your son's death. Well, I have them. I brought them along in case I'd catch you either in San Francisco or here."

"Why, thank you, John. I'll want to make notes of this." I remembered that John had come to see me at Diocesan House on what happened to be my last day in my office in

San Francisco. He had called Myrtle for an appointment. Thinking he was coming about Minute for Peace, and being quite overburdened with last-minute responsibilities, I at first told Myrtle I felt I was just too busy to see him.

"He seemed to have something personal to talk over with you, Bishop," Myrtle commented, knowing that I don't turn away persons who seem to want to see me pastorally.

"Then go ahead and set it up," I said. "I'll make time somehow."

I remembered that it turned out that John had come not for help for himself, but to share with me some experiences—both his and others—which occurred in the early morning of the day Jim took his life. John said he had awakened suddenly in the wee hours of Friday morning, February 4, with a terrible sense of dread—as though he were dying, he said. "I struggled in my mind to cling to life and to understand the meaning of the feeling. It then seemed to me that someone—not in my own family—was dying and I should pray for him. I wept and stayed in intercessory prayer for what seemed about two hours."

At that time John was living at the New York Theological Seminary. He told me that the next morning in the elevator he met a friend who was also staying there and that she could hardly wait to tell him what she described as a horrible experience during the night. She told John that in the early hours of the morning she had experienced being suddenly awakened by someone knocking at the door in the women's dormitory section. She went to open it and saw two awful faces of evil—and then she woke, knowing she had been in bed all along. But the nightmare had been so disturbing she could not go back to sleep and remained awake until daylight with a deep sense or feeling that something terrible had happened.

Before his friend (who has personally verified these facts by letter) learned of Jim's death, John had continued, she made a long-distance phone call—rather impulsively—to a friend of hers at an upstate college who had known Jim when I was Dean of the Cathedral of St. John the Divine in New York (she was the daughter of one of the canons). The two girls had not been in touch for some time.

From the papers John and his friend learned of Jim's death and connected their experiences with the time he died. She then realized what a strange thing it was—especially after her scary nighttime experience—that Jim had been mentioned in the course of that phone conversation the morning of his death. Neither John nor his friend had known Jim personally—John knew me; she knew of Jim only through that mutual friend.

Finally, John had reported that he had mentioned these strange experiences a week later during a prayer meeting at St. Mark's Lutheran Church in Brooklyn, and that the pastor reported he had been similarly awakened on the same morning at, it would appear, the same hour.

Upon hearing John and Pastor Prang's stories, another person present, a Miss Anna Marie Zacharias (later to become Mrs. John McConnell), recalled a strange episode in her life on the same morning. She told the group her story, assuming it was somehow also related to Jim's struggles.

Miss Zacharias reported that she woke around 3:00 A.M. on February 4, with a great fear. Then she continued: "I remember praying to Jesus to lift the fear. Also, I remember trying to pin-point who or what was the connection. Through a struggle of approximately an hour I was more and more consciously aware that something terrible was happening somewhere in the world. I did not know where, how or to whom. I kept repeating Jesus' name and asking that it be lifted. About an hour after this struggle started, I felt a lifting and went to sleep."

Now, on that afternoon in Santa Barbara, I remembered well all that John had related to me, for it seemed to corroborate the experience of two others who were also in New York on that fatal early morning.

Not long after Jim's death I received a letter from a man in New York reporting virtually the same experience. This concerned Nan and Billie, the two friends Jim was so eager to visit during that brief stopover in New York.

Knowing Jim's plans, I had dropped Nan a line before leaving Cambridge, saying Jim would be stopping off in New York by himself primarily because he wanted to see her and Billie, and that I hoped she could await a call from him late in the afternoon or early in the evening on February 2 as I still had some concern about his use of psychedelics. When she received no call from Jim by late evening on the second, Nan called Billie. Intuitively she felt all was not well, so between them she and Billie called some thirty hotels in New York, trying to find Jim.

They were unable to locate him. In the early morning of February 4, they were both awakened with a horrible feeling that tragedy had somehow struck. Nan again called Billie, who was in Brooklyn, from her Greenwich Village apartment. They shared their sense of horror and grief, but were unable, of course, to do anything about it. By the next evening the news of Jim's death reached them.

This all ran through my mind again as I talked to John McConnell. I wondered what mysterious connection of things could explain experiences like these. I had read accounts of persons who are dying or just dead appearing to loved ones or friends, and I later learned that some scientists feel such apparitions to be among the most convincing data available as to the survival of persons after death.*

But the experiences reported in connection with Jim's death did not include apparitions. Rather, these were reports of vicarious experiences of moods and feelings which must have been Jim's just before he died. I suppose they could be accounted for by ESP—though why, if that were the case, persons who didn't know Jim and whom he didn't know would also have been involved I couldn't understand. Or perhaps this was an example of the mediation of feeling through the collective unconscious. In that case, it could have been that those in the vicinity with some connection—even if remote—to me or to my son might have, because of their own openness, received these impressions. Whatever explanation could account for them, they were indeed mysterious events.

I remember thinking of my speculation in Cambridge that somehow disturbing energies could have been released by the events preceding the death and the death itself. Here seemed to be another example of a disruption of the "atmosphere"—as though unleashed and undirected impulses had sent their vibrations out in random disarray. These events seemed to point to an intertwining of lives at the unconscious level, as indeed Jung had suggested.

As John left to go to the conference room and set up his recorder for the taping of my brief message for his peace program, I returned to my desk and reached for the phone book. Two books which I had thought about, in meaningful con-

* See, e.g., Gardner Murphy, Ph.D., Director of Research, Menninger Foundation, "An Outline of Survival Evidence," *Journal* A.S.P.R., vol. 39, Jan. 1945, pp. 2–34, reprinted in *Three Papers of the Survival Problem* (New York: The American Society for Psychical Research).

texts, strangely appearing the night before; Irving Laucks' questions right after I arrived that morning; John McConnell's appearance, mentioning a Spiritual Frontiers minister and recalling those strange experiences of the morning of Jim's death; and the date being August 1—all this could have been pure coincidence or perhaps an example of what Dr. Jung identified as "synchronicity" (an acausal connecting principle)*; but for me it added up to time for another attempt to contact Jim. It had, after all, been nearly five months, and purportedly he had said, "I'll be in touch come August." I found in the directory the Rev. Mr. Daisley's phone number and address, wrote them on a slip of paper and tucked it in my pocket.

After the taping of the radio message for peace, I read the paper for the day's seminar. Then after the session and the pleasant staff buffet which followed, I spent the afternoon getting settled in, examining the library facilities of the Center and answering questions at a press conference which was called by the Center on the occasion of my first day there. That over, I drove down the hill home.

As soon as I got in the apartment and said hello to my mother, I pulled out the slip in my pocket and headed for the extension of the phone in my bedroom. But before I reached the receiver, the phone rang. I picked it up somewhat impatiently.

"Hello, Jim." It was David Barr calling from San Francisco.

"David! How are you?" I responded, glad to hear from him.

"Now be sure you're sitting down," he went right on, ignoring my question. "I waited to call you at home, not

* In C. G. Jung and W. Pauli, *The Interpretation of Nature and the Psyche* (Princeton University Press, 1955) and *The Structure and Dynamics of the Psyche* (collected works of C. G. Jung, New York: Bollingen Foundation, vol. 8); also see *If This Be Heresy*, pp. 140 ff., 143.

wanting to interrupt your getting rolling at the Center with a playback of Cambridge."

"You don't mean—" I really did sit down.

"Yes. Let me tell you." David's words came tumbling out: "Lynne and I were out to dinner, and we came home around eleven. When we opened the door and came in the living room we found *open safety pins* here and there—some of them in pairs, arranged in that same position."

"Eight-nineteen?" I asked.

"Eight-nineteen."

David was always an accurate observer, as was appropriate for one who had graduated from the University of California at Berkeley with honors in mathematics. But he was an enthusiast and colorful in his descriptions—and this news was a bit much. So I asked, "Did Lynne see this, too?"

"She sure did. She'd never seen anything like it before. She found it hard to take in what you and I had said about all that stuff that happened in Cambridge, but now she knows what we were talking about. Did you find any pins?"

"No, I didn't, but a number of other things happened," I answered and went on to tell about the appearance of the two books and the series of "coincidences" at the Center during the day. "I have a feeling Jim's trying to be in touch again," I remarked, telling David about my remembering the words promising to be in touch in August.

"Well, why don't you call the medium that fellow mentioned?" David urged.

"That's just what I was about to do when you called," I replied. Then after a little catching up on news and greetings to and from Lynne, we promptly ended that call so that I could make the other one.

As I dialed the number on the slip and waited for an

answer, my mind was back in England—David's helpfulness there—

"George Daisley here." The accent was such as to make me feel I was *still* in England. (He came to the United States in 1961, it turned out.)

"This is James Pike calling," I opened. "I understand you're —you're connected with the Spiritual Frontiers group."

"Oh. Bishop Pike. I'm so glad you called. If you hadn't, I would probably have been in touch with you before very long," Mr. Daisley responded in a warm but matter-of-fact way.

"Oh?" My voice must have revealed my puzzlement.

"You see, I rather expected your call," he explained. "Your son was in touch with me about two weeks ago."

"In touch?" I was taken aback. "I moved to Santa Barbara about two weeks ago, but—"

"No, it was your boy. Out of the blue a voice simply spoke to me from across the room, saying, 'I am Jim Pike, the Bishop's son.'"

"Oh, really?" I found his words difficult to believe even after my previous experiences. Was he talking about a supposed "materialization" apparition, or clairvoyance? In the former, the supposedly dead (or distant) person is said to appear in such a way as to be manifest to whomever is present. In the latter, rather than an actual presence objectively visible the medium receives through his unconscious mind a powerful mental impression which is projected by him to a given space. To illustrate the difference with two very familiar examples: the accounts seem to indicate that Jesus *appeared* to his disciples after his death, the apparition being testified to by more than one person in most instances.* St. Paul,

* Matt. 28:8–10, 17–20; Mark 16:9–18; Luke 24:13–32, 36–52; John 20:19–29, 21:1–23.

on the other hand, must have had a clairvoyant and/or clairaudient experience, for his companions in one account heard the voice but did not see the figure, and in the other saw the light but did not see anything else.*

Whichever variety of experience Daisley was talking about, his memory of it seemed pretty explicit.

"Yes. Well, I looked up to see a tall, thin young man across the room. 'I want you to help me get through to my father, around August 1,' he requested. But I told him, 'Your father would have to come to me first, Jim.' You see, Bishop, as you would understand, it would have seemed unprofessional for me to have—"

"Oh," I interrupted. As a lawyer I recalled that hearing of, say, an accident and approaching the strangers involved as potential clients was dubbed "ambulance chasing."

"Then your son said he'd work on it nearer the time. He sounded pretty self-confident, if I may say so. Had you not called I would have found it difficult not to call you eventually, but I prefer it this way," Mr. Daisley concluded.

I was, in one way, dumbfounded by what I had just heard. Yet at the same time it fit: *I'll be in touch come August.* It would seem he'd been working at making that promise good. The date with Mr. Daisley was set for a couple of days later at 9:30 in the morning so I could reach the Center in time for our regular 11 o'clock seminar.

I felt it was a good idea to have not only a witness but also someone to take notes, having found both to be helpful the first time, and since Maren Bergrud had been there then I asked her if she would accompany me again. She was glad to, and also suggested that it might be helpful to have two of

Ψ

* Acts 9:3–7, 22:6–11, 26:12–18; cf. 1 Cor. 9:1 and Gal. 1:15–17.

us there who would be able to make some comparison between the functioning of the two mediums.

Calle Fresno, the quiet street where Mr. Daisley lives, is reached by turning right off a wider, more well-traveled road which ascends toward the mountains. In that part of Santa Barbara the street names are just stenciled on the curb, so we missed his street at first. When that became completely evident we turned around and went back—and were somewhat delayed in arriving.

Mr. Daisley greeted us at the door of his relatively new, tract-house-style home. He was a man about my age, and in a rather typical British manner of respectful friendliness he ushered us into his living room. His home was attractively decorated with modern furniture. There were many paintings around (I later learned oil painting and tennis were Mr. Daisley's hobbies), and a substantial library of books, primarily in the psi field, was much in evidence. We settled down to a get-acquainted chat in the course of which I learned a great deal about Mr. Daisley himself.

He was born in London's East End, the son of poor parents. His powers emerged at age ten, but they only created difficulty in a family which knew nothing of such "nonsense." He began to keep to himself, feeling that he was somehow "different." Finally, in his teens, he happened to meet someone who did know about such powers and who, in turn, introduced him to a group of sensitives who helped train him. From then on he began to take part in public demonstrations and to give private sittings in the course of which he came to know various well-known mediums and various clergy interested in the field. He had only been in Santa Barbara five years, but already had a fairly full schedule of group meetings, training sessions and appointments for spiritual healing and mediumship.

Then Mr. Daisley himself shifted the attention to me. "I had read about your son's death, of course, and I was so sorry. I can assure you," he went on, "that the lad will manifest himself through me today." Though he said no more than this about the suicide, Mr. Daisley's manner and expression gave me the feeling that his response was one of genuine sympathy and understanding.

"Good," I said non-committally. He then proceeded to explain that he had clairvoyant powers and could "see" my son, and that he also had clairaudient powers, meaning he could "hear" my son speak. Not having the same powers, however, I would not "see" or "hear" the messages except as he was able to relay them to me. That sounded very much like my first session with Mrs. Twigg, so I felt comfortable enough. We were silent. I remember sort of bowing my head. Then I looked up just as the direction of his head changed abruptly.

"Your son is standing just behind you and slightly to your left," Mr. Daisley asserted. " 'Hello, Dad,' he says. 'I'm so pleased to see you today. I was with you recently when you did not think you could find a book in your library that you really wanted to consult. After you left the room and returned, you were startled to find the book on the desk where I put it in your absence. You know, Dad, I've been trying to bring about a great deal of physical phenomena in your surroundings.' "

A great deal. I pondered the words. Only two physical phenomena had seemed to occur. But then something fairly obvious dawned on me for the first time: if a deceased person can move things at all it is more than likely that a good many more such happenings occur than are noticed—especially by one like the author, who does not always have things around in perfect tidiness.

Mr. Daisley was leaning slightly forward in his chair, his

eyes opened wide as if he were watching someone beyond me as he addressed me. His face was bright—almost illuminated. His words seemed to confirm my inference that Jim had wanted to be in touch with me again. Even though the one detail—mentioning that it was on my desk instead of on the coffee table—was in error, the essence of the matter was accurate enough. Either Mr. Daisley pulled the event out of my subconscious by ESP and then attributed a motive to it on Jim's part—and this without knowing about the Cambridge events—or he was in fact in touch in some way with my son who had apparently used physical phenomena to get my attention.

"When you missed the street and went on up the hill," Mr. Daisley went on, purporting to speak for my son, "I was afraid you wouldn't get here at all."

"How did you know that?" I asked—mainly to see what kind of response I would get.

"Oh, I was along," the answer came back. The mood seemed almost playful, but I was not overly impressed by this exchange. After all, we did arrive a few minutes late, and I would imagine we were not the first to miss Mr. Daisley's street. That remark could well represent a good guess on the part of the medium.

"I have Elisha here," the medium's voice continued. "He will help you in your quest. 'We've both been helping you,' he says." I thought of one line from the familiar ordination hymn which begins: "God of the prophets, bless the prophets' sons. Elijah's mantle on Elisha fell." Elisha is *not* Elijah, hence not Elias—though Elisha *sounds* more like Elias than Elijah does! Yet the reference pointed to a concurrence: the unknown minister telling me after the service at St. Thomas that Elias was teamed with my son standing behind me (in both senses of the phrase) as I preached unconventional doctrine. In a way the variance made it somewhat *more* convincing. But I doubted that Mr. Daisley knew that Elisha referred to Jim's grandfather. I nodded slightly in acknowledgment, without raising my eyes. On the other hand, there was a parallel between this presumed entity and the next mentioned—Jim's other grandfather.

"Your father is here also," George Daisley commented. "He says, 'Your mother and I are different.'" That seemed a very safe observation—and hardly profound! Then Mr. Daisley went on to observe, "Elisha and Jim were great friends in life. Elisha says Jim is exhibiting anxiety because he doesn't want you to grieve for him." That seemed strange to me. George Daisley didn't seem to hesitate to say "Elisha" and Jim were good friends in life. That was true, but I wondered if Mr. Daisley knew who this "Elisha" was. And the comment which had followed sounded a little like some pastoral reassurance of the kind with which I am very familiar from my own counseling. I appreciated the concern which it revealed—either on the part of the medium or of Jim and his grandfather or whoever—but I was not overly moved by it. I wasn't "grieving" much any more, so it didn't really fit my circumstances too well.

Ψ

Daisley spoke rapidly, as if he could hardly keep up with all he seemed to be hearing and seeing. "He is finding himself and is trying to create a sense of presence in the room. You have mediumship ability," he suddenly said to me. Then he went on.

"Your son is much taller than you. He certainly is a clever-looking boy. He cannot express his sorrow for the great grief he brought but it was a shock to him also and a surprise to find himself living. He has tried to speak to his father in his father's sleep but his father will not recognize it. He will continue to try and reach you so that no doubt exists in anyone's mind, but he is not satisfied with this mediumship and this sitting and feels he can do better."

The last remark seemed to represent a feeling of insecurity on the medium's part. He needn't have felt insecure, though, for I had no preconceived notions as to what I wanted to come through. I was there because it appeared Jim had "called." The movement of objects was rather like having someone leave an operator's number and a request to return the call. I felt the responsibility to make the next move, so there I was. But I had in mind no particular message.

I was impressed by the observation that Jim was surprised to find himself living. If Mr. Daisley had been guessing—or trying to please me by saying what he thought I would want to hear—I would have thought he would have portrayed Jim as believing in life after death. But these words fit with what was actually true: he thought there was a way out. To find that there was none would indeed have been a surprise.

I was also impressed that Mr. Daisley could "see" that Jim was much taller than I, just as earlier he had purportedly observed a "tall, thin young man." Jim had been that: and if there had been news reports which indicated his height, I had not seen them.

There was something different about this sitting than those with Ena Twigg. It seemed more like a pastoral counseling session. Mr. Daisley's manner was very kind and sensitively concerned, manifesting a warm personal interest. He was very much the minister and pastor—his awareness doubtless expanded by ESP—and, having myself always regarded the pastoral role as the first priority, this was a positive reaction. Much that had been said was general and comforting but not solely explicable in terms of Jim as the source. In good measure, I am sure, the medium's own concern was being reflected.

Mr. Daisley next commented: "Jim is a clever and a very thoughtful boy. It will not be too long until he is completely with life again. I believe you spent many long weeks with your son because Jim is looking back to the times he spent with his father talking about life and meaning."

Then Mr. Daisley turned to Maren and said, "Jim is looking at the lady present at the sitting, who has been looking at pictures of him. He says he has brought someone to speak to the lady. It's Edgar Cayce," Daisley asserted.

"He says, 'You have been reading books about me—one in paperback and one in hard cover—as you have been moving books around in the library.'" Maren told me later that in unpacking her books she had come across *There Is a River* and *Many Mansions*, both of which tell the life story of Edgar Cayce, and both in paperback editions. She had in fact glanced through them both and, finding them of great interest, had been reading one. She had not, however, been looking at pictures of Jim. That had perhaps been a "bad guess."

Edgar Cayce seemed to go on, addressing his remarks to Maren. "I want to help you develop spiritual healing, and I want you to read *Many Mansions*. You are now reading a book on reincarnation which you do not understand. *Many Mansions* will be a help to you." Then Mr. Daisley commented that Cayce seemed to have taken an unusual interest in Maren.

I was not familiar with any of the books about Cayce, nor did I know anything about him, so that part of the conversation was almost entirely lost on me. I later learned that Cayce was a medium who was able to prescribe treatment for illnesses and give "life-readings" for people while in a deep trance. The life-readings seemed to tell the history of a living person's previous incarnations, the very suggestion of which had been disturbing to Edgar Cayce himself while in a waking state because of his strong orthodox Christian upbringing. I didn't know what his comments to Maren about developing healing power might mean, but I kept in mind that Edgar Cayce would be fallible in the matter of predictions—along with everyone else, both "living" and "dead."

Daisley went on at his same rapid-fire pace. "Jim sends you a kiss, Maren," he said. We were both startled since neither of us had mentioned Maren's rather unusual first name; we had simply introduced her as Mrs. Bergrud. "Jim says you look pretty and your hair is better than it used to be."

My mind returned immediately to those bizarre events of several months before when Maren's bangs had been burned three days running, and to the recollection that Jim had said once the summer before in San Francisco that he didn't like her bangs. She had no bangs on this occasion. That seemed to corroborate my suspicion that Jim was somehow responsible for burning them off.

Ψ

My thoughts raced to keep up with Mr. Daisley. "Jim says he expects that you are wearing blue because he first saw you in a blue dress," he continued, still addressing himself to Maren. I tried to remember that occasion and couldn't think when it might have been. Later Maren and I were able to reconstruct it and she recalled that she had indeed been in blue, though it had been a different dress.

Then Edgar Cayce was quoted again as speaking to Maren. "You and he [Mr. Daisley pointed to me] have used a ouija board. That only leads to confusion." How remarkable, I thought! That was several months before and only on that one occasion in Cambridge when at the suggestion of Canon

Pearce-Higgins, David Barr, Maren and I had put together that homemade version. And the result *was* confusing. I was unable to see how George Daisley could have known of that isolated, and unimportant, incidence of experimentation—and its dubious outcome. He might have just been guessing, but somehow that seemed unlikely to me. One does not automatically associate bishops with ouija boards. Was this depth ESP at work?

Daisley went on, "Give my love to all the family—I love them all dearly." These were what I would call "safe" remarks, but hardly evidential either way.

Then Mr. Daisley said, with a smile, "He is asking which wall did you finally put that TV on? You need a bigger place." I thought back to several days ago when the carpenter had been in and my mother and I were trying to decide where to put the TV—whether against the wall where the special TV outlet was provided, but where it would crowd the piano, or whether to have a place built in for it in the bookshelves and have an extension from the outlet run under the rug.

"He thinks you'd better either get another room, or start getting rid of some books and furniture," George went on, reflecting on his face a pixie-like look that would be natural to Jim talking like this. The medium hadn't seen the current state of disorder in my new residence; and the observation that there didn't seem to be enough room for all the furniture and books was all too true. I was quite impressed with what, at the least, was effective extrasensory perception. He appeared to be able to grasp the recent past quite accurately.

Mr. Daisley's voice went on, his comments moving quickly from one subject to another.

"Someone in the spirit world whom I do not know says he heard you discussing going to a dentist with a lady in the hall yesterday," he said to Maren.

"That's right," Maren said. She later told me she had just talked to the landlady, requesting the name of a dentist. Another perception of a recent event.

"Jim says there will be an interchange of books between the two of you," Mr. Daisley continued. A fair assumption, I thought, since each of us read a lot. He went on, "Jim is becoming happy. Also he has been trying to move things again." Apparently not just trying! I thought.

Ψ

"Elijah [*Elijah* now: Elijah = Elias, the right name] says to tell you that the greatest part of your career as a useful man lies ahead, and you will . . ." Mr. Daisley reported. Then, as if interrupting himself, "Someone here keeps insisting there are clergy in your family. I don't know who this is."

And, the subject again changing, Daisley spoke to Maren: "Jim wonders if the watch you found is working. He says you certainly didn't get the prettiest one."

Maren had lost a watch and had just purchased a new one that was quite inexpensive. The remark made me think: How blunt—how unnecessarily blunt—and how typical of Jim it was to say such a thing. It certainly seemed unlikely that these could be Daisley's words. The polite Englishman with whom we were just getting acquainted would not have made a remark like that on his own.

"Edgar Cayce is speaking to you now, Bishop." Daisley turned back to me. "He says that your Uncle Will is in the spirit world."

"No," I demurred. "No, he's not. I have no such uncle in the spirit world."

"Uncle Will is either here or very nearly here. We are

watching for him. He is giving you his greetings and says he will stay close to your son."

The remark puzzled me, but I gave no further thought to it until October when word reached me that my Uncle Bill of Campbellsville, Kentucky, had passed away after a long period of illness. My mother and I flew to Kentucky, and I preached at the Requiem Mass at the request of the Roman Catholic pastor who had obtained permission for this from the Archbishop of Louisville.

I talked with Aunt Ethyl about Bill's death and mentioned the words that had come through in the séance. She asked when the sitting had taken place, and upon comparing calendars, we discovered that it was the very day when Uncle Bill had gone into a deep coma from which his doctors, and Aunt Ethyl, really did not expect him to recover. He had come out of it, however, and when he did, he told my aunt, "I saw Jesus, and with him others who are over there waiting for me."

Uncle Bill's "vision," as reported by Aunt Ethyl, was of a type not unfrequently experienced. It did not correspond precisely to the comments made by Jim. He did not mention Jesus. It is not surprising, however, that a person steeped in the Christian tradition (Uncle Bill was a convert and a seriously devout Roman Catholic) should "identify" someone on the other side as Jesus more readily than he would identify someone he had known personally on this plane, because of the customary teaching that we will "meet Jesus" after death. There is no doubt that Uncle Bill really expected to. In any case, the coincidence of the message which came through in the sitting with Uncle Bill's vision is an impressive one.

Ψ

The voice of George Daisley went on impatiently, as if trying to cover the ground as quickly as possible so as not to miss any comments which he was apparently hearing. "Dad," he reported my son as saying, "I will use your hand. Speak for the clergy. Some of them look on you as being a prophet on earth right now. It doesn't matter how much 'they' bug you," he seemed to say with urgency. That was consistent with Jim's mood all along. It rang true.

"Edgar Cayce is speaking to you again," Daisley said to Maren. "He says you must get new glasses for distant use. Your eyes are irritated and the irritation will never cease until you get new glasses. Your eyes are changing. You are getting older."

I later came to realize that there are certain standard phrases or comments that seem to come through frequently in sittings. I call them "fill," for it's as if they hold a space open until further "messages" can come through. One such remark is that the sitter needs new glasses; another, when addressed to a lady sitter, is, "I saw you going through your stockings this morning," or "I saw you trying to choose which lipstick to wear this morning." Such comments, as is not surprising, quite frequently hit the mark and in any case are certainly harmless, but they can seem so unconvincing that the skeptical sitter is likely to react very negatively—perhaps even rejecting the whole sitting because of a few seemingly empty comments.

That does not seem to me an appropriate response. Being an extemporaneous preacher and speaker, I know that there are short "records" one unconsciously plays, when occasionally in need of regrouping one's thoughts, which—though they doubtless contribute little or nothing to the theme of the address—at least avoid awkward silences. That something like this process may well occur in the extemporaneous speaking of mediums is not surprising, nor does it, as such, negate the experience as a whole—any more than does (hopefully not!) the analogous process in my own public presentations.

Then, turning to Maren, "He says he watched you trying to choose which lipstick to wear this morning. He says there are three in the bathroom."

I felt Mr. Daisley was really just keeping the conversation going now, so I decided to try to evoke some more content. Thinking of the previous occasion when Paul Tillich had seemed to come through, I said, "Jim, how about Paul?"

"I should get a lot of volume." Daisley (or Jim) seemed to think I was referring to someone not deceased. He paused and then said, "He is not on earth, but there is great difficulty in communication. He has fairly recently gone over."

I gathered we were not able to be in touch with Paul Tillich. Then he quickly reverted to Edgar Cayce, who purportedly resumed his conversation with Maren. "We can unfold mediumship in you, if you are not impatient, but one for healing power as I had on earth."

This did not impress me positively or negatively. But I noticed that Maren raised her eyebrows. She commented later as we drove away that this had certainly struck a responsive chord in her. She told me that she had completed pre-med with all A's and even taken graduate work in biochemistry, but had been blocked from going to medical school by a series of misfortunes over the years: first the need to support and care for a slowly dying husband, next a shortage of funds and finally her own ill-health. Her frustration in this regard had been—and still was—acute, I realized for the first time. She had engaged in spiritual healing in association with a priest of the Diocese of California who stressed this aspect of the ministry.

I wished I knew more about who this Edgar Cayce was. He then seemed to say to me, "There is some confusion of conditions in and around your life that will come to a very happy period." I was not *un*happy now, I reflected. In fact, I was doing fine—though one could not have called the conditions of my life at that time "a very happy period." The latter was to come. It in fact has—and quite some time ago. But at the time I didn't receive this prediction as convincing. I automatically categorized as neutral all evaluative statements which represented what one would *want* to hear.

Ψ

These reflections were interrupted as George Daisley spoke again. "Jim says, 'Don't use all those pens that don't work.' "

I had to smile to myself. Trivial as it seemed, the injunction did have a point. I had been sorting through a box of old ball-point pens while unpacking, wondering where on earth I had accumulated them all. I tried a couple which didn't work; but rather than sort them I tucked the lot of them into a drawer in the buffet, in case I should ever need them for something.

I spoke up. "Jim," I said, "is there anything about this fall for the others in the family?"

"No, I can't tell, Dad," was the answer. Not an illuminating answer but at least not unverifiedly prophetic!

Then Daisley turned to Maren and said, "Jim wants to talk but doesn't know how to to you."

I thought I would try another question to see if I could get more information to indicate that my son was really communicating. "Cathy is coming to stay for a couple of days, Jim," I said, without giving any indication to George Daisley that I was referring to one of my son's sisters. "What about this?"

The answer came back, "Give her my love. They want to believe. I don't know if they will, but tell Cathy." The comments were too imprecise to establish real identity, and yet I had the intuitive feeling of conversation. So when I recalled that comment several days later, I felt a sort of obligation to tell Cathy about my experiences of supposed communication with Jim, though I wasn't sure how Cathy would receive such a report. She and Jim had been very close. I felt she had a right to know, and even if there was a small percentage of a chance that such communication was real, I wanted to comply with what seemed to be the wishes of my son, especially when it was so easy to do.

Mr. Daisley sat on the edge of his chair and looked at me intensely, "Jim is saying to me, 'Some exciting emotion is standing in my way now, but tell Dad that we will work with him. Tell Dad I did not premeditate my passing at all. Tell him it had to be; the manner was not promoted by evil forces but my time on earth was done. I am going to be much more help to Dad from here. Tell Dad to feel no sense of shame.' "

The words tumbled out, and there was a kind of earnestness in George Daisley's expression which again reinforced the pastoral tone of the sitting. The words were not inconsistent with what had come through Mrs. Twigg, nor with what I knew of Jim while he was alive, but they did seem somewhat overdrawn. He went on, "You will experience more physical manifestations. You will have to struggle with the clergy . . . You will write an important book with much help from Elijah . . . We will all help you."

The string of predictions poured out; but it was not until two months later that I saw any particular significance in them. By that time a draft heresy presentment signed by a dozen bishops had been circulated to all the bishops and released to the press; I had been censured (without a semblance of due process) by the House of Bishops at Wheeling, West Virginia; a trial for heresy was in the offing; I began writing my most substantial book on theology (published by Harper & Row in the fall of 1967, a year later, under the title of *If This Be Heresy*)—much of the thought of which would accord with my late stepfather's; and I had occasion several times to sense Jim's presence because of physical phenomena which occurred.

But these things I had no way of knowing as Mr. Daisley closed the session with the words, "All of them are sending their love and blessing. Many more wanted to speak . . . wanted to get through."

"Thank you very much," I told George Daisley. And then, rather tentatively—but very sincerely—"Thank you, Jim. It was good to be in touch again." That was mainly on the faith that—or just in case—this was really Jim. I realized that to state it that way was an oversimplified response, perhaps, but that was how I intuitively felt. The following words, published as a part of the majority report of the Church of England's Commission on this subject, express that feeling:

> We accept many things as certain in the realm of personal relationships upon the basis of direct insight.
>
> When we say that we know our friends, we mean something very different from saying that we can give a scientific and verifiable account of them. But we are none the less sure of our knowledge. Similar certainties are to be found in the sphere of mystical experience.
>
> It may well be that in this matter of the evidence of the survival of the human personality after death, we are dependent exactly upon this same kind of insight, and that a scientific verification,

though valuable where it can be obtained, is of secondary importance, and only partially relevant.

And this is precisely the situation in which we find ourselves in our assurance of Christianity itself. "We walk by faith, and not by sight."*

We rose to go.

* From *The Church of England and Spiritualism* (London: Psychic Press, 1949).

8

It is because of the Divine Spirit *within us* that we seek truth: it is because of the Divine Spirit *without us* that there is truth to discover.

—*Lily Dougall*

The essence of these more stubborn objections is the *virtually unlimited range* of the telepathy with which the automatist's or medium's subconscious mind has to be gifted. It must be such as to have access to the minds of any persons who possess the recondite items of information communicated, no matter where those persons happen to be at the time. Furthermore, the telepathy postulated must be assumed somehow capable of *selecting*, out of all the minds to which its immense range gives it access, the particular one or ones that contain the specific bits of information brought into the communications. But this is not all. The immediate understanding of, and apposite response to, allusive remarks in the course of the communicator's conversation with the sitter (or sometimes with another communicator) requires that the above selecting of the person or persons having the information, and the establishing and relinquishing of telepathic rapport with the mind of the appropriate one, be virtually *instantaneous*. And then, of course, the information thus telepathically obtained must, *instantly* again, be put into the form of a dramatic, highly verisimilar impersonation of the deceased purported communicator as he would have acted in animated conversational give-and-take.

—*Prof. C. J. Ducasse*

Single facts can never be "proved" except by their coherence in a system. But, as all facts come singly, anyone who dismisses them one by one is destroying the conditions under which the conviction of new truth could arise in his mind.

—*Prof. F. C. S. Schiller*

About three weeks later, on September 9, 1966, I made another appointment to see Mr. Daisley. I felt quite certain that there had been another movement of books in my apartment, and I felt that Jim might want to be in contact again.

Much of the content of that sitting repeated themes from the previous three occasions when it appeared that Jim had communicated with me, but on this particular day I had a feeling that what came through was far more related to my current activities than to facts about Jim, information about others or "big thoughts." For example, reference was made to certain somewhat insignificant recent events, which it seemed Jim had observed. "Jim says that he saw you going over those notes from the sitting in England," Mr. Daisley said. I had, in fact, read them just the night before in preparation for that day's sitting. George also reported Jim as having asked if I remembered that he was helping me find a book I was looking for on a shelf. This seemed to have reference to the event which led me to make another appointment: a book which I had wanted, but had been unable to locate, turned up inexplicably.

These incidents could have been pulled out of my conscious mind—or at least would have been accessible from my unconscious mind—by ESP, of course, and thus are not at all probative of the survival hypothesis. Nevertheless, in the over-all impact of a sitting, such references give a distinct feeling of "presence."

In addition, however, a great deal of material came through which revealed a marked sensitivity to the state of my personal affairs. Much of what Jim purportedly said was personal, revealing an awareness of the tensions, confusion and even conflict which I was experiencing in a number of contexts, and his comments about my new work—in which I was rejoicing—and about the various members of the family were particularly astute. Whether the sensitivity was George Daisley's or Jim's, it was at the least accurate.

Mr. Daisley reported Jim as being very anxious to be of help to me. "Jim says to tell you that he is going to work with you as a team. He says that you will have a lot of help from many wonderful people in a new phase of your work which is to come . . . you will be led into great public work, but of a different nature than what you have done so far," the medium said, relaying the message to me. "Jim says that some people will love you, but a lot will criticize and hate you for the time being."

Although I found the words somewhat reassuring at the time, they seemed rather vague and general until, as in the case of the predictions made in the preceding séance, I received word of the new heresy charges against me by some brother bishops. Then, after I was denied my right to present evidence or cross-examine my episcopal accusers at the Wheeling censure proceeding, I felt the necessity of taking my case "to the people"—a far more "public" work than I had ever done before. I decided to accept far more speaking dates throughout the country than I otherwise would have. In the year which followed I traveled all over the country, speaking to people with television, radio and press—readily and at their own initiative—aiding in the cause almost everywhere. Rarely had theology been given such comprehensive coverage.

From time to time I recalled Jim's purported words and felt a kind of encouragement and strength in them. Again, those comments could have come from the medium as precognition. Their impact toward the survival hypothesis only takes on importance in the light of the accumulation of evidence and the consistency and continuity of the comments which purportedly came from Jim not only through this medium, but through others. Jim appeared to be "tracking" me at every point, wanting to be of help—a consistent portrayal in the light of our common experiences in Cambridge.

Ψ

In that sitting, I asked for the first time about a good friend who had just died to see if it would be reported that Jim had seen him or heard of him. (In the light of what follows he will have to remain anonymous.) The answers: "Jim says that he saw A., but that A. didn't believe he was seeing Jim. Later on, Jim says, they will try to bring him into the power." And, when I asked how A. died: "Jim feels that he must have taken his own life because he came there the same way Jim did."

A.'s death was not officially declared to be suicide; but the immediate background and the mysterious circumstances of the fatal "accident" strongly pointed to that hypothesis. If it is the correct one, there is an impressive consistency between the reported state of A., Jim's own apparent inability to function for a fortnight or so and numerous other reports of the bewildering effect of sudden death (one recalls the petition in the Prayer Book litany: *From sudden death, good Lord deliver us*).

One of the most evidentiary items of communication which came through in that sitting was the following: "Jim says that the first sitting with George was assigned before you met George—while still in England. Jim says he tried to put the lady [I presumed the reference was to Mrs. Twigg] into a trance and he tried to foretell that you would be sitting with me," George said, pointing to himself. I recalled vividly, after the assurance "I'll be in touch come August," the response to my query as to how I could be in touch: "Spiritual Frontiers."

It was on August 1 that I learned from John McConnell that George Daisley was a member of the Spiritual Frontiers Fellowship, and this prompted me to call him when, in effect, I wanted to return Jim's "call," the two poltergeist phenomena in the apartment the night before. I also remembered that Mr. Daisley reported Jim had been in touch with him, wanting to get the two of us together. I had not told George about the fact that at the second sitting in London when Ena Twigg was in trance (in the earlier one she was not) Jim seemed to be able to give me instructions as to how to get in touch with him in the United States.

The fact that all of this had been tied together in the second sitting with George Daisley impressed me very much indeed. Again, he could have, by ESP, gotten all of that out of my unconscious—but, if so, that in itself was remarkable.

There were other messages in the September sitting: a suggestion that I read *The Betty Book*, by Stuart Edward White, with the suggestion, purportedly coming from the author, that I should not take too seriously the long-accepted assumption that those who take their own lives are wicked; an apology (though quite unnecessary) for the grief and anxiety which Jim had caused those who love him; an assurance that Jim was feeling better, more at home and happier; a recollection of our long talks in Cambridge and of the help we were able to give one another; and a strong encouragement that I "tell the world" about my experience with communication. While none of these latter comments are evidentiary as such, they fit.

All in all, the sitting that day left me with the same feeling of closeness and loving friendship which Jim and I had in fact shared during those months in Cambridge. Jim—if indeed I was in touch with him—seemed to have made real progress; he was apparently able for the first time to give more thought to other persons than to his own situation.

Ψ

In the rush of my busy schedule, I did not follow up the recommendations made to me that day. I did not look up *The Betty Book* nor did I begin to share my experiences of apparent communication with more than members of my immediate family, a few close friends, two relatively small clergy conferences where it was relevant to the question of life after death, and with my colleagues at the Center during a seminar to which it was relevant. That seminar was led by Irving Laucks,* who had asked me to follow his introductory presentation with a summary of my psi experiences.

In none of the scores and scores of public addresses and sermons during the next year in which I spoke of belief in the life to come on an empirical basis did I refer to my personal experiences. Nor did I mention these experiences in the fifty-page chapter on that subject in *If This Be Heresy*. This closemouthedness was not an intentional dodging of words of advice; rather it was the outward sign of my inward conviction that, granting that the survival hypothesis could be affirmed, we were still dealing only with human personalities. Any counsel was only the advice of another finite being, as

* Mr. Laucks, consultant at the Center, is author of a very helpful book in this field: *A Speculation in Reality* (New York: Philosophical Library, 1953).

I had previously concluded, and the fact of his being "on the other side" did not automatically make his words true or wise.

Communication through a medium, in other words, could more properly be compared to talking with a friend on the telephone than to receiving a revelation from God: a friend's opinions and advice are certainly worth listening to and taking into consideration, but the responsibility for any decisions still rests upon one's own shoulders, and I personally didn't feel the time was right to "tell the world." I wanted ample opportunity for further study and quiet reflection for a good stretch of time after my son's death. And I knew that, in any case, word of this, no matter how carefully stated, would not be easily received by "the world."

Ψ

Only a few days after that second sitting with Mr. Daisley the pace and scheduling of my hours and days was changed radically. This was because the charges of heresy leveled against me by the Bishop of South Florida were made public. There was an immediate increase in the amount of "fan mail" (including of course some "negative" fan mail) which flowed in. Also, the number of invitations I received for speaking engagements increased. Above all, there was suddenly before me the task of defending myself against the charges. I became aware that my secretary, Miss Goodwin, and I were not going to be able to cope with all this in addition to my work at the Center for the Study of Democratic Institutions.

In my previous post I was an example of that rather rare legal species known as the corporation sole and thus had—indeed was!—a non-profit foundation which could receive, from me and others, and expend funds for the furthering of causes and concerns relevant to my sphere of activity and to my hopes for creative change in the Church and society. Now suddenly I was without such an entity, and it occurred to me that there should be formed a new non-profit foundation which could fulfill those roles and, quite congruently with them, act, in effect, as my agent for speaking engagements and writing contracts, sort out TV and radio invitations, assist in answering the deluge of mail, aid in the research for books and articles and help in the preparation of manuscripts. It would receive, along with contributions from others who share my concerns, a good portion of my honoraria and royalties. And although at this point I made a policy of declining tenders of heresy defense funds until an actual "presentment" (like an indictment) should be rendered, a non-profit repository of such funds would have enabled many clergy and laymen who had offered financial help have the advantage of a proper tax deduction. So it was, with three distinguished friends of quite divergent backgrounds serving as the Board of Directors, that New Focus Foundation was organized.

Mrs. Maren Bergrud, who by now was feeling ready to take on regular employment, became its first director, and quickly assembled a small but highly competent and loyal staff.

Ψ

The October House of Bishops meeting in Wheeling, West Virginia, far from clearing up the heresy issue, only made things more complex. In order to avoid a heresy trial, a majority of my brother bishops voted a censure resolution. This had been prepared by a committee to which the Presiding Bishop appointed three of my accusers, but I was denied a hearing before that committee. So with two other bishops (as required by canon law)—my successor and the Bishop of Indianapolis—as my co-signers, I filed a formal demand for the full judicial process with reference to both the cruel denigrations of my ministry hurled at me in the censure and on the heresy charges in the draft presentment —which though bypassed, had been widely circulated. "I put my miter on the line; clear my cause or unfrock me," I stated as I took this step, and concluded, "as an honorable man and as a bishop of the Catholic Church I cannot do otherwise."

In addition to giving the green light to New Focus to step up the acceptance of speaking engagements in various parts of the country, I resolved to "get with" the book on doctrine which I had only just begun, in time for it to be published before the General Convention in September of 1967. I had planned to call the book *Fewer Beliefs—More Belief*. In the light of the new situation in which I found myself, I changed the title to *If This Be Heresy*.

The weeks and months rushed by and I had very little time to think about the psi field. My interest and attention were focused on the heresy issue. I recall only one unusual incident during the whole fall and winter. However, that event was impressive, personally helpful—and dramatic enough to be a jolting reminder of the unusual experiences in Cambridge.

I had arrived in Wheeling on a Saturday, early for the House of Bishops meeting but in time for an advance session of the Committee on Theology, of which I am a member. I knew, of course, that the committee "on me" was meeting over the weekend, and, since my repeated requests for hearing had been denied, I was feeling rather uncomfortable. On Monday the Presiding Bishop announced that the committee would report to the House the next day, Tuesday, at 3:30.

While I tried hard to stay with the business of the Monday morning meeting, I was naturally pondering the possibilities of what was coming up the next day and what my possible responses might be. I decided to glance through a new book on theological freedom by the Roman Catholic theologian Father Hans Küng, looking for material that I might use if I got a chance to say anything.

A little after eleven I closed the book, slipped out of my row and left the meeting to go to the rest room. On my way through the lobby I passed a nurse who was stationed there at a small table and saw a pair of small scissors among her equipment. This reminded me that a couple of long hairs from my left nostril needed clipping. I asked her if I might borrow the scissors for a moment. Before leaving the men's room I went to the mirror to clip the hairs and then noticed that on the left side of the parting of my hair there was an overly long lock about an eighth of an inch wide. It really belonged on the other side of the part, but since I did not have a comb with me I simply clipped about three quarters of an inch of it off with the scissors. I smoothed down the rest of my hair with my hand, brushed off my coat and returned to the meeting, leaving the scissors with the nurse as I passed her.

When I got back to my seat, there was on top of the other things on my desk a mimeographed copy of a press release which had been passed around. It was on a subject in which I had neither involvements nor interest, and I wanted to get back to my exploration of Father Küng, so I laid the report aside, and, raising the book a little from the desk, started to open it looking for the page I had last been reading. The book opened at pages 90 and 91. There was something there between the pages. On the outside margin of the right-hand page, about two thirds of the way down, was a narrow lock of hair. Odd, I thought. Then I realized that it was just like the lock of my own hair I had clipped off a few moments before.

As usual my first reaction was skeptical. I immediately left my seat again (mumbling to my good friend who sits on my left in the House, Bishop Daniel Corrigan, Director of the National Church's Home Department, as I passed behind him, "Something funny here!") and headed rapidly back to the rest room.

I looked at the left flat edge of the washbowl, where the portion of the lock clipped off would have landed. It was not there—except for three hairs the same length, which were moist because they had fallen on the edge of a wet spot on the porcelain.

This time I returned to the meeting much more slowly, trying to figure it out, and when I slipped past Bishop Corrigan's seat to settle in my own, he asked *sotto voce*, "What's up, Jim?"

Since we have been very close over the years and since I was so astonished, I started to tell him what had happened.

"*Thrix!*" he interrupted. I knew that θρίξ was Greek for "hair," but I failed to get the point.

"And so?" was my puzzled response.

"Don't you remember," he smiled, "that *thrix* also suggests an 'omen'?"

"Thanks Dan," I replied, as my thoughts immediately turned to Jim and the indication, at the last session with George Daisley, that he would be with me in the struggle and wanted to be of help. I suddenly felt a resurgence of courage and a new sense of calm.

Then my eye fell on the passage in the book to which the strand of hair was pointing:

Freedom in theology is a necessary condition for multiplicity in theology. Compulsion gives birth to uniformity, narrowness and vacuity; freedom to variety, multiplicity, breadth and richness. If there were in the Church only one united theology in the sense of one united party, only one single theological tendency in the sense of one single theological party line, this would be a sign not of Catholic freedom but of uncatholic compulsion. "*One* Lord, *one* faith, *one* baptism" (Eph. 4:5)—but *different theologies*.*

These words were read as a key quotation in the brief response I was allowed to make toward the end of the debate on the censure. Its crucial insight went out over the airways to many people all over the land—people of many different churches and of none. Its counsel was the one which prevailed a year later at the Seattle General Convention where things were put to rights.†

Ψ

By December I was focusing my work on the chapter in *If This Be Heresy* entitled "Life after Death." Although I had been picking up some knowledge of the studies which have been conducted regarding the various manifestations of the power of the human psyche to transcend the space-time continuum even here and now, I felt the need to broaden my studies before again making a faith-affirmation of survival in print. The method of *facts* + *faith* required a familiarity with a representative number of facts, analyses and critiques in this broad field of study.

* Hans Küng, *Freedom Today* (New York: Sheed & Ward, 1966), p. 91.

† See *Theological Freedom and Social Responsibility*, Report of the Special Committee to the Presiding Bishop (New York: Seabury Press, 1967). A portion of the quotation itself I used in my position paper for the committee (see pp. 127–28).

After reading a large variety of books and articles, I adopted the generic symbol for the transcendent aspect of the human personality, coming into more and more common use by scientists in the field: ψ, the Greek letter psi (the first letter of ψυχή, psyche). For me to use this symbol was not a mere matter of convenience. It was a recognition of the hypothesis that there is a unity, however inadequately grasped as yet, behind a score of categories on which there are data. For example: extrasensory perception in its various forms, including telepathy, precognition, retrocognition and clairvoyance; mystical experiences, with and without psychedelic drugs; speaking with tongues; the collective or universal unconscious as well as synchronicity; telekinesis; and psychic phenomena, or apparent communication with deceased persons.* To these should also be added spiritual healing, intercessory prayer, exorcism, and even ordinary dreams.

Once I began to read seriously in the psi field, I was absolutely amazed at the amount of literature available. There is an abundance of material reporting spontaneous events of different kinds—some quite unverified, others with considerable corroboration by witnesses. This book would fall in that category. But also there is a growing number of scientific studies reporting a wide variety of experiments and investigations under carefully controlled conditions and using, in appropriate cases, such adjuncts as the electroencephalograph and the computer. At the least, as I was able to report in my book, there is no poverty of facts in this area; what faith-affirmation is to be made on the basis of these facts, however, is a matter of personal decision. There are various

* These various areas are briefly discussed, with selected references to responsible studies, in *If This Be Heresy*, ch. 7. See, more fully, the bibliography at the end of this book.

explanations and one must decide for himself which are the most plausible.

My own experiences, together with the facts which I was led to search out as a result of them—as well as the analyses of scientists respected in their fields who had *also* given careful attention to data in one or more of the psi areas—enabled me to affirm life after death as the "natural" thing to expect of the human psyche, which already seems to be in eternal life. This was one of the three affirmations I was able to make in my book: fewer beliefs indeed but, hopefully, beliefs based on far sounder, more empirical foundations.

Ψ

As the year was nearing its end the Presiding Bishop still had not made a move to initiate the proceedings required under the canon law, as I had formally demanded. He and I were among the many in the Church hoping to find an alternative to a heresy trial since quite obviously the censure had not succeeded as such an alternative. Finally the Presiding Bishop appointed a new, broad-based committee on theological freedom and social responsibility (with Bishop Stephen F. Bayne, Jr., as chairman) and I publicly indicated that I was content with further deferment of judicial proceedings until the committee had made its report and, if the report were sufficiently corrective of Wheeling, until the General Convention the next fall had had an opportunity to take action in regard to it.

When the committee met, I was invited to serve as one of its theological advisors along with such respected friends as Bishop John Robinson, Professor John Knox and the late Father John Courtney Murray, S.J. I prepared my position paper with great interest and enthusiasm, and I was glad that I was invited to meet with the committee in Boston in March.

At last, I thought, there was going to be some theological dialogue in official circles of our Church. And indeed there was.

Not long before I was to go East to meet with the committee, however, an event occurred which caused me to return to George Daisley for another sitting—scheduled, it happened, the day before I was to fly to Boston. I was a leader, in dialogue with Father William DuBay, of a weekend conference at a center in Southern California called Kairos. Fairly well along in the Saturday evening discussion, the subject of life after death came up. A scientist present who knew something of psi data gave a brief summary of the field. Someone else then said that he thought all such data was nonsense. At that point a Mrs. Wendy Fellows, who hadn't said anything that evening, spoke up: "I hadn't wanted to interrupt to mention it before, Bishop, but since we're on the subject, there was standing behind you for a while a man about your height, in Church vestments, who repeated several times 'You're right.' Or at least that's what I thought he was saying. It was red around his chest area. I don't know if that was in the design of the vestments or what."

"That's very curious," I remarked. "And was he in a clerical collar?"

"Yes," she replied, "and in what appeared to be the vestments a priest wears for Mass or the Eucharist—as if he was all ready to take a service, or just had."

"And you thought he was saying 'You're right'?" I asked, just to be sure.

"That's what it seemed to be," she declared.

This added up to precisely zero so far as I was concerned—and I said so to the whole group. But the next morning as I awoke it suddenly dawned on me that the words which Mrs. Fellows thought she heard could have been "Hugh Wright."

Father Wright was a priest of the Diocese of California who had come over from another ministry midway in my episcopate. I was very fond of him and had every reason to believe that the feeling was mutual. Just a short time before, when I was in Pennsylvania for a college lecture, word had been passed to me of his tragic death as a result of the capsizing of a boat in which he was fishing on Lake Shasta.

I immediately called his widow in Santa Clara County. It turned out that when the boat turned over he and his fellow fisherman had been able to swim to shore—but at a remote, wooded spot. Hugh had evidently collapsed while walking for help. A hemorrhaging had filled his lungs with blood, suffocating him.

It obviously was quite remarkable that Mrs. Fellows—a complete stranger to both Hugh Wright and me—should have reported such an experience. This seemed to be an impressive example of clairvoyance and clairaudience, since no one else in the room saw or heard anything out of the ordinary. It occurred to me—since that is how I had come to interpret phenomena seemingly connected with Jim—that this might be an attempt on Hugh's part to be in communication with me. Therefore I made another appointment to see George Daisley.

The sitting was a cipher as far as the intended purpose went. The only one who seemed to come through was Jim. Although I was glad for that, I had somehow felt an urgency from the other direction. I asked Jim whether he had been in touch with Hugh Wright and what came through as the answer was not very helpful: "No, I haven't. I have sort of moved on and I'm not much in touch with who comes. I'm sorry. I can ask."

I realized that, even granting both the hypotheses of survival and of communication, it would be naïve to expect that every person on the other side would know about the passing of every other person. But the way in which persons who had been close to me had seemingly managed to get together on other occasions had led me to assume that—if all this be so—Jim would be alert to the "arrival" of persons related to me. However, nothing came through. In fact, even the ESP process wasn't working.

The same was true of another try: "A good friend of yours recently died in Mexico. He was also on a psychedelic drug. [I was referring to the instance mentioned in the first chapter.] Have you talked with him?"

The answer I got seemed to be a dodge: "We must talk about real things—like drugs. My generation wants to try everything. There is an alternative in the mental process in the brain cells, but the drug is different. Everything is altered, but it's either Nirvana or it's sheer hell." The remark seemed consistent with what I knew about drugs, and the references to altering the mental processes were certainly not irrelevant. I also knew that many young people take drugs hoping to experience Nirvana, or enlightenment, but instead get caught in a kind of hell scene. Moreover, both Jim and his friend had apparently died while on hallucinogenics, and it would not seem farfetched to guess they were caught in the first and horrible act of a trip. Yet there had been no answer to my direct question about Jim's friend.

Here is an example of two persons about whom—if what is operative is ESP—the medium could have pulled information out of my conscious and unconscious minds and didn't. Because he didn't, and because Jim—or whoever is the source of his remarks—didn't seem to know much either, I tended to be skeptical and somewhat suspicious of all my supposed "experiences."

Then there followed something which has come through in several sittings and which, to one coming from the Christian tradition, sounds very much like a cliché. As a consequence, though it comes through as one of the most commonly repeated phrases, I must confess I do not receive it as much more than a "professional jargon" type of comment from the medium. I don't say this pejoratively, for certainly we clergymen use an abundance of such phrases. The words were, "I died that you might live."

The only possible meaning I can conceive of for such a statement from my son would be that somehow he considered himself a burden and therefore felt that by taking his own life he would in some sense free me. But even if this were his message, I doubt very seriously that he would have used those words to communicate it. Moreover, it strikes me as the kind of piety which Christian ministers so easily fall into when trying to be helpful. It is not something I strongly object to, but I certainly don't think it adds to the credibility of psychic communication.

At the same time, I was struck by the accuracy of one small segment of the séance which related to one person I was not at all thinking about and to another I didn't know about (or at least had completely forgotten). It came "out of the blue."

"There have been four Jameses, and four in four generations," Mr. Daisley asserted.

"No," I countered, "only three. Jim, me and my father. *His* father—I can't recall his name at the moment—but it wasn't James."

"But I sense another clergyman James, like you—in a generation ahead of your father."

I simply demurred that I did not know of such (my father died when I was two years old).

When I returned to my office at the Center, I called my mother to ask if she knew if in my father's family there was a priest (if clergyman, priest he would be: my father's forebears were Roman Catholic all the way back to the time of their coming over to Maryland from the part of Kent County around Canterbury in the mid-eighteenth century—having been Anglican before that).

"Why, yes," she answered promptly. "Father James Pike, your father's uncle—whom he was named after and whom he was very fond of."

Too, much that came through, apparently from Jim, had direct relevance to my current situation, and thus it was difficult simply to dismiss the sitting. For example, he was reported as saying: "I met Paul (one of your friends who fought for freedom in the Church and who is helping you) and he says to give yourself time to grow. Don't let them pressure you, he says. Give yourself some time." Then later in the sitting: "As son to father I have a word of caution—do not pursue this heresy thing. The bishops have been given their warning, and now greater powers will take control. Bishop or not, you have a task to fulfill."

I did not consider such messages to be oracles, of course, yet I received them in a mood of careful contemplation. Jim seemed to have more to say about the same subject: "Don't force anything in September. It's up to them. Don't you do it. Paul says the same thing, and I don't mean St. Paul either. The wise ones in the hierarchy are using their intermediaries to bring about as much as can be given. It's a question of choice."

The remark about using intermediaries reminded me of a friend of mine in touch with the Presiding Bishop who had come just before Christmas to try to work out some way of avoiding a heresy trial. It was that conference which led to the establishment of the Bayne Committee on Theological Freedom. As for the remark about leaving it up to "them" at the General Convention in September, this merely reflected my own thought. I felt that I had done all I could to help get the Church out of the bind the House of Bishops had created, and that from here on it was the Church's problem, not mine. If a heresy trial had to be, I was ready for it. If they were willing to vote for greater freedom of thought and for due process in the Church, I would be even more pleased about that.

In any case, what seemed to be coming through from Jim was very much in keeping with my current scene. I was to meet with the Bayne Committee the very next morning, and these words were apparently addressed to that forthcoming event: "I know you will not speak dogmatically. It's actions that count, not words. I'll be with you tomorrow morning, helping to give you strength to cope."

And then the last words in the séance: "Safe return . . . and courage."

Much of this could have been ESP again, of course—even ESP of my own wishful thinking, though I had not shared any of the "inside story" with Mr. Daisley. Or it could have been that, plus good pastoral advice from the medium. However, the indication that Jim was following my affairs closely and felt a sense of involvement with me in them seemed a persistent theme in all these sittings.

Ψ

There were two other sections of conversation which were of great interest to me in the sitting that day. First of all, I had recently arranged for a conference with Mr. Alexander Liepa, the Doubleday religion editor, regarding two old book contracts on topics not currently of great interest to me. In order to relieve myself of my sense of obligation, I was hoping to make a deal: I would, at some time in the future, tell the full story of my experiences with psychic phenomena to Mrs. Maren Bergrud and let her write a book about it all which they could publish in exchange for my other contracts. It was not easy to convince him that someone else should be the author of such a story, but I wanted my main focus for research and writing to be on Christian origins, so I "passed" and promised that I would cooperate with her on it. He and his colleagues were kind enough to agree.

In that sitting with George Daisley, the following words seemed to come through: "I'm so glad you have decided to issue the challenge . . . to urge others to go out and find their own loved ones. Tell them to be extremely selective about where they find their verification of facts. I created that hullabaloo at Cambridge. I brought you here . . . I'm working real hard at learning that being dead is really being more alive. It's an excellent idea to let the story be told. It's long overdue. This gives freedom . . . do you know how hard I've worked? Santa Barbara was to be a stimulus, too. Listen, Dad, don't be bothered . . . go on fulfilling yourself . . . don't let any sense of persecution, prejudgment, prealigning stop you. Present your case . . . the public will listen even if the Church doesn't. And anyway, we're looking for truth, not popularity. You're in on the sensing of the spiritual implications of this field."

George Daisley knew nothing of the book. He could have gotten by ESP the information that its publication was planned; and the advice could have been his pastoral addition. But the remark "And anyway, we're looking for truth, not popularity" was entirely consistent with the mood Jim and I had shared in Cambridge. It might have come out of me; but if the survival hypothesis is true, this was certainly expressive of Jim's stance.

Secondly, I pressed a little on the matter of what Jim was learning on the other side. I asked, "Have you by now heard anything about Jesus?"

His answer was a rather lengthy "dissertation" on the nature of spiritual development, something like the following: "I haven't heard anything personally about Jesus. Nobody around me seems to talk about him. When we come over here we have a choice: to remain as we are, or to grow in our understanding. Some still seem to be Church-minded and are waiting for a Judgment Day, but these seem to be the unenlightened ones. Others seem to be expanding their mind and self toward more Eastern understandings. I have talked to someone of Chinese origin who offered to help me. He said, 'All of life is a process of evolution and growth.' It seems that the more intellect used, the better—but we're dealing with a 'mind self' which we are fusing with the 'spirit self.' They tell me it will take much endeavor to find the truth.

"A man came to earth who was Jesus, I am sure, and I would assume he came from the sphere where the purified are. I am in the sphere where those who've made mistakes are, but there seems to be no reason why at some period of eternity we can't all be a part of what some call the 'Christ sphere.' "

Remembering some of the reading I had done in this area, I pursued the matter a little further. "Have those in this 'Christ sphere' existed before?" I was thinking of the reincarnation hypothesis, such as that set forth in the Edgar Cayce life readings.

"Yes," seemed to be the response. "Now receive this correctly—in the present state on earth there is great need for such a person."

"Couldn't there be several such persons?" I asked.

"Yes. They voluntarily come back. That seems to be the point of the universe."

It is difficult to tell in such a discussion how much of the medium's own understanding is being expressed and how much is the understanding of the surviving personality who is purportedly in communication. In addition, it is possible that the ideas one brings into the séance could be picked up through ESP by the medium and reflected back as thoughts congenial to the sitter. In any case, I myself tend to be less receptive to philosophical or theological generalizations which seem to come through than I am to any other material. What is said could very well be true—in fact, it often seems all too true, and thus of very limited probative value.

Ψ

I did, indeed, meet with the Presiding Bishop's Committee the following day in Boston. There I was given an opportunity, in company with a group of men with excellent minds, to discuss the matter of doctrinal norms and of the due process of law for bishops brought under charges of heresy or threatened with censure. The Committee was most cordial to me, and we were able to carry on a fruitful theological discussion. For the first time I was very much encouraged in my hopes for reform in the Church.

Having thus made my contribution to the investigation of the possibility of theological freedom in the Episcopal Church, and having mailed off the manuscript of *If This Be Heresy* to the publisher, I left for Europe to attend the Pacem in Terris II Conference, sponsored by the Center for the Study of Democratic Institutions, to be held in Geneva. On my way there and back—now free of those other pressures and able to return to what had been my major field of interest:

the study of Christian origins and the Dead Sea Scrolls—I consulted at length with various scholars in England and France, and was much stimulated to get right on with the further study these talks pointed to—and then the writing —soon after my return to Santa Barbara.

Then, only two weeks after returning to the United States, I was again struck with tragedy: Maren Bergrud, Director of New Focus Foundation, took her own life by an overdose of sleeping pills.

Her death came as a great shock to me. She had shared several of my experiences of what seemed to be communication with Jim after his death, and she had done quite a bit of studying in the field of psychic phenomena in preparation for the writing of the book for Doubleday. She knew the circumstances of Jim's death and appeared to accept not only the fact that there was "no way out" but also the assumption that Jim's adjustment had been more difficult because he did not die a natural death. So in one way it was surprising that Maren would take her own life.

On the other hand, I know, that she had had two operations for cancer, and that she tended to equate any illness involving internal pain with another cancerous growth. Moreover, from the information I was able to gather from her family and the secretaries who worked daily with her at New Focus, as well as from my own observation, it was apparent that her health and her emotional stability had been steadily declining and that over a period of time she had been taking increasingly more medicines of various kinds. Nevertheless, Mrs. Bergrud's death came as a terrible shock to all of us.

Another suicide on the part of one with whom I had been closely associated was more painful than I can readily describe; it carried not only its own impact but also the burden of the recall of Jim's death. In this case, however, I felt it likely that I would be able to communicate with Maren as soon as she had recovered, on the other side, from the trauma of her death. She had believed in the communication with Jim and I was sure, granting survival and psi communication, that when she "woke up" on the other side she would make every attempt to come through. So it was that fifteen days after Maren's death I went to see George Daisley in the hope that I would be able to communicate with her, be of help and learn something about her frame of mind at the time of her suicide.

Ψ

The session was both frustrating and disturbing. It was frustrating because Maren did not seem to be able to come through at all. Jim seemed to be there assuring me that he was with Maren. "She is confused and numb—unable to talk yet," Mr. Daisley reported Jim as saying.

I asked whether Jim had been able to learn anything about her death. The response was, "We are all with her, ready to help her adjust, but she is suffering a great deal and is still in a state of great confusion." This latter was disturbing, but it reflected what I had learned was often the case—that those who die violent deaths or take their own lives have more difficulty adjusting on the other side.

It was in mid-August, upon my return from Colorado where I spent a month as a Resident Scholar at the Aspen Institute of Humanistic Studies, that I went again to George Daisley to see if it were possible for Maren to come through. I felt it almost as an obligation—like the feeling that one should visit a friend in the hospital. On that occasion nothing seemed to come through from Maren, but Mr. Daisley reported that Jim had been able to talk with her. "She is still confused and is still suffering," were the words that came, "but she is beginning to be able to talk with us some."

"Has she said why she took her own life?" I asked.

"She says she was feeling very good that day and she had hoped that if she died feeling that way she could perpetuate the feeling. She knew the high would not last. She wanted to stay on it," was the response.

That was indeed what those of us who had seen Maren on the day of her death had observed. She had not looked as well in months. She seemed full of life and on top of everything. The secretaries reported that she had spent nearly all morning dictating to answer a whole pile of mail—more than she had done in one sitting for a long time. She had met a visitor from Belgium at the airport, driven him around Santa Barbara and joined him and me for a late dinner. When she left us, she was most pleasant and cheerful. Thus it seemed entirely possible that she had hoped somehow to perpetuate the good feeling she had enjoyed that day.

In fact, I had speculated just that. It was the theory about Maren's death that I myself had held—and others tended to concur in it. Thus, I was far from sure that anything was really coming through from either Jim or Maren. It seemed quite possible that Mr. Daisley was picking up my own thoughts, speculations and feelings by ESP and was reflecting them.

Ψ

All this seemed ironical. Whereas after Jim's death I had not believed he would live on, had known almost nothing about the field of psychic communication and therefore would never even have thought of trying to be in communication with him, and a series of events had almost forced me to seek out a medium; yet now that I really believed such contact to be possible—and knew Maren also thought so—nothing seemed to come through at all. Of course there were several possible explanations for that, even granting the survival hypothesis. It is possible, for example, that Jim could be one of the few persons on the other side with the gifted ability to communicate. Not all are able to, if any of this is to be believed; and those who can, become "guides" and apparently help others to come through by relaying messages for them. This was apparently the role Jim was developing.

Secondly, it is possible that Jim found it relatively easy to communicate with me because of the very close relationship we had established in the months we were continually together before his death so that channels were obviously "open."

Third, it is possible that Maren would not have the gift of communication from the other side in spite of her interest in the whole process while she was alive.

Still, the thought that there was not only no communication but also no survival suggested itself strongly. After all, it would have been relatively easy for any medium to know enough basic facts about my son to be convincing, whereas to find out anything about Maren Bergrud would have been another story. Moreover, a great deal more could have been pulled out of me about Jim by the use of ESP than would have been possible about Maren. And finally, it would have been more difficult to make good guesses about Maren, since much less was known about her, whereas to make some safe guesses about Jim would not be too difficult.

So once again I was left with the uncomfortable feeling that maybe the whole business of communication with the dead was less than plausible, after all. And this is spite of the fact that Jim had seemed to continue to come through in the sessions with comments and suggestions that were entirely relevant to current events in my life and consistent with his personality.

However, as the summer was coming to an end, I was focusing more toward the imminent meeting of the General Convention in Seattle, where the Bayne Committee report would be presented and some action taken on it. This would determine my future course regarding the heresy trial, and thus the shape of the next year—perhaps of several years to come.

9

To conclude, the position as I see it is this. In the known relevant *normal and abnormal* facts there is nothing to suggest, and much to counter-suggest, the possibility of any kind of persistence of the psychical aspect of a human being after the death of his body. On the other hand, there are many quite well attested *paranormal* phenomena which strongly suggest such persistence, and a few which strongly suggest the full-blown survival of a human personality. Most people manage to turn a blind eye to one or the other of these two relevant sets of data, but it is part of the business of a professional philosopher to try and envisage steadily both of them together. The result is naturally a state of hesitation and scepticism (in the correct, as opposed to the popular, sense of that word). I think I may say that for my part I should be slightly more annoyed than surprised if I should find myself in some sense persisting immediately after the death of my present body. One can only wait and see, or alternately (which is no less likely) wait and not see.

—*Prof. C. D. Broad*

The terror which shaped primitive theologies still tinges for the populace every hint of communication with disembodied souls. The transmutation of savage fear into scientific curiosity is of the essence of civilisation. Towards that transmutation each separate fragment of our evidence, *with undesigned concordance*, indisputably tends.

—*Prof. F. W. H. Myers*

Evolution is the product of knowledge acquired by personal experience. One only knows what one has experienced. Beyond this there is only belief. So long as you have not gone to Versailles you do not *know* that Versailles exists; you may *believe* it from reports, but you will not know it from experience.

—*P. E. Cornillier*

In preparation for the release of *If This Be Heresy,* as is customary my publisher arranged for a number of television and radio appearances in which I would be interviewed about the book. At the same time, Mr. Allen Spraggett, religion editor of the Toronto *Star,* conceived of an idea for a program on the CTV network known as "W-5" (Who, What, Why, When and Where). Mr. Spraggett knew of my Cambridge experiences and of my sittings with Ena Twigg and George Daisley, for while at our Center's Pacem in Terris Conference in Geneva (which he had covered for his paper) we had had a discussion about them in connection with the foreword I had just written for his book *The Unexplained.** Though that discussion had been in confidence, Mr. Spraggett also knew that my chapter on "Life after Death" in *If This Be Heresy* was to include the category of psychic phenomena as part of the data-basis upon which one could affirm ongoing life.

It occurred to Mr. Spraggett that it would be experimentally and pedagogically useful to invite a leading and responsible medium to appear on a program with me. It was his thought that if such a medium could go into a trance during the taping and "bring through" some entities, data would be directly provided for analytical discussion in the last part of the dialogue. Because he himself had carried out considerable investigation in the area of psychic phenomena he was most eager to give it a try. When Allen put the proposal to me I responded with interest and agreed to do it, knowing that since it would not be a live show we could decide at

* New York: New American Library, 1967.

the end of the video-taping how much of it should be aired, if any. In fact we knew that it would be all right if the medium chosen didn't "produce" in this particular context, since we were relatively sure of a fruitful discussion program anyway—whether the attempted séance came off or not.

Allen then invited the Rev. Arthur Ford, Disciples of Christ minister and well-known American medium, to appear on the program with me. The plan was that we would start off with a dialogue about the ideas in the books written by the three of us, each of which dealt with the psi field to a greater or lesser degree: Mr. Ford's *Nothing So Strange,** Spraggett's *The Unexplained,* and my *If This Be Heresy* (ch. 7). Then Mr. Ford would attempt to go into a trance and we would see what—if anything—happened. Whether he did or didn't, we would then go on with the discussion.

I arrived in Toronto late in the afternoon on September 2, 1967, and was taken to the hotel by a young lady from CTV. There I had a brief visit about the next day's plans with Allen Spraggett in the lobby of the hotel. When Allen closed by saying that he had similarly briefed the Rev. Mr. Ford, who was staying in the same hotel, I said I'd give him a ring and see if he could have dinner with me so that we could get acquainted. I told Allen I would be most interested to have a good visit with the man who alone had successfully met the challenge to mediumship the late Harry Houdini laid down before he died, namely, to come up after his death with the secret code he and his wife used in their "mind-reading" performances,† and who was thought by many to be the most outstanding medium in the United States today.

Mr. Spraggett told me that Arthur Ford preferred not to see me until before the taping, since if he were able to go

* New York: Harper & Row, 1958.
† Ibid., pp. 67–75.

into a trance and if the content were significant, any judgment as to its quality should not have to weigh in the fact of a visit by the two of us before the taping of the program. I was sorry, since much as I saw the value of the scheduled dialogue, I somehow didn't really believe that anything beyond that was going to happen—especially under the bright lights of a television studio crowded with personnel and moving equipment. But I was not unduly disappointed about not seeing Mr. Ford, for a free evening provided a welcome opportunity to catch up on some work.

It somehow never occurred to me that if Mr. Spraggett's small hope worked out it would draw national—indeed international—news coverage. I have done so many hundreds of television programs in the past twenty years that I have long ago come to be very relaxed about them, to the point that I am quite unself-conscious about the viewing audience. I do not think of "putting on a show," but rather I respond to the programs as opportunities to learn and grow and communicate, concentrating on and enjoying the persons with whom I am directly in conversation. Once the taping is over—that being the personal encounter—I give the program no further thought (never taking time to view the program itself) unless mail comes in about it. Then I answer the letters calling for pastoral advice and as many of the others as I can manage.

So without either trepidation or high hopes I reported to the television studio on Sunday afternoon, September 3, 1967, for what turned out to be not only a remarkable experience for me personally, but also one which was to bring to public attention—prematurely for my own preference—my experiences with psychic phenomena.

Ψ

The program began with Mr. Spraggett interviewing Mr. Ford. The two of them were seated on a platform in the center of a very large studio, surrounded by lights and cameras. Sitting around the periphery of the room were about twenty onlookers, including crewmen and studio staff members.

Allen asked a number of questions of Arthur Ford to draw him out as to the discovery of his mediumistic powers, some of the highlights of his career and the kinds of psychological and physiological tests to which he has been subjected over the years in order to determine the validity of his powers. One portion of their conversation (taken directly from the tape transcript) will, I think, be of particular interest:

SPRAGGETT: What is a medium?

FORD: It simply means that I am able to use for others the spiritual gifts which made the Church possible in the beginning, and am able somehow to function mentally and spiritually without regard to my body. I don't know how to put it.

SPRAGGETT: But when you're a medium, does this mean that you act as a kind of transmitter between the living and the dead?

FORD: I think so, yes.

SPRAGGETT: Although you don't think they're dead?

FORD: I don't think they're dead. They are much more vibrantly alive, I think, than we are.

SPRAGGETT: How does this communication take place?

FORD: It can take place in many ways but in my particular case it requires me to go into what is known as a yogi trance in which I am completely unconscious and another personality who calls himself Fletcher (and there was such a person; we've checked him out) speaks and he claims to be interpreting the ideas and the thoughts of people who are drawn to a particular group or a particular person because they're there and are needing help.

SPRAGGETT: Fletcher, in other words, is a kind of telephone operator who passes on messages through you from people who are dead?

FORD: That's right. And he's known as a "control" in psychic circles.

SPRAGGETT: I see. Now who was this Fletcher?

FORD: Fletcher is a French Canadian who was killed in the First World War and he's been working through me since 1924 and that's all I know about him, except that I do know his family, and I did at the time that I met Fletcher when I was about five years old.

SPRAGGETT: What evidence do you have that this personality that manifests itself through you in trance is really the spirit of a dead person? How do you know it isn't just a phase of your own unconscious mind?

FORD: Well, we're not altogether sure of that and there are many different ideas about it, but we have to judge what comes through by its evidential content, and I work with a great many people who are experienced at this sort of thing who investigate carefully and they check out the materials and they find that even if it was myself unconsciously, I couldn't possibly give the material I get.

SPRAGGETT: In other words, when you go into a trance the voice that comes from your mouth is not your own voice. Is this what you're saying?

FORD: I think it is my voice because Fletcher is a discarnate and we ask a discarnate—

SPRAGGETT: Discarnate. Do you mean out of the body?

FORD: A spirit if you like. And if we ask one to come back he has to use some person who's willing to be used, and so I provide the vocal chords through which Fletcher is able to put their ideas into words. And if you look back through the Bible and through history and study the history of psychism, you'll find that people have always been necessary as instruments for those in the spirit, or discarnates, to communicate.

Ψ

When I was invited onto the platform Allen Spraggett engaged me in conversation about chapter 7 of my then new book *If This Be Heresy*, in which, after covering a host of other kinds of experiences which point to the psi factor in the human personality, I dealt with the field of psychic phenomena. In that chapter I asserted that I could affirm life after death because of the vast amount of data available in these different fields suggesting that man is able to transcend the space-time continuum even now—and thus is already in eternal life. In addition, I said that for me the data in the field of psychic phenomena and research pointed to the likelihood that from time to time we are able to communicate with those who have died but live on.

Earlier Mr. Spraggett had asked Arthur Ford if he remained a skeptic and an agnostic about many aspects of this field, and Mr. Ford had replied that he thought agnosticism was the most direct road to truth. In discussing my affirmation of the possibility of communicating with deceased persons, therefore, I pointed out that my method of *facts + faith* is an attempt to implement the agnostic spirit in arriving at theological truth. If there are no facts available, a leap of faith is certainly blind and therefore of little real significance. If, on the other hand, we have genuine facts which are relevant, then the appropriate theological response is to seek a reasonable hypothesis to explain them, and—without freighting on an undue amount of "belief"—to make a leap of faith which would enable one to live and act on a basis of the hypothesis.

Mr. Spraggett then asked if I would have made the same affirmations ten years ago. I admitted that I would have affirmed life after death as one of the basic tenets of the Christian faith—but on a quite different basis: at that time I still accepted without much question the authority of the Creeds of the Church. The possibility of communication with the dead, however, would have been a different matter. Though I would have been open to it—it was, in fact, on the basis of such an openness that I had been willing to become a sponsor of the Churches' Fellowship for Psychical and Spiritual Research—I would not have affirmed it: I did not have sufficient evidence of my own, and the Church was not teaching it, except with regard to Jesus and his disciples, and, in the case of the more Biblically "faithful," a few other instances in the Old and New Testaments.

Then Allen asked if I had had any personal experiences of communication through a trance medium. I remember being hesitant to answer the question, for I was not yet ready to talk publicly about my experiences. I can see now that even that reaction on my part was odd in the light of my presence there. After all, if Mr. Ford were to go into a trance it would then be public knowledge—in Canada anyway—that I had been at what would, after the fact, be tagged as a séance. Yet somehow I was not putting all of this together.

So I answered, "Yes, some personal experiences, but I have approached it in the broader way for this reason. I think that many of our viewers today probably are reflecting on experiences of extrasensory perception, precognition, or perhaps even the sense of the presence of someone deceased. But if they are fairly skeptical—and we are in a scientific age —they are probably rejecting those experiences as not proving very much because they are just isolated instances . . . I don't believe people ought to draw great big conclusions from isolated events, but if they will study and read, they will find that there are dozens of others who have had similar experiences. If they will see how broad a base of data there is, how many instances in all of these different fields have been checked out objectively, then they will be able to take their own personal experiences seriously and say, 'That fits in,'" I explained.

But Mr. Spraggett was not content with my answer, and he persisted: "Now in your case, have you received any messages through mediums that you regard as factual?"

Being one who, though a churchman, had increasingly come to believe in speaking the truth, and in saying it the way it is (and to learn to endure "respectable" churchly rebuke for my pains!), I really felt cornered. "Yes, I have had this occur," I conceded. "It, as I say, is credible to me in the light of the larger context. You see, otherwise I would probably strain very hard, lean over backward, to find every possible way to explain away some of the phenomena. And, indeed, that is probably a good discipline anyway. If it is explainable some other way, fine. We are not reaching for it. We don't want to overbelieve."

The three of us then went on to discuss some of the narratives in the Bible which would seem to reflect psychic events: examples of clairvoyance, messages delivered by angels (who seem to act in the role of "guides"), the Resurrection appearances, etc.

Mr. Spraggett asked what kind of evidence I would require to be convinced that a purported communication from the dead really was such, and not just guessing or fraud on the part of the medium. I put forth my belief that the gift of mediumship should not be dismissed offhand because there are frauds in the field. Instead, I pointed out, the approach of the scientist is to evaluate the data which are before him and on that basis to draw his conclusions. To dismiss as impossible something which has not yet been investigated is most unscientific.

I then went on to say that I have no doubt that some things which come through in a sitting can be accounted for under the category of extrasensory perception, but that I found it interesting that many people who five years ago would not have believed in ESP now would explain purported communication with the dead as "just extrasensory perception," as though that were a commonplace thing. "That is a gain, anyway," I commented.

"And second," I went on, "to me extrasensory perception is a profound and wonderful mystery and gives beautiful evidence of the synchronicity of the universe—the Unus in the universe, namely, God. So that is fine anyway. I am not unimpressed if it is extrasensory perception. I have seen an awful lot that I could reduce to that.

"On the other hand, when the data which comes through the medium is something which was not known already to you or to anyone present—and especially if it is known to no one but the person who is deceased and you have to check it out—then we are dealing with a level beyond the ESP possibilities which is impressive indeed." I had a more limited understanding of the possibilities at that time: I thought ESP took us to a certain level, and that from there on only the existence of a surviving conscious personality could adequately account for the perception and reception of information. I know now that to conceive the alternative in only this one way was too simplistic a view.

"To me explanations apart from the affirmation that communication focuses and centers upon the person on the other side," I went on, "get so complex that they begin to violate the principle of parsimony—you know, the rule that you don't take the more complicated explanation if the simpler one is available. In other words, sometimes the simplest explanation is that this is a surviving human being."

Ψ

The conversation was in that mood when the time came for Mr. Ford's attempt to function as a medium. As an added agnostic observer, a previously unintroduced member of the studio staff—a woman who did not believe in the possibility of communication with the dead—joined us. Although I was not sure anything would really happen, I was most interested to experience firsthand the mediumistic gifts of Arthur Ford. I watched closely as he prepared to go into a trance.

Allen Spraggett had asked him to describe what he was going to do as he did it, so as Arthur Ford took out of his pocket a dark handkerchief and began to tie it around his head, he said, "Yes, I'm going into a trance or a sleep. It may be another form of self-hypnotism. Anyway, I become unconscious, and I put this handkerchief over my eyes simply because it's easier to go to sleep if you don't have the light. I don't like a dark room. Anything that takes place in the dark can generally take place in the light. I'll go to sleep, and if Fletcher comes, I hope something happens . . ."

Mr. Ford adjusted his posture to a more comfortable position and began breathing very deeply. His head fell to his chest and the deep breathing continued. After several minutes of dead air time, his head jerked and lifted up into a normal waking position and we heard:

"Hello."

"Is it Fletcher?" Allen asked. The response came (excised from the condensed version aired, I understand):

"Yes, my name is Fletcher. I have spoken to you before."

"Yes, that's true," Allen replied.

"These other two people I have not spoken to, but I'm very happy to speak to you. [The comment seemed to be addressed to me and the young lady from the CTV staff.] The only people I can talk to are people who come because you are here, and they don't walk in the room like you do. I can see a great light . . . light, a great massive light, if light can be a mass, and I watch this light, and suddenly it begins to take form, and it takes the form of people. They're taking form now. I can see several. Sometimes if they are able to build up very definite bodies and come very close I can almost read their lips. Other times I have to depend upon thought projection from them. And I have to put it into other words, and sometimes it is difficult. But I have developed for myself a sort of system by which I'm able to get pictures of sound."

I was interested in this rather lengthy explanation of the process of communication we were apparently about to experience. I had never had it explained in quite those terms, though it had occurred to me that a medium serves as kind of an "instrument" through which—if the process is what it is purported to be—messages are transmitted from entities on the other side and that the instrument is not a perfected one at all. In fact, being in a séance is comparable to listening to an old-fashioned crystal radio: what comes through is spotty, disjointed and often difficult to decipher.

"The first person who comes is someone—and there's two, there's a young man and an elderly man. There are others in the background, but the young man seems radiantly happy, and very clear, though I get the impression that he was helped by this other man to make the adjustment. Death does not do anything to a person except to free him, it doesn't change their character, or their thinking, but it does remove the limitation."

An interesting observation, I thought. I had always believed this to be the case, but customary Christian beliefs are quite different in this regard.

"And this boy says that before he came over he was confused and mentally disturbed, but more a sense of fear and frustration. It seems like there's a Slavic background: maybe Russian, Polish, or something, I don't know what it is. Anyway, he says, he's glad to speak to his father, and he has learned that when people come over suddenly, and quite often they come violently, they do still retain enough of their former life in the body—anyway, it's a crisis experience, and they're able to do things that they cannot do later. He says that he was able to give some—what you're talking about, he was listening when you were talking about that, what he did was a telepathic thing, or telekinetic."

We had been discussing telekinetic and psychokinetic phenomena earlier. Apparently the reference was to that, and implicit was an inference that Jim was responsible for the phenomena in the Cambridge apartment. This could well have been pulled out of my mind by ESP, for in the discussion I had been thinking about the Cambridge events, or out of Allen Spraggett's, for he also knew in general about my experiences.

The voice of the medium came haltingly. The feeling conveyed was that something like a process of translation was going on which caused the control—or the medium—to grope for words which would adequately express the feelings, ideas and images seemingly being impressed on him. The words frequently came in spurts and sometimes without logical connection with the preceding sentence.

As for my son's Slavic background, the most elemental

research could have uncovered that, for his mother's Russian maiden name (Yanovsky) was hardly deceptive in that regard. And the words about his mental condition before death could well have represented a safe guess, since Jim did, after all, take his own life.

Then Allen asked, "Who is this message for, Fletcher?"

Arthur Ford's voice came back: "It seems to be for the clergyman. I haven't got the boy's name yet, but I will in a moment. I've got senior and junior. Is that right?"

"That's right, Fletcher," I responded.

I had, by then, become adjusted to the concept of a control and thus addressed "Fletcher," whatever in fact this might represent in the total process, as I had grown accustomed to addressing "Jim" in the same context. No matter how iconoclastic one might be about the results of such sessions, when in the context itself it seems appropriate to go along with the process, taking it at face value and responding as personally as seems appropriate to the dialogue. This I would call "getting with it." It is not unlike saying the Creed in church in order to go along with the congregation's corporate worship, even though one, if alone, might be unsure about affirming each individual item thereof.

Just out of common courtesy, really, one should have a cooperative spirit and respond on the medium's terms while in a sitting. After all, whatever one might—from an agnostic posture—make of it all, here is a man using his gifts in the most effective and beneficial way he knows. The least one can do is receive his contribution with respect. In any ordinary conversation communication can be effectively blocked by a person who picks apart sentence after sentence and complicatedly qualifies every response. No less so would this be true when a medium is trying to bring through messages in a séance.

So when Arthur Ford's voice went on, I tried to be helpful.

"And he talks about having a Slavic background: What's that mean . . ."

"That's right," I acknowledged. "He is one quarter [*sc.*, half] Russian. And you referred, Fletcher, to an older man with him, or . . . I gather from the image . . ." I was trying to elicit more information.

"Well, this older man looks like . . . he doesn't look like a Biblical character, but the Biblical name, like an old prophet, or something. Quite old when he came over but his spiritual body doesn't take on the defects of the physical, you know, and in the spiritual body they're mature and perfect. I would say he was maybe very old, and a very good man. But this boy seems to be very close to him, and this boy says that I am not going to go over a lot of ground that has already been covered, I could say many things, to prove my identity but I will not say them on television, but he wants you to remember what he . . . and Elijah, or something—"

I was struck by the fact that what seemed to come from Jim broke through in the first person. I wondered what this meant in terms of the role Fletcher was supposed to be playing.

"Elias," I corrected, "the Greek Septuagint and Latin Vulgate name for the prophet Elijah. This is his grandfather."

When Arthur Ford reminded me after the program that it had been he who spoke to me at St. Thomas in New York about my son and Elias, I recalled the attempt by the purported Fletcher to find the right name for Jim's grandfather, when, in a waking state, Mr. Ford had not had any difficulty with the name, apparently. Perhaps, then, the trance state really did enable another "person" to come through. If so, the Fletcher personality apparently did not have ready access to—or had forgotten—the message which Arthur Ford gave me that day in New York.

This made me more convinced—not less—that something really paranormal was going on. On a normal level of communication there would have been no problem with the names. If, as had been explained at the beginning of the séance, there was involved here a kind of translation process —of images, impressions and ideas to words—then it could have been much more difficult.

Ford's voice continued: "That's right, and in their earth life they seem to have been quite fond of each other."

"Right," I affirmed.

The flow of words continued: "And they are now. I should say that the grandfather preceded him here. This boy says that he is not, he does not know, he cannot remember, the circumstances of his death, it was some tragic way, but he says that he knows now that he was falling into the state of mind of, a, I don't know, condition, and he doesn't remember how or why, except he knows that he was not able to think straight, and he wasn't . . . but he says 'I will tell you this much, Dad'—he called you Dad—the beginning was someone whom he calls Halverston. I don't know, is the name like Halverston, or Halbertson?"

"In this life or the next?" I asked. I remembered a Marvin Halverson—I thought, at least—but I had not heard anything about him for years, so I had no way of knowing whether he was living or dead. The answer came.

"He's here now, this Halverston. I've seen him here; he seems to have come over about the same time the boy did. Do you remember such a person?"

"I think I do. I didn't connect him," I responded. I did not know whether Jim even knew Marvin Halverson—or if the man I was thinking of was the one being referred to.

Ford's voice went on: "Wait a minute, wait, check it out. He had, his name was Marvin, and uh, something about some modern music, or modern dancing, or art or something, in the church. And, uh . . ."

"There's such a person," I interrupted. I was sure now we were talking about the same one.

My last recollection of Marvin Halverson was that he had been director of the National Council of Churches' department dealing with the relation of the Church to various art forms and architecture. That evening, while waiting to take a plane to Philadelphia to appear on the Mike Douglas show, I made a telephone call from the Kennedy International Airport to a friend in New York City about another matter, and was given information about Marvin Halverson which began to clear up the mystery of his connection with my son. The very fact that the next "outside" person I talked to after leaving the Toronto group had this information about the most puzzling item in the séance would seem an instance of synchronicity!

"I'd have to check out any connections with my son. Though now we're talking about connections on the other side."

"Yeah, Halverson's here. On this side."

Then Allen broke in for the first time in several minutes. "Did Halverson know Bishop Pike's son? On earth?" The answer: "Mm, hmm, and he knew Bishop Pike, not intimately, but had done some things in connection with the church, or Cathedral, and he was trying to bring back into the church modern music and the updated . . . so to speak, that's what Jim says."

For the first time my son's name was used—so casually I almost missed it.

(I later recalled one thing which Mr. Halverson had done in connection with the Cathedral years before. Between 1955 and 1958 a weekly ABC network program of mine originated from the Cathedral of St. John the Divine. Marvin Halverson had been my guest on a program which dealt with the history of the cross in church art and which was filmed in the Cathedral building itself. So the words ". . . he knew Bishop Pike, not intimately, but had done some things in connection with the church or Cathedral" were correct, but left a mystery in what his connection may have been with Jim.)

Ψ

The focus then seemed to shift to another person, as if someone else had stepped forward: "Now, then, another person has come and said, 'I want to speak to you, because I more or less followed, you more or less followed the same path I did, I was older than you.' This man says that he was a chaplain at some university, before you were. I guess you took his place. Goes quite a ways back. He tried, or people tried twice to make a bishop of him, but failed. And he studied in the same seminary you did, and got to be very much interested in what you were doing, you succeeded him as chaplain. Name is—I don't get the last name—I get the first name, is Louis. Louis is an older man, doesn't look so old now. Louis, Pitt, I think, Pitt. Do you remember such a person?"

"Yes, I do," I said, reaching back into my memory. It had been a long time since I had thought about him or heard of him.

"And he has with him someone who says that—he said, I feel a little bit responsible in a way for your present condition, because, he said, I was interested in studying the background of religion, the history of the Churches. The name starts with "Z." Sounds like another Russian name, Zalinsky, or Zabrisky, or something."

"Yes," I nodded. Again in the back of my memory I recalled a Zabriskie, though I had not thought of him for years.

"And he said, 'The reason I'm coming here, that Jim asked me to do so is because your life also parallels something in my family. Before you became a minister or clergyman, even a bishop, you were a lawyer and my father was a lawyer, and at one time many years ago, was the chancellor of the diocese from which, where you used to be.' Do you remember anything about that?"

"Yes I do," I said, "I think we're talking about the Dean of the Virginia Theological Seminary, when I first took courses there, and the lawyer we're talking about is a George Zabriskie, I think, or maybe not." It was so long since I had thought about Alexander or George Zabriskie, Sr., that I wasn't certain if I remembered correctly. And then again, I wasn't certain how much speculating I should do as to what was being said.

"'Yeah,' he smiled, 'that's right.' And he said that the course you took under him more or less shaped your thinking."

"More what?" I asked. Sometimes it was difficult to understand the words.

"More or less shaped your thinking."

"Influenced my thinking, indeed." I was trying to be polite, for I couldn't remember, frankly, what course I took from Zab, as we called him, though I had a feeling that I might well have taken one. Yet during a sitting I have the subjective feeling that I am talking with someone, and if I am, or if there is chance that I am, I want to be at least as polite as I would be under ordinary conversational circumstances. Yet there is also an air of unreality which stems from the fact that there is no one to be seen while conversing except the medium—and he appears not to be the communicator.

"He was teaching in the field of Church history, at Virginia Theological Seminary, as well as being the Dean," I replied. Then I tried to move on, since I couldn't recall the course I was supposed to have taken from him.

(I later remembered: I in fact had been a member of a small seminar of his in the thought of selected American figures such as Jonathan Edwards, Horace Bushnell, etc. I also recalled important ways in which my work on Edwards and our seminar discussions of his writings had brought about the sharp focusing of certain psychological/theological issues enabling me to enter my studies at Union with Paul Tillich and Reinhold Niebuhr with significant [to me, at least] questions to the fore. *More or less shaped your thinking.* Correct.)

"The Louis Pitt you're referring to, I think—I'll have to verify this later—was Acting Chaplain for a while, or in some way connected with the chaplaincy at Columbia University, at some point before I came there as chaplain, as head of the Department of Religion. He was involved in the chaplaincy somehow while Rector of Grace Church in New York City. He wasn't in the episcopate; there's a long story there, but there's an involvement," I finished.

Again I was avoiding a statement which might offend. I was beginning to recall the biography of this priest, who had appeared to be a likely candidate for bishop at least twice, but who each time lost out by a surprise turn of events. Arthur Ford's voice then broke in on us again: "Anyway, he just wants to tie it in, because in both these cases there was an outreach, and a parallel, do you understand . . . Now, then, Jim says he wants you to definitely understand that neither you nor any other member of the family has any right to feel any sense of guilt or have any feelings that you failed him in any way."

I wasn't impressed one way or the other by such reassurances. If really from Jim, it was kind but not oracular and not determinative of the complicated question of the relative degrees of parental, societal and personal responsibility. Some have said, "That's what he wanted to hear." Actually it wasn't (though I didn't mind, of course). One who has studied and written on the ethics of responsibility in the light of psychology,* has counseled extensively over the years and has been psychoanalyzed himself is unlikely to accept either simplistic clearances or simplistic faultings for himself or for anyone else.

Now what followed was of a different character—not on the opinion level but on the fact level. "It was a physiological condition, and the mind, or the psyche, cannot manifest on the earth plane, except through the brain, which is a transmissive instrument. If that brain is damaged by some kind of a shock or by an organic condition, then there's no clear thinking, do you understand?"

"Right. Right. Thank you, Jim," I answered. The words came close to a statement about the use of psychedelic drugs and I was beginning to feel uncomfortable. I was not ready to reveal the fact of Jim's involvement with drugs and though I knew we could edit the tape, I was not eager even for the small audience that was there in the studio to know the facts about the details of his death. So I hoped another subject would be opened up. These words followed: "'And I

* E.g., *Beyond Anxiety* (New York: Scribners, 1953); *The Next Day* (New York: Doubleday, 1957; rev. ed., under the title *Facing the Next Day*, Macmillan, 1968); *Doing the Truth* (Doubleday, 1955; rev. ed., Macmillan, 1965); *Beyond the Law* (New York: Doubleday, 1963); *Teen-agers and Sex* (Englewood Cliffs, New Jersey: Prentice-Hall, 1965); *You and the New Morality: 74 Cases*, cited above.

want you to realize this, that I enjoyed the time I was with you.' Was he with you in some other country?"

Again, words as from Jim seemed to come through directly for a moment, but I responded to the question which had been put.

"He was indeed, when I was on leave at Cambridge University."

"Well, we're speaking about . . . He said that he used to meet there with some people who were interested in ESP, or psychic things, met some. But he used to sneak in to hear the lecture that someone was giving. And there's an old gentleman and your son; and that man, the man that was giving the lectures, has the same name as his father. Seems like a Scotch name, but the interesting thing is that the old man, and he wants you to check this out, because there is something that could . . . prove, that the old man has two cats, which had formerly belonged to his son. And there was something about Corpus Christi. Wonder what he means, Corpus Christi?"

"There's a college of Cambridge University called Corpus Christi," I proposed. What a groping, rambling message that was, I thought. I didn't know of any interest on the part of my son in ESP or psychic things. Could this stand for psychedelic? If so, the rest of the sentence held up. But as to the lectures, I drew a blank. Moreover, what could two cats have to do with anything?

"Do you get this man's name, Fletcher?" Allen Spraggett asked. The reply: "Sounded like Donald, something, Mac, I think it is, Donald Mac."

"Is he the younger, or the older?" Spraggett went on.

"He's the younger. The old man is here and has the same name. Do you know anything about that?"

"The old man is deceased?" I asked. I thought I knew who

might be the living referent, but I didn't know anything about his father.

"Yeah, he's with your boy here."

"Really?" I was trying to figure this all out.

"But he says that he knows nothing about theology but his son does. And, uh . . ."

"And the son has two cats that belonged to the older man?" Allen tried again to get it straight.

"That we could check out," I offered, not really being able to imagine how. But a correction came: "No, the older man has two cats that once belonged to his son. Seems like his son has, maybe a weakness for cats. You don't know about that, do you? You can check it."

"The old man is deceased?" I asked again.

"Yeah, and he was Scotch, and uh . . ."

"Where are his cats now?" For the first time the CTV staff member entered the conversation. Ford's head turned slightly toward her, as if to acknowledge her presence: "They're in the spirit world . . . animal, there's only one life in the universe, and it takes every form of life in a tree, and the life in an animal, the life in a person. The same creative force but it manifests through different vehicles."

"Can you try for the name, Fletcher?" Allen made one more attempt, entering into the spirit of the questioning as I had. The name seemed difficult to get.

"Sounded like McKenny. McKenny, or something, McKinnon, Donald McKinnon."

"Donald MacKinnon is a professor in the Faculty of Divinity at Cambridge; I knew him quite well. He was the principal influence on my thinking there," I said, relieved that the name had finally come out.

"How about the cats?" Allen asked me.

"This I don't know about, but we could check it," I replied.

Cats seemed like an almost ludicrous subject for discussion, somehow. Although Donald MacKinnon had had a great deal of influence on my thinking during my sabbatical, I knew nothing about his personal habits and certainly knew nothing about his father. I wondered how one could even find out about the cats, but Ford's voice went on: "Another thing, this old man says that when he was on the earth plane he was very—well—he was a Socialist, or laborer, or something and not into church business . . . church."

I had thought we were through with the MacKinnons. Now I entered in—speculating—in order to get on to something else. "The father must have been of the Church of Scotland. He'd be Presbyterian. [I don't know why I said this; I had never heard a word about Professor MacKinnon's father. Was something coming through to me directly?] The son is a layman, but a professor of Divinity, nevertheless. I think the Episcopal Church of Scotland. We can check on that."

My interruption did not seem to help. On went the same theme: " . . . laborite, now there's very definitely, and this boy who says he's your son, says that he, on one or two occasions, either met this professor or listened to him, but he didn't spend all his time where you were, you see."

"No, that's right." This latter comment seemed rather obvious, considering it was supposed to be about a twenty-year-old, even if Arthur Ford himself were making it. But it seemed important enough to go on with: "Did he walk around, go on a sort of walking trip, or bicycles, something, horses? hostels and things?"

"He, he . . ." Again I was hesitating. This seemed like guessing, for the question could have been about any young student.

"Making a tour? But anyway, he's there and speaks about it."

This feeble last try called forth my helpful side and I decided to be more cooperative.

"He used a bike and he was there at another college, Cambridgeshire College, something like a junior college," I offered, hoping we would move on to something more interesting.

Ψ

Shortly after the taping, Allen Spraggett was able to contact Professor Donald MacKinnon in Cambridge by long-distance telephone. He told the professor a little about the séance and the message that had purportedly came through from his father.

"Did you ever have two cats?" Mr. Spraggett inquired.

"That's extraordinary," Donald MacKinnon responded. "I did have two cats as pets when I was a boy, one black and the other gray. One was named Mewger. The gray disappeared about three years after my father's death in 1933—and the black one acted strangely the day of my father's funeral. It darted out someplace in front of the coffin as it was being carried out of the house."

Such a response on the part of Professor MacKinnon would appear to confirm the information that came through from Arthur Ford. However, shortly thereafter, a staff member from *Newsweek* contacted the Cambridge professor and called to his attention the fact that much of what was said about him was readily available, or inferable from, the *International Who's Who* (1966–67, page 1955), which gives the following information, along with a lot more that didn't come through:

MacKINNON, PROFESSOR DONALD MacKENZIE, M.A., Norris-Hulse Professor of Divinity, Cambridge University, since 1960; Fellow of Corpus Christi College, Cambridge, since 1960 . . . s. of late D. M. MacKinnon, Procurator Fiscal . . . Member of Scottish Episcopal Church and of Labour Party . . . *Recreations:* walking, cats, the cinema . . .

But still at first blush it seemed that by making a few guesses—especially with regard to the late Mr. MacKinnon's interests and affiliations, and to the cats which he purportedly had with him—Arthur Ford could well have brought through some "remarkable" material, needing only a little help from *Who's Who.*

Actually, on the church side there was a hit; on the political, a miss. The deceased Mr. MacKinnon was a member of the established Church (Presbyterian), the Church of Scotland, unlike his son who, as *Who's Who* indicates, is a member of the branch of the Anglican Communion found in Scotland, the Scottish Episcopal Church. On the other hand there is also a divergence between the two on political party. Professor MacKinnon is, as *Who's Who* says, a member of the Labor Party, but, according to the latter, his father, far from being "socialist" or "laborite," belonged to the Conservative, i.e., "Tory" Party.

As for the deceased felines, while the biographical paragraph uses simply the word "cats," as one of three present "hobbies," there came through Mr. Ford explicit reference, as from the Professor's deceased father, to two particular cats who had died. It was this, not just the bare reference to "cats," which Professor MacKinnon readily connected with two cats he had owned years before and which were associated with his father, the second of them in a particularly mysterious way.

In any case, there is no way of proving that this material was researched. Even if the reference to the *Who's Who* entry had been complete—which it certainly was not—all that would actually have been proved was that the information Professor MacKinnon had supplied to the publishers of the reference book was reflective of the same facts which by *some* process—research or psi—received expression through Mr. Ford. Now if the totality of individual items which were voiced that Sunday afternoon had been embraced in various available sources, either the reductionist method or the principle of parsimony would make it appropriate to discard the functioning of psi as a viable hypothesis. If, on the other hand, there are items which turn out to be true but which were highly unlikely to have been researched, then the fact that some items in a total sitting have been published somewhere does not automatically disqualify the psi hypothesis. But even if this material about the MacKinnons was researched, that does not in and of itself call into question all the other data. An otherwise valid séance *could* have been bolstered by some research. It is possible.

Donald MacKinnon immediately dropped me a note telling me of the *Who's Who* entry, suggesting that Mr. Ford might have researched that part of the séance which referred to him—and perhaps more. I was grateful for his tip-off, since I would not have thought of looking in *Who's Who* myself. But when I read Professor MacKinnon's response to Allen Spraggett, I felt that there was more to it than that—along the lines of the reasoning just spelled out.

Ψ

At last the scene seemed to shift: "Now, then, there's another man, as I said. He was glad that you took up the fight where he left it off, or something to that effect, and he said that his name is Hope, Holt, and uh, something about women delegates, or women, certain privileges of women in the Church. He was working on that many, many years and was rebuffed. Wonder what it means?"

"Hm, this we could check out; I have been active in this area," I responded. The name meant nothing to me. As if to help out came these words: "He says Charlie Kaye could answer that for you."

"Charlie Haig? Living or dead?" I asked. The response was a correction of the name:

"No, Charlie Kaye."

"Charlie Kaye?" I was almost amused at what appeared to be an earnest effort to get the information straight.

"It's a long name, I don't get it. It's a preacher of some kind."

"Charlie Kaye Holt?" I was really guessing now. Everything seemed so remote. It was hard to follow it all.

"No, Charlie Kin something, Kin . . ."

"Charlie Kinsolving." The words popped out of my mouth before I could catch them. I was sorry at once that I had let slip a name before it had come through clearly. I knew that ruined any opportunity to determine whether the name would have been given without my help. But it was too late now. The question was now being addressed to me.

"Could there be such a person?"

"Maybe I led too strongly on that name," I said apologetically. And after all that came this:

"Anyway it doesn't matter. Check that out on the Holt. And the first name is either Howard or Harry, or something, starts with an 'H.' "

"Howard, or Harry, Holt, who was involved with fighting for women's rights in the church." I had been distracted by the "Charlie Kaye" thing and was trying to recall what had been said about this Holt.

"Right. In the church."

I never did find out who was being referred to. With so many other things on my mind, I only checked out the items which mattered to me personally; to test the validity of the purported message about a Harry Holt would have been interesting, but frankly, I just never got to it.

Ψ

It appeared that someone else had stepped forward, if that's what was going on.

"Now he said to tell you that the last person who comes here for you is someone who calls himself the, what is it, ecclesiastical, ecclesiastical panhandler. What's that mean?"

"Ecclesiastical panhandler," I repeated noncommittally. I wondered if the implication was that my son Jim was bringing all these people forward. Did that mean he was acting as a "guide?"

"Begging Bishop, wouldn't it be?" Allen chipped in.

"No, begging or ecclesiastical," I suggested. "Let's find out who it is."

This time I felt Allen Spraggett was leading too strongly. It's very difficult while in a sitting to restrain yourself from responding to the medium's voice in the same candid way one would respond in any other conversation, holding up his end of the conversation by filling in information where possible—even to the extent of finishing sentences for people or "second-guessing" their thoughts. Yet I knew that we should not be offering too much information if we wanted to test the process itself to see whether veridical information could come through. Instead, we needed to wait, no matter how hard that was to do. Ford's voice continued: "Wait a minute, he says he died in the act of baptizing, or some rite of the church; he had a heart attack, and you succeeded him, wherever it is. But he said, that was what some people called him."

"That's indeed what he was called. He called himself this," I agreed. I knew who was being referred to.

"Do you get a name, Fletcher?" Allen was being careful again—trying to draw out information.

"Oh, like Black or something. Charl, Carl, Black, Block."

"Karl Morgan Block, the fourth Bishop of California, my predecessor. I was Bishop Coadjutor and then succeeded on his death at an ordination. In the midst of an ordination he had a heart attack."

All of that could have easily been researched, although it seems to me it would have been difficult to know of the nickname "ecclesiastical panhandler." It may have been widely known, but I had only heard of it from one person, a Canon to the Ordinary (a senior aide to the Bishop) who served under both Bishop Block and me, the Rev. Richard E. Byfield.

Meanwhile, Mr. Ford's voice went on: "But he says that you know that you have a great many friends among the prophets. Now, he seems to be talking about prophets on the earth plane. A school of prophets . . ."

"He founded a School of Prophets at the Cathedral for postgraduate training in preaching for clergy." That made me feel somewhat uncomfortable. It was a program that had been quite dear to his heart, but, because of the vicissitudes of shortage of income, I had not carried forward the original idea and had instead put the income to more modest, but related, clergy-education purposes. I sensed the underlying meaning of the expression "rising up to haunt." It was out of this somewhat embarrassed feeling that I responded within the context.

"Karl, or rather, Fletcher, could you speak to Karl, if that's the way it is. I did change things a bit, you know, and we'd never been in touch very much. You were ill when I came out, and we didn't talk but a couple of times, but . . ."

The response was an interruption: "Things needed changing."

I felt relieved and said so. "It makes me feel good to hear that, because I admired and respected you, and yet I hoped you weren't feeling too badly about some changes." Intuitively and subjectively I felt that I was indeed talking to Karl Block—but as much when he had seemed to be embarking on something I didn't much want to hear as when the word was personally reassuring. I found myself addressing him directly, and the answers also seemed to come back in the first person.

"No, here we soon realize that we have to get things into perspective, so easy to get into a rut and go around in a circle, repeating, repeating, repeating. You did a magnificent job, and you have magnificent work yet to do. He says, 'I think that in the future, maybe the distant future, that book you have in your hands, your book, will be almost as important as the theses that Luther nailed onto the church door.'"

"Thank you. I hope it's useful," I said quietly. I felt he was overstating it a bit and I was almost embarrassed. I hadn't intended to turn the conversation back to me and surely not in such an elaborately complimentary way. But Karl had been capable of that. A big man in both senses of the word, he was a Virginia gentleman of the old school, with ready enthusiasms expressed in a ready flow of fulsome words and phrases and vivid analogies. That was Bishop Block.

But the words continued to come: "And do not feel that you are going to suffer any more indignities. You are putting into words what the majority of your fellows think,* but dare not speak because they are afraid to jeopardize themselves. You've never been afraid to do that." (The style—and elegant it is—was certainly that of the fourth Bishop of California.)

Determined to change the subject to one of my own choice, I said: "May I say to Karl—and this comes right from the shoulder for my predecessor, through Fletcher—that he built a very strong foundation. And, Karl, you had a great gift for picking out land, ahead of the procession, for some of the churches I've built and congregations I've founded. You've missed only once and that's a place, I think, called El Sobrante. You got on the wrong side of the freeway, and landed out there in sort of a cow pasture. But that's a pretty good record, missing only once. You were a great land buyer."

The response seemed to be highly informed: "The most, he says . . . This might give you a clue . . . he said that one of the best pieces of land I got was, uh, at Obispo, or something. Do you know anything about that?"

"Yes, I do, indeed," I agreed, surprised that this should come up. "Now," I urged, "this is quite remarkable . . . One of

* Supportive of this is the research headed by Professor Charles Y. Glock and Dr. Rodney Stark of the University of California at Berkeley. Their statistics on the subject, with citations of their works, are summarized in *If This Be Heresy*, pp. 70–72. In a recent article, "Will Ethics Be the Death of Christianity?" *Trans-action*, June 1968, pp. 7–14, they say ". . . during the recent attempts to try him for heresy, Episcopalian Bishop James A. Pike defended himself by saying he had merely told the laity what the clergy had taken for granted for years. Moreover, the majority of Episcopalian church members hold theological views quite similar to Bishop Pike's. This presents an ironic picture of Sunday services in many churches. Both pastor and congregation reject or at least doubt the theological assumptions of the creeds they recite and the rituals in which they participate, but neither acknowledges this fact."

the best pieces of land you've bought . . ." I wasn't going to give it away this time if I could help it, but Ford's voice completed the sentence for me: ". . . was Obispo."

"Well, Obispo was [part of what] you named it. You named it half modestly and half immodestly. I liked the name. Obispo is part of the Spanish name for the place you bought. A magnificent buy indeed. Can Fletcher spell that out a little bit?"

I was most interested to see what he could come up with and was trying very hard not to give away any more clues. When I initiated the topic of property I was thinking about land for churches. Now suddenly we were talking about a different kind of property altogether. Arthur Ford could not have picked this up from me by direct ESP, for I hadn't even been thinking about El Rancho del Obispo.

In response to my request came these words: "Well, he said, I wanted a place where one could think without interruption. And I wanted a place which was almost like a monastery or a retreat."

"Right." Perhaps I was too readily convinced, but this seemed remarkable indeed. I went on in confirmation of the remarks: "It's the Diocesan Conference Center (ranch land north of the diocese) up on the Russian River. It is a ranch named El Rancho del Obispo, the Bishop's Ranch."

It impressed me a great deal that information which I knew to be absolutely accurate had come through on a point far from my mind but related by "association of ideas" to a topic of conversation I myself had initiated. It could have been pulled out of my unconscious by ESP; but, if so, even at that it was very impressive.

Ψ

The conversation moved on and I couldn't imagine where all these different characters were coming from. It was like watching selected short subjects at the movies. Whether arranged by Arthur Ford and/or Allen Spraggett on this side or by Jim and/or Fletcher on the other side—or whether just by coincidence—this was turning out to be quite a production. Next in line came: "Do you know an old lady who, well, she doesn't look old now, she's very nice-looking, she used to be a thorn in your side, when you were the Dean. But she won't give us any more than that. But Jim says, he has a delightful old lady with him, named Carol, who you were associated with in some way . . . Carol Rede or something."

"Carol Rede?" I asked in surprise. I couldn't remember that name. The response was: "Yes."

"When I was the Dean? In New York?" I was seeking further information.

"She had some official position and you were the Bishop or something in the Cathedral, she says."

The information was a little jumbled, but it jogged my memory. "My goodness." I suddenly remembered who Carol Rede was. "Is she on the other side?"

"Yes, she's here anyway."

I guessed that meant she was on the other side. "Really." I was still waiting for more.

"Is there something, uh . . ."

There was a pause, so I said, "I think she was the Bishop's secretary, very dignified, rather formidable . . ." I was trying some pump-priming.

"But you're not aware that she's dead?" It was Mr. Spraggett who asked the question.

"I was not aware that she was dead." I nodded assent, to which there was a quick reply through Ford: "Well, she isn't. She says, 'I'm not dead, I'm more alive than ever.'"

Both Allen and I felt self-conscious for having suggested that she was "dead" when we were purportedly in communication with her at that very moment . . . "Oh, excuse me," I said quickly, "I didn't know . . ."

"It's a manner of speech we have here, you know," Mr. Spraggett tried to explain. "We didn't mean to insinuate . . ." But the medium's voice went right on.

"But some day when you go back to California . . . I have a brother there who is retired . . . He is a major."

"Now is this Carol Rede; is this word from Carol Rede?" I asked, somewhat perplexed. It was hard to imagine why she would be coming through to me. I hadn't seen her since I left the New York Cathedral Close for San Francisco to be consecrated on May 15, 1958. Nine, nine and a half years, I thought. But even more to the point, the five years I was there as Dean I never felt at all close to her, for the principal impression she made on me was that of one protecting the Bishop from those of us who felt we needed some of his time. Later, when I myself became a bishop, I could appreciate much more a rigorous attitude on the part of a secretary, but while a dean, I found it a real block. The answer didn't help much: "And she speaks about Carmel."

"I'm very distressed to hear she's passed on. We got along very well, kind of at arm's length, but we got along. But formidable . . ." Again, I felt somewhat awkward, not knowing quite what to say to Carol Rede, if it were indeed she.

"Do you know of her brother in Carmel?" Allen Spraggett inquired.

"No. I don't." I replied.

Upon inquiry we later learned that not only had Carol Rede been dead—or perhaps I should say "on the other side"—for nearly four years, but also that her brother Ross, who was mentioned, died two months after she did. Thus we had an example of an obvious error on the part of the medium or of his control, or a somewhat surprising lack of information on the part of Carol Rede if she were the one communicating. I have seldom during sessions encountered such a flat contradiction in fact, but occasionally they do come through.

Ψ

It seemed Arthur Ford had been in a trance for hours—a very long sitting—but at last it appeared to be coming to a close: "There's only one other person left here who says that if he were on the earth plane, he would be right here, standing with you and happy to be counted as a friend. This man was killed in an automobile accident, or died as a result of automobile injuries, and, I got the name: I thought it was Reggie, or Reginald, or Reg, or something. Something like Seiger, and he's in robes like a priest would wear, and he said he went to the same college in England you did, came over here and he became something, I don't know, president or dean or something, of an Anglican school, or college, here. And he was killed in an automobile accident. Not too long ago. He's a young man, about forty-five. Name is Seiger."

"Does this ring a bell?" Allen asked me.

"It doesn't," I responded, "but it could be verified, I would think. When you say 'here,' Fletcher, we're talking about . . . we are, of course, in Toronto . . . in Canada, and would you also include in that 'here' the United States?"

The response was immediate: "No, this man was in this town here. And he met you long ago. You wouldn't remember him, because it wasn't necessary but, something called Provost . . . and there's some college here . . . and this man was a theologian, and he came from Cambridge, and he was in the west and he came here, and there's some . . . is there a Trinity?"

Allen answered at once, "Yes."

"There is a Trinity College [one of the Anglican institutions which is part of the University of Toronto]." I agreed before Ford's voice went on: "And he died in an automobile accident."

"Was the name Reginald Seiger?" I noticed Mr. Spraggett was making a note of the name, doubtless so he could check it later.

"It starts with 'R.' I think it's Reginald, but it's Seeger. 'S' double 'e,' something. That's the best I can do."

Again we had an example of an apparent difficulty in communicating names. But later investigation by Mr. Spraggett revealed that there was in fact a Reginald Seager from Toronto, who had been Provost of Trinity College, Toronto, 1925–26, was Bishop of Ontario from 1926–32 and then Bishop of Huron, 1932–48. He could well have met me on some church occasion when I was in Toronto or elsewhere (from early in my ministry I was invited around quite a bit); but I certainly had no recollection of it. He was, however, as far as his daughter could recall, never in an automobile accident. He did die of pneumonia in 1948 shortly after attending the Lambeth Conference.

Here seemed to be another example of a "mistake" on the part of the medium or his guide. The message was to a large extent in agreement with facts that could be verified, but the report on the mode of death was clearly in error. If an entity was indeed trying to communicate, it is possible that this was an example of a misunderstanding on the part of either the control or the medium of what a "Reginald Seager" was trying to say. If, on the other hand, we assume that here we were dealing with material drawn out of the collective unconscious by extrasensory perception, then it is possible that recollections of someone who died in an automobile accident were surrounding the memory traces of Reginald Seager. In that case, the medium could easily have "confused" the facts. But in any case the material does not bear the marks of being researched for my benefit (since there would be no way to establish a connection between us)—or researched at all, so much did it miss the mark.

Ψ

The next comment was extremely interesting.

"I've got a lot of things to say, that I have deliberately suppressed or put into cryptic form. You understand? I feel this must be checked—all of these things must be checked out—before this goes on the air. Everything must be clear."

I did understand. Several times material had come through which made me feel most uncomfortable because it came so close to matters I didn't want made public. In fact, there were one or two instances when more was said than I would have preferred, even though I was glad to have the purported information. I fully agreed that everything needed to be checked out before it was aired, and there were parts which I really felt should not be shown on television. Those same items have been deliberately left out of the account given here because the implications directly affect living persons.

It did strike me as rather remarkable that the same sensitivity and sense of caution which I myself was feeling should be demonstrated by and/or through the medium. At several points I had noted pauses and what seemed to be a groping for words which would be appropriate. In each case I was aware—because of the subject-matter—that such "screening" could be necessary.

After the taping I asked Arthur Ford about Fletcher's purported role in this regard and he informed me that it seemed to be very characteristic. Many a time, Mr. Ford reported, after a sitting persons would tell him how Fletcher tried to find a form of words which would take into consideration the feelings of the person in the room. Such sensitivity would seem to me to be very important; for if, in fact, communication between persons is going on, then the ability of the sitter to receive the messages being passed on—and, in the case of a séance in public, the appropriateness of offering particular information for general consumption—would simply be characteristic of good interpersonal relations.

In any case, we appeared to be nearing the end: "Now then, uh, Jim says too, it is, uh, it is almost as if this is the thing you came into the world to do. And all the experiences that you've had in your life have been preparing you and giving you experience at different levels so that you could interpret and speak to the new day, and he said the thing you must remember is that thinking alone is not important, and feeling alone is not important, but when feeling and thinking are married, then there is an integrated person. But thinking alone leads to confusion—to manic-depressive conditions. And feeling alone leads to the same thing. One is either married to all of life or else he's isolated. And he says, on occasion, or an example of what it means to center everything on thinking alone, the atomic bomb resulted from that. Feeling married to thinking would have turned it into constructive uses . . . Anyway, he says you're properly balanced and that is good."

As soon as the "speech" about thinking and feeling began, I felt sure Mr. Ford was beginning to come out of his trance. This was another example of what I have come to describe as "fill" in a sitting: that is, material more than likely coming out of the unconscious of the medium, meaningful but not in any significant way specifically relevant—usually material that is "all too true" and therefore can certainly do no harm. At the same time, it seems to me that—like advice from the other side—it should be taken no more seriously than would any other "good idea" one might read or hear under other circumstances.

On the assumption, then, that we were nearing the end of the séance, I said: "Send my thanks to Jim and all the others . . . and Donald MacKinnon's father, whom I'll have to learn more about. And the others who have come, and Louis Pitt. And thank you, Fletcher."

Arthur Ford fell silent. His head dropped to his chest again. He appeared to be asleep. Then, in a matter of seconds, he gave a little start, raised his head, pulled the handkerchief down and rubbed his eyes. Allen Spraggett asked him, "How do you feel?"

"All right. Did you get the results?"

Allen nodded affirmatively, and then turned to me. "Bishop, can we talk about some of these details?"

We then launched into a rather lengthy discussion of the material which had come through, assessing its validity and making notes about the items we would want to check out in order to verify them. I had been moved by the experience. Perhaps that is difficult for someone to understand who has never been in a séance, for what can be an intuitive sense of the reality of the communication is not something which can be duplicated in an oral or written account of the experience. Yet I felt something very real in the way of communication had been going on here.

In the discussion we acknowledged that several kinds of information came through. Some of it could have been known to the medium through published reports, in which case the data could have come directly from the memory of Arthur Ford. Some of it would have been in my conscious memory, or Mr. Spraggett's, and much of it was in my unconscious memory—so long unrecalled that in several instances I had difficulty identifying the persons and the details about their lives. Either way, ESP could have accounted for the purported communication.

Some of the information, however, was not known to me or to Mr. Spraggett. For example, I did not know of Carol Rede's death, I knew nothing about Donald MacKinnon's father, nor of any cats important long ago to the MacKinnons, and I knew nothing about a Reginald Seager or a Harry Holt. In addition, two rather significant items of information seemed to come through from my son which I am not able to reveal here, and both of these were completely new to me.

Although the information about the MacKinnons, Carol Rede and Mr. Seager could possibly have been researched, I do not see how the more personal items could have been. Moreover, I myself brought up the matter of land purchases in relation to Bishop Block. The medium would have had no way of knowing I was going to talk about real estate and, therefore, could not have anticipated what information he would have needed to gather through research. Thus it seemed unlikely he would have learned about Bishop Block's acquiring of El Rancho del Obispo through research.

During that discussion following the session, I mentioned one thing that puzzled me then and has puzzled me a great deal since. Even if we did agree that much of the information that came through could have been dug up by research, it would remain difficult to imagine *how* that could have been done. For example, in order to find out that Carol Rede was a "thorn in my side," I presume a research assistant would have had to talk to the persons who worked with me during the time I was indirectly associated with her, for such an assessment is a subjective one and would not be found in written records. Now just how one would find the right person to ask, and why one would have inquired about Carol Rede anyway—since she was not my secretary but the Bishop's—is very difficult to understand. Moreover, if someone were to have gone to the Cathedral of St. John the Divine to inquire about my associations while I was Dean there, I would be very surprised indeed if anyone had mentioned Carol Rede as being an important person to know about.

This raises the question, then, as to why the particular persons who came through would have been the ones investigated. Far more evidential, for example—and more appropriate in terms of the "unifying" theme: those who had an influence on me or were in some way associated with me in the course of my various careers—would have been some kind of communication from Paul Tillich. Not only was he the principal influence on my theological development, but he had purportedly come through in previous séances with Mrs. Twigg and with George Daisley. Surely the researcher would have talked to the other mediums who had seen me. Then why not bring through an imposing figure such as Dr. Tillich? Or, to put the question in another way, why bring through someone as insignificant to my career and development as Miss Rede?

The same question could be raised with regard to several of the other persons who seemed to come through. Had I myself been suggesting the persons I would like to have heard from, I suspect the list would have been quite different. Therefore, even if one granted a possibility of garnering the facts through research, the mystery as to how or why that particular selection was made would remain unsolved.

Finally, suppose someone did go about finding out bits of information connected with my past. To do so they would have had to talk to persons who knew me—and therefore know me. Why, then, would not at least some of those persons have contacted me immediately following the publicity about the program to say: "Why, Jim, just last month a fellow was in asking me about you and I gave him that very bit of information."

I got no such word. If it could be proven now that all that information was indeed researched, then it was done in a most elaborate and sophisticated way. My recommendation in such an instance would be a direct one: let's make whoever was responsible for gathering the information the head of the CIA!

Ψ

There remains an intuitive perception of personality which is impossible to dismiss when one is analyzing any such experience piece by piece. It is not difficult to forget it, and I often do, for it is an all-encompassing feeling rather than a set of facts or a series of statements. Nevertheless, the sense that one is communicating with persons is so strong as to be almost the most convincing single factor leading to the affirmation of communication with the deceased.

During the discussion following the séance that day in Toronto, I used the illustration of a telephone conversation to point to that intuitive feeling—an analogy I have used many times since. I said, "For example, if I were to call you by long-distance telephone and you were to be skeptical about whether it was really me, I would try to convince you. I would presumably try to identify myself by citing joint memories which no one else would know. I might say to you, Allen, for example—'what about the time we met in Geneva at the Pacem in Terris Conference?' And you might say, 'Well, that doesn't prove it's you. It was reported in the newspapers. You might have read it.' So then I might try again and say, 'What about the fact that we both had cheeseburgers that night? Do you remember? And I couldn't find the napkin and it was under the tray.' And you might say, 'Yes, but someone could have come in the room at that moment and have seen us.' And thus we would continue our conversation. It would be almost impossible for me to *prove* that it was I on the other end of the line. Yet I suspect that after talking with me for some time and asking a number of questions, you would be willing to gamble one way or the other regarding my identity."

Communicating through a medium presents the same kind of problem. Though one cannot prove anything, yet after a certain amount of communication one intuits either that the source is or isn't the purported personality. As I said that day in Toronto, "I think asking for definite proof is asking almost too much, because in most realms of life—even in those we call sciences—we use facts *plus* faith . . . Proof is not the word, but I would say we can speak of a highly plausible inference enabling an affirmation."

After nearly two hours of taping, Mr. Spraggett reluctantly brought our discussion to a close. The lights went out, and as we stepped down from the platform we were met by the director of the program, who said with enthusiasm, "*That* is what I call good television!"

10

We cannot but speak the things we have seen and heard.

—*SS. Peter and John* (ACTS 4:20)

Whatever the humblest men affirm from their own experience is always worth listening to, but what even the cleverest of men, in their ignorance, deny, is never worth a moment's attention.

—*Sir William Barrett*

There is a principle which is a bar against all information, which is proof against all arguments and which cannot fail to keep a man in everlasting ignorance. That principle is contempt prior to investigation.

—*Herbert Spencer*

The supreme importance, as I see it, of the labors of Dr. Rhine and his fellow parapsychologists lies in this: that they are providing a slow, painful but sure demonstration by the methods of science of a truth that the religions of the world have grasped intuitively or that is seen only vaguely through the eyes of faith. I mean the truth that man is more than a physical organism responding to stimuli—that while living in this world he is yet in contact with an extrasensory order of existence whose relations to time and space transcend those of the world of matter.

—*S. G. Soal*

It could be folly to attack a man who offers tangible evidence of life after death. It is all very easy to sneer at medium-media "contacts" with persons who have died, but woe unto the cleric who does so. Perhaps 99 99/100 per cent of his flock wants to be reassured on that subject. The fact is that much of Christianity has rather pussyfooted around with death. There has been a sort of conspiracy to "pretty-up" death and to speak of it as "passing on," or "going on," or just "passing." But for those who have "passed" or "died," and for their families, the big question mark is, "What's next? What is immortal life?" What is the how and why of "immortality?" What is it like? Will we know each other? Is there a consciousness in the "immortal spirit"?

—*Ralph McGill*

Whether or not the séance we taped that day made good television, I cannot say. I never had an opportunity to see it. But that it made news can certainly not be denied. The show was taped on September 3, 1967. Shortly after that I left for Seattle for the triennial General Convention of the Episcopal Church. My mind was on legislative and policy issues—not the least the issues of doctrinal breadth, heresy, and due process in censure of bishops; so I had not particularly thought about the Toronto séance since the day we taped it.

After a long and busy week at Convention the report of the Committee on Theological Freedom was finally presented and adopted with only one dissenting vote. It extended the borders of theological inquiry sufficiently to leave inside them the views for which I had been charged with heresy and consequently censured. Further, it made clear that bishops shouldn't be censured (as I had been) without due process. And it recommended future legislation to make the starting of heresy proceedings much more difficult. As much as I would like to tell the full story of the dramatic twenty-four hours following the presentation of the report, it is not directly to the point of this present writing. Suffice it to say that I was advised by a caucus of liberal bishops not to withdraw my demand for trial until action was taken right at that very Convention on heresy proceedings and censure actions. Such action took place the next morning, September 26.

Both houses of the Convention voted into canon law (by special action made effective immediately rather than, as would be usual, the first of the next year) changes which made it virtually impossible to have heresy trials in the future. The House of Bishops voted explicitly that due process of law is essential when considering the censure of a bishop. I forthwith handed to the Presiding Bishop a withdrawal (co-signed by Bishops Myers and Craine, who had signed on with me at Wheeling) of the demand requiring heresy proceedings, Bishop Hines read it to the House and applause greeted the ending of a difficult chapter in our Church's contemporary history. It was a real victory for freedom of thought and teaching, and gave a green light to efforts to bring the Church into the twentieth century. And as for proper hearing in connection with censure proposals, our House of Bishops is now as moral as the U. S. Senate.

When I arrived back at the House, after a "celebration luncheon" with friends, I took my seat with a new sense of freedom and relaxation. My mind wandered to thoughts of how nice it would be finally to settle down at the Center for the Study of Democratic Institutions, greatly reduce my time away from its daily expression of "the civilization of the dialogue" and get on with the study of Christian origins, the field of scholarship at the heart of my interest and concern. The past year had been a hectic one indeed, one in which I had fulfilled more than three hundred speaking dates all over the country—reaching (quite apart from numerous network and local TV and radio audiences) more than 150,000 persons. As Dr. Hutchins put it understandingly, I had been "taking the issue to the people." Now I could more fully live the life of a scholar for which I had left my post in the Diocese of California. The fight was over. The victory had been won. I was relieved.

While lost in reverie about the year ahead in which I would

be finally free from special tensions and pressures, a page delivered a message to me asking that I return a long-distance phone call to Mr. John Leo of the New York *Times*. During the next routine-type report I left my seat in the House and found a telephone.

"Bishop Pike," John Leo's voice came from the other end of the line, "I have just received word about a television show you made in Toronto, and the word I have says that you were in communication with your late son. I wonder if you would be willing to verify this."

The words hit me with such force that I was almost unable to respond. I had an overwhelming sinking feeling, and I thought, Oh, no, here we go again . . . ! My thoughts raced over the events of recent weeks and I tried to imagine how news of the Canadian program—which at this point seemed ages ago—could have *now* reached the New York *Times*. And anyway, in my almost twenty years of being on television (including a weekly ABC network program for five of those years) I couldn't remember a newspaper covering a program—I assumed it was because the press regarded TV as a competing medium. While this was going through my mind, John Leo went on to describe to me the report he had received, including details I recalled from the program.

"Yes," I said reluctantly, "we did tape a show for CTV on which, after some discussion, Arthur Ford tried to go into a trance—in fact, succeeded—and some remarkable things seemed to come through." I tried to explain, without saying more than I had to, what had happened during the taping and how I understood the phenomena. I was not happy to have the story come out as news, with the inevitable oversimplification of headlines, the implicit sensationalism and the understandable lack of space for the *whole* story and for all the ifs and buts appropriate to careful analysis and interpretation of psi phenomena. Yet the story obviously *was* out, and I preferred to tell about it myself than to have a story written up on the basis of word second- or third-hand.

"Do you believe you were in communication with your son?" Mr. Leo pressed.

"Since you didn't say 'know' but said 'believe,'" I answered, "yes, I believe that to be the most plausible explanation of the phenomena which occurred." I must have repeated those words a hundred times in the days that followed. Yet what I felt to be a careful statement did not make good headline material. Thus, the reporting of the story took on quite a different flavor.

Ψ

PIKE CLAIMS 'TALK' WITH DEAD SON

The headline in the Seattle *Post-Intelligencer* the next morning had all the subtlety of a meat chopper. I shuddered when I thought of the reaction of my brother bishops, who must, like myself, have felt very relieved the day before when we were finally past the awkward, tension-producing struggle about heresy. And some of those less enthusiastic about my theological views had doubted my motives regarding that issue, not infrequently accusing me of being a publicity seeker. I could imagine their various reactions to this morning's headline. Some of them, I was sure, would attribute the initiation of this to me, and the headline certainly gave them cause to do so.

"That's just like Pike to seek some other sensational issue to keep himself in the public eye," I could hear them say. "He is never content to take a back seat—not even for a few hours." The headline was so offensive that I was furious, but I knew there was little that could be done at this point to remedy the damage. Had I myself been ready to release the story, I certainly would not have said it anything like that. I was not *claiming* anything.

My mind went back to a conversation I had had with two reporters in October 1966—soon after Wheeling. During a clergy conference in the Diocese of Delaware, I had shared, in confidence, some of my experiences with psychic phenomena and had stated rather tentatively that I felt such data could be used as a part of the basis for a leap of faith regarding the affirmation of life after death. News of my "confidential" story had reached reporters of both the New York *Times* and the Baltimore *Sun*, but when they contacted me I was able to convince them that this was not the time to release such news: I was far from ready in terms of my own inquiry and study, and we had just been thrown into a heresy struggle by the Wheeling meeting of the House of Bishops. With a promise that I would give the two of them a break on the release of the story when the time came, and in connection with the publication of the contemplated book, they graciously agreed to leave it in confidence.

Now here it was in bold print. I realized, with genuine regret, that I had demonstrated a distressing lack of foresight in agreeing to participate in the Toronto program. I would have been glad enough—and was—to have a TV dialogue with Allen Spraggett and Arthur Ford on the psi field in relation to the theological affirmation of eternal life. That was covered in a long chapter in *If This Be Heresy*, just out, and I had often used this approach in university and college lectures during the year. But I hadn't really believed Arthur Ford could go into a trance in such a setting even if, once before the strong lights, he should feel moved to try to. If he did try and could succeed, I figured we would have learned something valuable. My mind never connected such a full-blown happening with mass media—other than the one being used, in which time, moving pictures and sound combine to communicate the nuances and interpretative dialogue, with open-endedness as to options. But seeing it all in print, I recognized that I had not taken into account what a "good story" this would make. Had I anticipated such a result, I would surely not have agreed to participate in the television discussion of what might turn out to include a séance.

Reporters, writers and interviewers representing all of the mass media immediately besieged me with phone calls and descended on Santa Barbara. Feeling a certain obligation to the newsmen from the New York *Times* and the Baltimore *Sun* who had been good enough not to release the story a year before, I was in touch with them to apologize for this unplanned "leak" and to give them an opportunity to print some follow-up stories, including references to some of my experiences before the Toronto taping. Then, when more of the story was out, more calls came asking more questions. Contrary to my expectations and hopes, my first few days back at the Center for the Study of Democratic Institutions were hectic and strained, with hardly a moment to catch my breath between interviews.

I kept hoping to clear up false impressions and misunderstandings, but nothing I could say seemed very effectively to dispel the image which some stories seemed to give: that of a credulous, bewildered and grieving father desperately seeking to absolve himself of guilt by "claiming" to have been in communication with his dead son.

PIKE'S SÉANCE PROVIDES MESSAGE FROM SON

BISHOP PIKE'S TALK WITH HIS DEAD SON

PIKE AT SÉANCE HEARD SON'S VOICE

PIKE'S SÉANCE: VOICES, CATS LINKED TO SON

Though I understood full well that the aim of the headline writer, in addition to the mechanical problem of fitting content to a predetermined typographical space, is to capture the interest of the reader, I was most distressed at the implications. It was not very long before I had to face the fact that I would have to slow up again the study which most interested me, Christian origins, in order to write the book which I had promised to do "someday" for Doubleday & Company. That seemed to be the only way my affirmation could be set in proper perspective. The length of this book is written testimony of what I knew to be true: the fairest headline, the most careful newspaper story—or even magazine article—could not come near to setting forth the particularities of the context, the complexity of the events and of my responses thereto, and the plausible analyses thereof.

Ψ

Mail flooded in from all quarters and editorial and feature writers in newspapers and magazines had a heyday. Syndicated columnists had their say. The more letters I read and the more articles I saw, the more aware I became of both the fascination with and the hostility toward this whole field. Though the genuinely positive reactions far exceeded the hostile ones—in letters, by about eight to one—I was outraged by the dogmatism of "liberals" who dismissed outright any possibility that there could be reality to psychic phenomena without even so much as considering the evidence or reading even one of the many scientific works in the field. On the other hand, I was equally put off by the almost fundamentalist credulity of the many who were willing to believe anything anyone reported in this field, whether it could be substantiated or not.

Falling in between those two responses were the largest number of people. Many of them had experiences of their own to share; a significant number sought pastoral help in their own bereavement, wanting to believe on a factual basis that it is possible both to affirm life after death and to be in communication with departed loved ones; many merely wanted to express their thanks for my courage in having been frank in an area which is still *verboten* among many people. They basically trusted me and the report of my experiences, and wrote to me out of their confidence.

In a category by itself was a smattering of extremely hostile mail. Some of it came from Christians who fully accepted the reality of the phenomena, but attributed it to the work of the Devil—literally. The remainder came from persons who speak of "the Devil" in psychological terms and had quite readily concluded that I was mentally ill.

Needless to say, I was now confronted with a direct challenge to go deeper into my study of the literature of the whole psi field, to complete my analysis of my own experiences and then to tell the full story and share candidly my own far from simple response to it.

Ψ

The extreme hostility was probably the easiest response to deal with, though that may seem strange to some, for it was so obviously an unreflective reaction to data which called forth well-learned "explanations" of unfamiliar phenomena.

Whether the response was to quote Scripture in order to prove that one should not "consort with mediums," or whether the person sought to psychoanalyze me from afar (by ESP?!), the basic response was the same: without knowing any of the facts they already knew what was what and were quite willing and able to tell me so.

Such letters revealed the most acute kind of fear of the new. No facts which would disturb their neat systems and frames of reference could possibly be taken in by these persons, and anyone professing such facts could not be simply ignored, but had to be "set straight."

> If thou dost not speak to warn the wicked from his way, that wicked man shall die in his iniquity; but his blood will I require at thine hand. (Ezek. 32:8)

This Biblical quotation, sent to me by several well-meaning persons, is perhaps the best summary of the spirit which seemed to motivate the Bible-centered critic. He felt he was doing me a real favor to "save me from the Devil."

"God's precepts do not change and seeking the spirit of the Devil is not tolerated by God," one woman was good enough to point out to me. The most commonly referred to example of someone punished by God for consulting a medium was the story of King Saul, who asked advice through the Witch of Endor (1 Sam. 28). Samuel appeared to speak to Saul through the medium, predicting that Saul would be destroyed and his kingdom would be given over to David.

Overlooked by most was Saul's reason for going to the medium: "And when Saul inquired of the Lord, the Lord did not answer him, either by dreams, or by Urim [a sacred object for determining the divine will by lot], or by the prophets."

(1 Sam. 28:6) Therefore he sought the aid of a medium in order to consult Samuel, who had been his friend and counselor while still alive.

It would appear that Saul was already "cut off from the Lord" before he made that decision. In fact, Samuel himself appeared to say to Saul, through the medium, "Why then do you ask me, since the Lord has turned from you and become your enemy? The Lord has done to you as he spoke by me: for the Lord has torn the kingdom out of your hand, and given it to your neighbor, David. Because you did not obey the voice of the Lord, and did not carry out his fierce wrath against Amalek, therefore the Lord has done this thing to you this day." (1 Sam. 28:16–18)

The implication of my critics' letters was that to see a medium is automatically to turn from God. Saul's story neither proves nor disproves that assumption. It merely implies that once cut off from God, no amount of advice—even through a medium—could save him; it only confirmed his fate. That his downfall in the account in the much later and highly stylized First Chronicles was attributed to the fact that "he did not keep the command of the Lord, and *also consulted a medium, seeking guidance,* and would not seek guidance from the Lord" (1 Chron. 10:13, 14a) reflects the bias of the unknown chronicler, who retold the story about a millennium after the purported events. It would appear that Saul did in fact first seek guidance directly from the Lord—and received none.

In several other passages of the Old Testament there are rather strong condemnations of those who seek advice through mediums. For example, Leviticus 19:31 says: "Do not turn to mediums or wizards; do not seek them out, to be defiled by them: I am the Lord your God."* Two things

* See also Lev. 20:6; Deut. 18:10, 11; Isa. 8:19.

are important to understand about such passages. First of all, such denunciations reflect a conflict between two competing religious systems prevalent during the early history of Israel: Judaism and the paganism of the Egyptians, the Canaanites and the Babylonians. Belief in pagan gods permeated the culture in which the Jews were immersed and dispersed. Consequently, the admonitions to be faithful to the God of Israel were frequent and harsh.

Diviners, soothsayers, augurs, sorcerers, charmers, mediums, wizards and necromancers were the pagan "professionals" who dealt with the gods: foretelling future events, attempting to manipulate the gods by magic, etc.

The Jewish religious professionals—the priests and prophets—had to protect their own roles as those who could reveal and interpret the Word of God, so they were quick to denounce with vehemence any competitors, like mediums and foretellers of the future.*

In this regard, those scriptural injunctions are of little help to us today, for our world view is so different. We no longer think in terms of competing gods. We seek to know instead the One—the all-encompassing, unifying reality. We are more and more open to truth, no matter what its source, and most Christians today would not assert that Buddhists, Muslims or even animists worship a *different* god, but rather that they worship the Ground of all Being in a different way. So any lingering uneasiness on the part of professionals regarding truth which might be revealed through other sources

* It is possible for a priest to have it both ways. Last May in Nablus (ancient Shechem) at the foot of Mt. Gerazim, in the portion of Israeli-occupied territory for which the name "Samaria" has been revived, after being shown the Samaritans' ancient Torah scroll inscribed in paleo-Hebrew I got acquainted with an impressive Samaritan priest at the entrance to whose office was a sign reading "Palms Read."

is less and less received by laymen as "God's Will" and more and more seen as the insecurity of finite men.

Ψ

Yet there is an important truth which is implied in these injunctions against seeking advice through mediums. The priests and prophets of Israel kept their priorities very clear: the Word of God is revealed *only* in the Law and the Prophets, and only that which proceeds from God is ultimate. Thus, they were careful to say: "When you come into the land which the Lord your God gives you, you shall not learn to follow the abominable practices of those nations." (Deut. 18:9) "And when they say to you, 'Consult the mediums and wizards who chirp and mutter,' should not a people consult their God?" (Isa. 8:19) In other words, the priests and prophets were admonishing the Israelites not to seek *oracles* from deceased individuals through mediums.

With this point I am in full agreement. As I have pointed out several times earlier in this narrative, I was aware from the very beginning that if there was any genuine communication going on here, it was communication with finite beings. Any advice received, therefore, would be taken only as seriously as its apparent source would make appropriate.

I would like to suggest that this reservation would apply equally to the messages received by the disciples from Jesus after his death: the words are received in accordance with our view of Jesus. For those who believe Jesus to be God, his words express the mind and will of God. Those who revere him as a prophet receive his words as prophecy. Those who hold him to be a great teacher and fine example study his sayings for the wisdom they impart, evaluating them as they would the words of any esteemed living man.

The caution which the scriptural passages cited above present against seeking ultimate truth through mediums is, therefore, an important one, I feel. It is for that reason I could never make an -ism of all this. I'm not saying how many bearing the name in fact do just that, but one reason why "spiritualism" or "spiritism" could not for me be an appropriate position, whatever facts or theories I might accept about psychic phenomena, is that I could never put at the center of my belief and life communication with any finite human being—even those on the other side. I would not so exalt anyone dead any more than I could so exalt the living. Instead, I would hold before the One—God—both the living and the dead, in the words of the Book of Common Prayer, that we might all "grow from strength to strength in the life of perfect service."

Ψ

Both the Old Testament and the New Testament are replete, however, with examples of purported communication between the living and "beings" from other realms through experiences which we would today categorize as paranormal or extrasensory. Messages delivered by angels were almost commonplace, dreams and visions provided guidance, prophecy was a highly prized gift and conversations with the Lord—in which voices were heard and physical phenomena occurred—were frequent. Such experiences of extrasensory communication were not distrusted, but rather were received as being from God. As long as these revelations came directly, and were unsolicited, they were to be received with gratitude and followed assiduously.

For a long time "sensible" people have denied the reality—and certainly the validity—of any communication that would be considered extrasensory. Thus a twentieth-century man is as suspicious of a message purportedly transmitted by an angel, or of a prophetic vision or dream, or of a revelation directly "from the Lord," as he would be of communication through a medium. But I feel that the time is fully upon us, as is demonstrated by the work being done in this field by reputable scientists and psychologists, when we are ready to examine all extrasensory phenomena with the same objectivity with which thoughtful people have sought to examine other aspects of our universe.*

Ψ

As has been indicated, many of those who are extremely hostile to the consultation of mediums *believe* in the communication. What alarms them is that they believe it is "of the Devil." One religious publication, for example, ran as the headline of an article on my experiences: NO, BISHOP PIKE, THAT WASN'T YOUR SON TALKING! Though the author had most of the facts wrong—including many of those which the daily newspapers had right—nevertheless he was able to conclude that the data can all be dismissed as being the work of "that old serpent called the devil and Satan, the seducer of the whole world."†

But there are, among Christians, many who do not believe such communication to be possible, and yet who themselves would profess a belief in the resurrection of Jesus and of his communication to his disciples following his death. The position of such "believers" poses two interesting problems:

* For a consideration of the question of the authority of the Bible, see *If This Be Heresy*, ch. 3.

† Richard H. Utt in *Signs of the Times*, a publication of the Seventh-day Adventists, vol. 95, no. 6, June 1968.

Is it possible to believe in the resurrection of Jesus while denying the possibility of conscious survival for other persons? Is it logical to believe that Jesus was in touch with his disciples if communication from the deceased is inherently impossible?

St. Paul addressed himself to the first of these questions in his first letter to the Corinthians:

> Now if Christ is preached as raised from the dead, how can some of you say that there is no resurrection of the dead? But if there is no resurrection of the dead, then Christ has not been raised; if Christ has not been raised, then our preaching is in vain and your faith is in vain. We are even found to be misrepresenting God, because we testify of God that he raised Christ, whom he did not raise if it is true that the dead are not raised. For if the dead are not raised then Christ has not been raised. (15:12–16)

It does seem strange that as to the second question—and the corollary matter of psychic phenomena—the very persons who profess a belief in Jesus' resurrection because of the accounts in the Gospels of his appearances to his disciples, most of which were written down from forty to eighty years after the events themselves, are the ones who rule out of court without examination any other evidence—no matter how promptly recorded or empirically verified—that death is not the last conqueror. One might expect that Christians would be delighted to have further evidence that their faith is not "in vain." But this has been far from my universal experience.

Not long after the news of my experiences with psychic phenomena broke in the press, for example, the rector of one of the largest Episcopal churches in the nation canceled his invitation to me to preach at his noonday services during Holy Week. Over a period of fifteen years I had been preaching from the pulpit of St. Thomas in New York City, and during my several struggles with heresy charges the Rev. Dr. Frederick M. Morris was always eager to have me express my views in sermons delivered there. When this very surprising cancellation came, my spontaneous response, when called by Ted Fiske of the New York *Times*, supplied for the next morning paper the "Quotation of the Day": *Having been under a cloud for believing too little, it's at least a change to be faulted for believing too much.*

Dr. Morris had explained the withdrawal of his invitation to preach with these words to the press: "The publicity has directed attention away from Bishop Pike's original message of reform and impatience with ecclesiastical officiousness. I don't want people coming to St. Thomas just because they might hear some sensational revelations."

There was a multiple irony in his remarks. First, one would wonder whether the disciples' reports of Jesus' resurrection appearances would not have struck people, on first hearing, as "sensational"; yet few pastors hesitate to encourage people to come to church to hear about them. Second, I had given no indication that I intended to talk about life after death this year—especially since the previous Lent while preaching at St. Thomas I devoted one of my sermons to the subject, giving an analysis of the various types of psi data, including purported communication with the dead, as the basis for making a faith-affirmation of ongoing life. (Incidentally, to that sermon there had been no negative reaction at all—not even from the Rector!) Third, when I did preach in New York during Holy Week, 1968 (at Central Presbyterian—they picked up the invitation which St. Thomas canceled), I preached—as contemplated all along—on an entirely different subject and never mentioned psychic phenomena. Yet on the Sunday after Easter, Dr. Morris preached on "Can We Talk with the Dead?" Not an appeal to expectations of "sensational revelations," I'm sure.*

The paradoxical reaction to evidence of survival on the part of professing Christians is perhaps typified by the Church of England's response to the findings of a committee appointed by the Archbishops of Canterbury and York in 1937 to investigate spiritualism (interest in which is more widespread in England than it is here). After two years of careful study, the committee of ten submitted two reports: a majority report signed by seven members and a minority report signed by three. Though the committee had been publicly appointed by both the Primate of All England and the Primate of England, no word reached the rank and file of the Church for nine years.

Finally, in some mysterious way, a copy of the majority report appeared on the desk of the editor of the weekly *Psychic News*. It was printed in full and was of course picked up by the national and world press and thus made available to the clergy and lay members of the Church and to the general public. It would appear that the report of the archiepiscopal committee was suppressed because, though quite cautious, it was basically a favorable report—and one all the more impressive because of such highly respected signators as the Very Rev. W. R. Matthews, then, and until he just recently retired, Dean of St. Paul's; the Rt. Rev. Francis Underhill, the Lord Bishop of Bath and Wells; Dr. William

* In the *St. Thomas Bulletin*, May 1968, Dr. Morris commented: "On the Sunday after Easter, when the preannounced subject of the sermon at 11:00 a.m. was 'Can We Talk with the Dead?' *an unusually large congregation was present as I had prophesied* [by ESP?]. I believe it was in no small part *due to the wide publicity* given the subject of séances in recent times . . . Copies of the sermon are available." (Italics mine.)

Brown, celebrated Harley Street psychologist; the Rev. L. W. Grensted, Nolloth Professor of the Christian Religion at Oxford and Canon of Christ Church; the Rev. Canon Harold Anson, Master of the Temple; and the distinguished barrister Mr. P. E. Sandlands, Queen's Counsel. Hence it was hardly a congeries of credulous and deluded fools hankering after sensational revelations who penned such words as these from the report:

> . . . certain outstanding psychic experiences of individuals, including certain experiences with mediums, make a strong prima facie case for survival and for the possibility of spirit communications while philosophical, ethical and religious consideration may be held to weigh heavily on the same side. When every possible explanation of these communications has been given, and all doubtful evidence set aside, it is very generally agreed that there remains some element as yet unexplained.
>
> We think that it is probable that the hypothesis that they proceed in some cases from discarnate spirits is the true one.*

It would seem that many of those who for years have been mouthing the words "I believe in . . . the Communion of Saints . . . the Resurrection of the Body; and the Life everlasting" and have been purporting to accept scriptural passages about these themes, including the communication of Jesus with his disciples, either do not really believe them or have never thought about their meaning at all. If the Church is to continue to make such affirmations, one would hope that more enlightened Church members will begin to take into account the rapid accumulation of scientific data which are supportive of them. If not, the Church may find itself in the very awkward position of being less believing with regard to

* *The Church of England and Spiritualism* (London: Psychic Press, 1949).

some of its basic doctrinal tenets than secularists who have objectively examined factual evidence pointing to their truth.

To quote again from the majority report:

> . . . it is clearly true that the recognition of the nearness of our friends who have died, and of their progress in the spiritual life, and of their continuing concern for us, cannot do otherwise, for those who have experienced it, than add a new immediacy and richness to their belief in the Communion of Saints. There seems to be no reason at all why the Church should regard this vital and personal enrichment of one of her central doctrines with disfavor . . .

Ψ

A few people wrote me hostile letters from another standpoint. They believe in the resurrection of the dead, but they believe that the dead remain asleep until the Last Judgment Day when all of the faithful will be raised to Glory and the sinners to an everlasting Hell. These people are expressing that understanding of the Resurrection which predominated through most of Christian history, and they are not to be faulted for failing to see beyond that which they have been taught.

I have long held* a radically different understanding of history and human destiny—one which my studies in the field of Christian origins (which reveal how historically conditioned the doctrine of the Second Coming is), together with my studies and explorations of the psi factor in the

* See *The Faith of the Church* (with W. Norman Pittenger), vol. 3, ch. 11; The Episcopal Church's Teaching Series (New York: Seabury Press, 1951); *Beyond Anxiety* (New York: Scribners, 1953), ch. 9; *The Next Day* (New York: Macmillan, 1957), chs. 14 and 15; *What Is This Treasure* (New York: Harper & Row, 1966), ch. 8; *If This Be Heresy* (New York: Harper & Row, 1967), pp. 156ff.

human personality, have confirmed for me. Though I can understand the expectation of an intervention into human history by the Christ who shall come to judge us, and though I know that many believe in it (including 24 per cent of the members of my own church*), I cannot accept it for myself. To give here all of the reasons, however, would not be possible—nor, in the light of my previous writings, necessary. But it is enough, I think, to point out again that when there are data which appear to contradict our hypotheses it is time to take a look at our working assumptions. Thus, I would not urge those who are preparing for the Day of Judgment to alter their convictions or expectations because I—or anyone else—suggest it, but I would encourage them to take a look at the facts made available by scientific studies in this field as to whether it would seem that "the dead" are "asleep" or "alive."

Ψ

"This time Pike's really gone off his rocker." "Isn't it sad—Bishop Pike is really slipping!" "The guy's nuts!" "He's gone out of his mind—he might kill somebody."

Such remarks came from those who sought to psychoanalyze me by remote control—again not knowing or investigating the facts or talking to me and/or to the various other co-observers of the phenomena. Several persons counseled me by letter on the assumption that they knew exactly what was going on inside of me. "You are someone crying for help." "You are searching for something that is not within your reach." "You are wracked with grief." "You have shocked me

* See Charles Y. Glock and Rodney Stark of the Survey Research Center, University of California, *Religion and Society in Tension* (Chicago: Rand McNally & Co., 1965), Table 5-3, p. 95.

in your desperate effort to rationalize your faith into a belief in communication with deceased loved ones."

Whatever validity there might be to such assessments of my psychological state, it has always amazed me that those who know the least about your inner life—or outer life, for that matter—are quickest to diagnose your condition. Most of us by now know enough about psychology and psychoanalysis to realize that even an analyst, after years of working with a counselee, would not be so bold as to state that he "knows" why his client did what he did in any given situation or believes what he believes about a given subject. Of course considerable insight can be gained, but even we ourselves do not know fully what motivates us. I am often reminded of that early medieval collect: "Almighty God, unto whom all hearts are open, all desires known and from whom no secrets are hid . . ." There is only One to whom all hearts are open, and it behooves the rest of us to acknowledge the finiteness and fallibility of our understanding of the state of a particular human personality.

Ψ

"Suppose in the séance your son had given you a good cursing and blamed you for the whole terrible deed. Now that would have been news. As it stands, the medium always tells the grief-stricken victim just what he wants most to hear . . . What if you had received a completely bad report. What would you have believed then? You would have discounted the whole thing, no doubt." Although I do not agree with the analysis which then followed, this introduction to a long piece of negative fan mail is worth consideration in its own right.

It is true that one seldom reads accounts of what might be called negative messages received through mediums. But this is not necessarily to say that all of what one hears is pleasing to the sitter. To take just one example in my own case, in the initial sitting with Mrs. Twigg my son did appear to come through, but he seemed to be in a state of great confusion. He regretted what he had done, he appeared to be having difficulty adjusting to his new surroundings, he was worried about what people here might be thinking of him and he even suggested that he was in what might be called "hell." This was certainly less than consoling for a father who would have liked to hear that, in spite of the suffering which preceded the death and the undoubtedly horrible experience of the suicide itself, his son had finally found some kind of peace. In fact, it was a long time until Jim appeared to come through in a séance reporting that he was genuinely "happy" and at peace.

And as for the remarks, purportedly from my son, indicating that neither I nor anyone else in the family was at fault, should feel responsible or should have any guilt with regard to Jim's death, there are two things to be said. First of all, I learned long ago to discount "reassuring" comments—being largely conditioned by my door-greeting experiences in the Church. General remarks such as "I so enjoyed your sermon" or "Your sermon was wonderful today" mean very little. After all, people have to say something. One can take heart, however, at a specific comment, such as "Bishop, today for the first time I understood the relationship between *x* and *y*." Such a remark is a direct and genuine response to the content of the message.

I have not been less discriminating in my reception of comments in the various sittings with mediums through whom my son purportedly communicated. General words of assurance have not seemed very important, but when they have been tied to specific remarks as to the circumstances surrounding events (as in the Toronto séance when Jim seemed to say, "I want you to know that neither you nor anyone else in the family should feel responsible for what happened," and then went on to *explain* what happened), I have received the communication as a genuine attempt to increase understanding.

Secondly, I would repeat my emphasis on the fact that whatever words come through a medium, whether one accepts the survival hypothesis or not, are fallible and finite, stemming from human personalities. No *person*, in this world or the next, can either condemn or absolve me for whatever responsibility I—or others—might bear for my son's death. God alone is the final judge of that, and though comforting words—or condemnatory ones—have come from many living persons, and though there have been several consoling remarks also in the context of séances, nevertheless the burden of assessment of my own role rests upon me, and between me and the One unto whom all hearts are open.

I would add the observation that it may well also be that in reporting messages received through mediums, the persons most directly involved, for whatever reasons of their own, screen out information which might have negative implications rather than reporting it frankly. If so, that would explain, at least in part, why sitters apparently receive the messages they "want to hear." Who knows: perhaps those are instead the only messages they want others to hear.

Ψ

There is another possibility—one which has been suggested to me on several occasions by persons who seem to know a great deal about this field and which has also come through in a couple of sittings. The suggestion is that those on the other side understand more clearly the nature of their earthly life once they have been released from their physical body.

They apparently function in still another dimension—four rather than three, possibly—and therefore are perhaps able to be more wise and sensitive than they would have been before death. What I am trying to suggest is that perhaps spirits on the other side would have less need to say negative things, having been freed from some of their former hang-ups, and would be better able to be sensitive to the needs of the person still living. They might, therefore, make comments which they feel will be helpful and freeing to the sitter. All this is, of course, assuming the survival hypothesis.

If, on the other hand, we are dealing here with a medium who speaks to please, then he would surely say what he thinks the sitter would want to hear. But in my own case, to take one example, I would have expected on that premise that Maren Bergrud would have been brought through with a few hopeful words about her progress, for surely the most insensitive (used with the more ordinary import) medium would know that I would be sad about her death. Yet the truth of the matter is that Maren did not seem to come through very clearly in the beginning; and what little information I have purportedly received from her reveals that she is not doing very well. For over a year now, and through four different mediums in different localities, I have been told that she has had difficulty adjusting—that she is still confused and numb, that she is not able to communicate well yet and that her progress is slow. I think one would have to consider this somewhat less than just "what one wants to hear."

I do not, however, consider the evidence any less convincing because it is not pleasing, as the author of the letter quoted charges. To the contrary: I have tended to be more convinced by facts which have either neutral emotional content or are somewhat unsettling than I am by platitudinous, seemingly reassuring remarks. From my experience, I am in rapport with the comment of the novelist Rosamond Lehman (who, after the death of her daughter, also had sessions with Mrs. Ena Twigg): "One of the reasons why, in the early days, I felt certain that I really was in touch with Sally was . . . that she wasn't 'in bliss' or 'at rest' or anything of that sort, but miserable, indignant and stubbornly reluctant to accept the fact that her stand on earth was over."*

Ψ

Over and over, the question has been raised, "Why is so much of the material that comes through in séances so trivial?" First of all, as I think the material in this book reveals, it is not all trivial. There has been, in my experience at least, a mixture of the trivial with comments of all kinds, including philosophical. Nevertheless, the question deserves at least some attention.

As I have said several times, if there is reality to psychic communication, then those on the other side with whom we are able to be in touch must be recognized as finite persons and not confused with supernatural beings. Thus it is to be expected, just as in ordinary human relationships, that from time to time those on the other side will comment on the trivial. To expect them to deal only with philosophical issues and ultimate questions would be to elevate them to a plane far beyond us, and the evidence thus far uncovered in psychical research does not suggest that those with whom we can communicate are that advanced. Nor would we necessarily want them to be: I am sure most of us would feel quite uncomfortable in the presence of anyone who was unable to

* *The Swan in the Evening: Fragments of an Inner Life* (New York: Harcourt, Brace & World, 1968), p. 148.

talk about anything but big and deeply significant matters.

In addition, it would appear that most of those who attempt communication—granted the survival hypothesis—are eager to prove that they are living. Strangely enough, the so-called trivial comments may seem the most convincing. Often the sitter can immediately recognize that they correspond to reality and thus feel closer to the supposed communicator because he seems to be directly in touch with common, everyday details of life. Occasionally, a seemingly trivial point is later discovered to be not only accurate but relevant—and thus adds to the conviction of the reality of the communication.

These observations are only relevant, however, within the framework of the survival hypothesis. If it is ESP we are dealing with, whether we could assume that the trivial is easier to perceive than the profound, I have no way of judging. In my experience, there has been no striking difference in the relative accuracy of the trivial as compared with the profound, but this might be a study worth the time of those interested in extrasensory perception.

In the category of guesswork, or what we have called fill, the broader the statement, the more likely it is to seem appropriate and applicable. Details—even trivial ones—can more readily be dismissed as inaccurate and thus would not be as safe in this regard.

In any case, as I hope the analysis thus far has shown, I have attempted to assess each item in a séance, whether trivial or not, by the same critical method in order to determine its import. Trivialities have been accepted or rejected by the same standards applied to what appears to be profound.

Ψ

The most persuasive of the challenges put to me during the weeks following the news stories about my purported communication with Jim was the suggestion that I was being taken in by a very clever plot on the part of mediums who wanted to convince me of the possibility of communication and of a medium's ability to facilitate it. The fact that so many spiritualists wrote me very supportive letters and published a number of articles lauding my stand and its "courage" contributed to my uneasiness. I could see that the spiritualists would have been most happy to have me "carry their banner" and I resented any implication that this was what I had stepped forward to do.

Thus it was particularly offensive when clergymen or columnists accused me of having become a spiritualist or of dabbling in spiritualism, both of which implied that I had put this whole field at the center of my interest (this, to me, is connoted by *-ist* and *-ism*). I had not, and have not. For good or ill, I am very much a here-and-now type. "One world at a time," words of the dying Thoreau to Emerson, has long been—and still is—a motto of mine. And what has long been one of my favorite lapel pins (the collecting and wearing of which is a hobby of mine) reads WE BELIEVE IN LIFE AFTER BIRTH.

Yet I was not so obtuse as not to recognize that my appearance on television with Arthur Ford, and the wide publicity attendant upon it, provided a perfect opportunity for spiritualists and professional mediums to "use" my name or the fact of my experiences to bolster their cause. Therefore, it did not seem impossible that I could have been "taken in" by some rather elaborate and clever planning.

11

We must indeed respect the attitude of those scientists who say "Now that fraud has been detected, not once, but again and again, I'm going to have nothing to do with it—to dabble in it is to damage the fair name of science." Yet we all know that the great science of chemistry sprang from the cradle of alchemy, some of whose exponents were genuinely striving after the transmutation of metals and the elixir of life, while others were as rank impostors as any false medium or fortune teller of today. This new branch of knowledge which is now struggling to be born will one day, I believe, look back to this period as the chemists of today look back to their own history.

—Sir Alister Hardy

When many coincide in their testimony (where no previous concert can have taken place), the probability resulting from this concurrence does not rest upon the supposed veracity of each considered separately, but on the improbability of such an agreement taking place by chance. For . . . *the chances would be infinite against their all agreeing in the same falsehood.*

—Archbishop Whateley

What does "proof" mean? A proof means destroying the isolation of an observed fact . . . the bringing it into its place in the system of knowledge.

—Sir Oliver Lodge

The possibility of fraud and the interest and criticism which the wide publicity evoked served as spurs to me, in the midst of much else to do, to set out to re-examine my notes in order to analyze in greater detail the various experiences I had had. To do so was no easy task, both because the notes were extensive and because to go over them brought back a host of memories, in part of course painful. Yet I felt an urgency now to write about the whole matter in order to correct the impression of credulity which had been given by the newspaper stories and to set forth my own conclusions, come to by the application of the theological method I was committed to—an empirical approach which I have referred to as *facts + faith*, along with an agnostic attitude toward questions when there is no known verified data.*

Because of the complexity of the phenomena to be analyzed and because of my emotional involvement in them, I asked Miss Diane Kennedy, by late August Mrs. Bergrud's successor as Director of New Focus Foundation, if she would work with me on the project. In spite of her unfamiliarity with psychic research, she agreed to join me in the effort, at first putting in a period of becoming acquainted with the scientific works in the field.

In mid-October we began in earnest a study of my notes in the light of the empirical criteria with which we were both by now acquainted. We gave special consideration to the possibility of fraud, and of conspiracy to that end—an option of explanation which I had frankly not taken into account

* See *If This Be Heresy*, ch. 5; also chs. 3 and 4.

until the issue was raised following the publicity. The two of us tried to put together the facts to see what they might reveal in that regard.

We were able to piece this much together as to how I became related to the field of psychic phenomena. A letter received right after the news of the Toronto program came out, from a Mrs. R. W. Hanna from Hillsborough, California —a laywoman in my diocese—reminded me that in 1963 she had, while in London, contacted the Rt. Rev. Mervyn Stockwood, Bishop of Southwark, in order to suggest that he invite me to become a sponsor of the Churches' Fellowship for Psychical and Spiritual Studies. This he had done, and, as indicated earlier, in the spirit of openmindedness toward a frontier of knowledge, I had agreed to be listed as a sponsor, along with a dozen or so other English bishops and the Bishop of Pittsburgh, the Rt. Rev. Austin Pardue, long an admired friend and author. I never took time to read the Fellowship's *Quarterly*, however, nor did it occur to me to make contact with anyone connected with the Fellowship on my next trip to England.

At the Anglican Congress in Toronto the summer of 1963 I had a couple of visits with Bishop Stockwood. We talked of many things connected with the need of the renewal of the Church and he invited me to come over to give a series of addresses at a clergy conference of his diocese, in which my good friend John Robinson (author of *Honest to God* and *Exploration into God*, and twice a visitor to my diocese) is a Suffragan Bishop.

It was during this gathering in May 1965, that I had dinner one night in Clacton-on-Sea with the Bishop and the Vice-Provost. I learned then about their interest in psychic phenomenon, and Canon Pearce-Higgins offered to guide me in learning more when I returned in the fall. But, as already explained, I didn't follow through.

Neither Mervyn Stockwood nor John Pearce-Higgins seemed overly anxious to get me involved either, for they didn't seek me out. In fact, when I did finally get in touch with Pearce-Higgins, he seemed rather diffident—as has already been mentioned—about my seeing Mrs. Twigg. Now I did learn later that the same Mrs. Hanna, while in London on a visit *before* Jim's death, had telephoned Bishop Stockwood to suggest that he arrange for me to have a sitting with Mrs. Twigg while I was in Cambridge. The Bishop, however, never contacted me to make such a suggestion. In the end it was Canon Pearce-Higgins to whom I turned, and it was at *my* suggestion—pressed after his substitute plan (the homemade ouija board) yielded little—that he arranged for a sitting with Mrs. Twigg.

The facts up to this point in the story would not seem to indicate a conspiracy to set me up to be "taken in." Genuine interest in the field of psychic phenomena and positive convictions about it are evidenced by the three persons thus far involved—Mrs. Hanna, Mervyn Stockwood and John Pearce-Higgins; but that's all. And certainly no one of them had anything personal to gain from my becoming a disciple.

The two clergy had long been active in the Churches' Fellowship for Psychical and Spiritual Studies—Bishop Stockwood is currently the Vice-President, and Canon Pearce-Higgins the Vice-Chairman. The latter lectures on the subject and is active in objective investigation in the field.

It appears that Mrs. Hanna had been interested in mediumship since 1959, following her husband's death, when she heard the Rev. Arthur Ford speak at the Alcazar Theatre in San Francisco as a lecturer on the "Town Hall" circuit. Afterward she read his book, *Nothing So Strange* (of which I was not aware until Mr. Ford gave me a copy at the time of the Toronto program) and decided that the knowledge revealed there was more important to her than anything else. In 1960 she went to New York, called at the Parapsychology Foundation, met Dr. Karlis Osis (now Director of Research for the American Society for Psychical Research) and had a sitting with a Mrs. Chapman in which her husband seemed clearly to come through.

In the fall of 1960 she went to London, made contact with the College of Psychic Science, and has continued to go there every year since. In 1963 she attempted to make an appointment with me, knowing, she said, of my courage and apparent belief that "the last result of wisdom marks it true." Since I was pressed for time and could not see her, she sent a book to me, entitled *Beyond the Horizon*, by Grace Rosher. She also enclosed a copy of the current *Quarterly* published by the Churches' Fellowship. I apparently wrote to thank her (or more likely my chaplain did), saying I would plan to read the book on a plane trip since it was a subject I knew little of. But, in fact, I never got around to reading the work.

Because of her conviction that the clergy should be better informed so that such important facts concerning life after death could be given out through Christian churches, she later tried—as I mentioned above—to get Bishop Stockwood to reach me.

To doubt the sincerity of these three persons would be most difficult indeed. Their interest in psychic phenomena grows out of their Christian belief in life after death, and they see direct experience of the phenomena and research in the field as a way of substantiating their faith. And, apart from that, certainly the Bishop and the Canon are estimable persons (they do not appear *less* honest in my eyes because the Canon at his installation service—newsworthily enough—declined to subscribe to the Articles of Religion and the Bishop went ahead and installed him anyway!); and I have no reason to regard Mrs. Hanna as other than honorable. I cannot believe they would be consciously involved in a plot with fraudulent mediums.

Ψ

We moved on in our analysis.

Since at the second sitting with Mrs. Ena Twigg it seemed to come through from Jim that I could find out how to be in touch with him in the United States through a Father Rauscher of the Spiritual Frontiers Fellowship, it might have been possible that Mrs. Twigg (still working on the assumption of possible fraud) then wrote to Father Rauscher, telling him of my two séances with her, giving him the content of the messages and suggesting that he see to it that I made some contact with a mediumistic member of the Spiritual Frontiers Fellowship.

However, I have in my files a letter from Father Rauscher written to me on August 5, 1966, nearly five months after that second sitting with Mrs. Twigg. In it he told me that he had just returned from southern France where he attended a special conference sponsored by the Parapsychology Foundation of New York City. He mentioned that he had been invited to the conference, along with another priest, the Rev. Robert J. Lewis, by the President of the Foundation, Mrs. Eileen J. Garrett. Mrs. Garrett, he explained, had for years sponsored research in the scientific disciplines and attempted to increase interest among scientists regarding the subject of ESP and all its related aspects. She herself, he asserted, is one of the greatest living mediums of our time. He suggested I try to meet her when she returned to New York in October.

He also sent me her address in France. (I failed to follow up on either lead and have yet to meet Mrs. Garrett.)

Then Father Rauscher went on to report that Canon Pearce-Higgins had told him of my interest in this field when he had passed through London on his way home from the conference, and had suggested I might be interested to know that there was also a priest here in America with similar interests. Father Rauscher then mentioned his participation in Spiritual Frontiers Fellowship and explained that it was the American counterpart of the Churches' Fellowship for Psychical and Spiritual Studies in Great Britain.

Canon Pearce-Higgins had not been with me at that second sitting with Ena Twigg, so he had no way of knowing (unless Mrs. Twigg had told him) I had received Father Rauscher's name that day "from Jim" while Mrs. Twigg was in trance. Had he known, he might well have contacted Father Rauscher sooner—were a plot afoot.

Moreover, there is no indication in that August 5 letter that Father Rauscher had heard directly from Mrs. Twigg about me either. Rather, he seemed to respond to the word from Pearce-Higgins rather promptly because of his own deep interest, as the rest of the letter reveals:

. . . I feel that these subjects have much to say in a scientific age and that there should be some interpretative link between the scientific findings and religion. I have tried to state these thoughts in the enclosed article. Arthur Ford, whom I have known for some twelve years, has helped greatly in forming some of the ideas which SFF wishes to express for our Christian heritage.

I look forward to the time when I can do more in this field of interest, but like so many things, the churchmen that we wish to speak with and share thoughts are some of the first to cast aside the entire subject. Especially here in America. Even though this situation exists I have been fortunate to be able to sponsor some interesting seminars, lectures, and do much of the same for others when invited.

If you are ever in the area and have a few minutes I would be most anxious to meet you for conversation. Please be assured of my prayers for your son.

I did not meet Father Rauscher until December of 1967—after all the post-Toronto publicity. Notation should also be made of the fact that Father Rauscher mentions knowing Arthur Ford well, yet he seemed to have no direct word from Arthur Ford about the contact he and I had had—although only briefly—in New York at St. Thomas. The Rev. Mr. Ford did not appear to have passed any word on to him so that he could help "pursue" me.

Thus Diane and I concluded that Father Rauscher was also more than likely very innocent of any "plot" on the part of the mediums to take me in. His genuine interest and conviction are evident, and he seemed not to have been in touch with either Ena Twigg or Arthur Ford about me.

Ψ

That brings us to the possibility that Mrs. Twigg might have written to Arthur Ford to pass on the word about my sittings with her, thinking that he could pick up where she left off. That, then, would explain how he just "happened" to be at St. Thomas in New York (Mr. Ford lives in Philadelphia) when I was preaching there.

I have no way of verifying or disproving that particular hypothesis. It seems unlikely, however, for two reasons: if Mrs. Twigg were trying consciously to convince me of the validity of the communication, it would have seemed more likely that she would have contacted Father Rauscher, since his was the name that came through. Or, if she wanted a medium to "continue on" with me, it would have seemed more logical to have written to someone on the West Coast. She had no way of being sure I would be in the East where Mr. Ford could contact me—though she might have been willing to chance that, assuming that I traveled a lot.

In addition, however, Arthur Ford certainly made no effort to latch on to me. He even let me "get away" without so much as catching his name. I was unaware that I had ever met Arthur Ford until he reminded me that Sunday in Toronto. Further, the door-greeting that day was taking so long that the Rev. Larry Williams, the curate there with whom Mr. Ford had the luncheon date, suggested they go ahead, saying that he could pass on to me later what Arthur Ford had wished to share with me, and it was at *my* insistence that they waited (I had not wanted to seem to "brush" a fellow minister who had said that there was something he wanted to tell me).

Ψ

My next contacts were in Santa Barbara. Now, the Rev. George Daisley is British by birth and could well have known Ena Twigg in London; so it is possible Mrs. Twigg might have written to him about my sittings with her. She had no way of knowing I would be moving to Santa Barbara, but he—being located in California—would at least be a more likely person than Arthur Ford, even though our state is now the most populous in the Union.

Again, there is no way I can prove that Mrs. Twigg was or wasn't in touch with George Daisley. If she was, he had concocted quite another story to tell me to cover it up.

Mr. Daisley says my son had come through to him on two occasions around July 15 (the date I moved to Santa Barbara): once when he was alone and once during a sitting with a group. He, however, did not try to reach me himself, but waited for me to contact him. It was through John McConnell, who just happened to be in Santa Barbara for a meeting in the interests of his peace movement, that I learned of Mr. Daisley, and *I* took the initiative in reaching George.

Now it is *possible* that George Daisley planned all of that: that he heard from Ena Twigg, later learned I was moving to Santa Barbara, waited to meet someone who knew me and played coy about getting me to come, having made up the story about my son's appearing to him.

As fragile as this reconstruction is, I suppose it is possible; but knowing George Daisley, it seems highly improbable. He is a very warm, sincere, uncomplicated person. It is difficult even to imagine him involved in fraud. A personal, intuitive response is not proof of integrity, but it is the basis on which we must generally operate unless we have proof to the contrary.

Ψ

If these mediums were using a soft sell, it was so indirect it might have been lost altogether on someone as iconoclastic as I had become. Their subtle game might well have gone unnoticed had it not been for the poltergeist phenomena, both in Cambridge and in Santa Barbara. My motivation for seeing both Mrs. Twigg and George Daisley was not simply that at different periods I learned about them (if that had been motivation enough, I would have gone to Ena Twigg long before, out of curiosity, or immediately upon my return to London following Jim's death). I was not—and am still not—

enough interested in the field to go to a medium "just to see." No, my motivation in both cases was simply that it appeared possible that Jim was trying to reach me—a possibility suggested by the phenomena which occurred in each of the apartments.

Were these attention-getting events a part of the fraud? We could not see how they could be, unless Maren (who had been both in Cambridge and in Santa Barbara) was somehow responsible for them. But she didn't know the mediums, had never been to one herself and didn't believe in life after death until *after* the phenomena occurred and we had had the sitting with Ena Twigg. Moreover, it was hard to see how she *could* have made some of the phenomena happen. Often the objects were moved while we were all three out of the apartment, and many of them seemed most difficult to "produce": e.g., dream states (though I've since learned it is possible*); a half-dozen bottles of milk souring without the caps being removed; the burning off of Maren's own hair in a fashion we still haven't figured out; and the slow moving of the mirror off the high shelf before our very eyes.

Then, even if Maren had been able to make the various phenomena happen, it is hard to see what motive she could have had. Not believing in life after death, it would not likely have occurred to her to try to convince me that Jim was alive and doing these things. And not having had any previous experience with mediums—and not knowing either

* See Lawrence LeShan, Ph.D., Research Consultant, Program in Psychiatry and Religion, Union Theological Seminary, "The Scientific Facts about ESP," *Ladies' Home Journal*, February 1968, p. 50; "A Manifestation of Spirits?" an interview with Montague Ullman, M.D., Director of Community Mental Health, Maimonides Hospital, Brooklyn, and Professor of Psychiatry, University of the State of New York, Downstate Medical Center, *Jubilee* [Roman Catholic], January 1968, pp. 9–13; and Martin Cohen, "Strangers Can Influence, Control, and Invade Your Dreams," *Pageant*, January 1968, pp. 76–82—articles about experiments correlating dreams, EEGs and ESP.

Canon Pearce-Higgins or Mrs. Twigg—it also seems improbable that she thought that by means of a series of contrived mysteries she could drive me eventually to a medium—and to a particular one who was part of the cabal.

Now it *would* have been possible for Maren to place the two books in their strategic places that July evening in Santa Barbara, for she knew of the other events and by then believed that Jim was responsible for them. But in order to put the right book out on the coffee table open to the proper page, she would have had to read my mind—for I had not mentioned to her that I wanted it. (The placement of the UNESCO volume would have been easier, since I had spoken of it to her.)

And in *all* of these cases, Maren would have had to find the time and opportunity to do each thing without being observed. It seems unlikely to me that she was consciously attempting to "fool" me, and even less likely that she was in cahoots with a group of mediums in some master plot.

David Barr is an even more unlikely candidate for the role of "poltergeister." Not only, as in the case of Maren, did he not believe in survival or know the two who would have to be the London "confederates," but also he was in San Francisco not Santa Barbara when the two telekinetic events happened there. In fact it was from San Francisco that he told me on the phone about the 8:19 safety pins episode he and Lynne witnessed in their home—before I told him of the Santa Barbara experiences.

Ψ

Finally, then, we come to the CTV program in Toronto. Many critics have suggested that this could have been staged —and indeed one correspondent even suggested that *I* was a part of the fraud, together with Arthur Ford. And I must admit that because of the astonishing way the program turned out, it is not difficult to understand why people have been suspicious.

I have known Allen Spraggett for five years. As religion editor of the Toronto *Star*, he first interviewed me at the Anglican Congress in 1963. When Allen had completed a book called *The Unexplained*, in which he explores all manner of psi phenomena, he wrote me in Santa Barbara to ask if I would write the foreword. This was really a long shot, for he knew nothing of any special interest of mine in this field; but he knew me to be a person open to new ideas, and he thought I "just might . . ."

I responded to his request—partly because his approach is iconoclastic, as mine is, and partly for reasons expressed in the foreword I wrote for his book, which it will be useful to quote at some length at this point. It expresses my outlook of about a year and a half ago, before I had reviewed again all the data, had read as many serious works and had conferred with as many scientifically qualified experts in the psi field as I have since.

Characteristic of the history of science has been the resistance —both on the part of professionals in the already accepted disciplines and on the part of members of the general public—to the recognition of new emerging fields of inquiry. An obvious example is the conflict and struggle over the recognition of psychiatry as a medical science. Similarly, psychology and, later, sociology, had a hard time.

Apart from the commonplace undifferentiated opposition to anything new, there have been two more specific bases for reactions ranging from diffidence to scorn toward those who are pioneers in new areas of investigation. First, it is asserted that there is no reality to the claimed facts which would fall within the purported scientific discipline: a dogmatic "it can't be so." Or, alternatively, it is asserted, a priori, that whatever facts there are which are undeniable as facts, *must* have to be explained in categories already accepted in recognized sciences or by "common sense." Second, it is assumed that the purported new discipline fails to embody modes of analysis which qualify under the category of the "scientific method"; therefore, whatever the data, conclusions drawn therefrom cannot be taken seriously.

Psychiatry, psychology, sociology and nuclear physics have successfully run these twin gauntlets. The same cannot yet be said of a number of areas (which are more and more being seen as related) which have to do with the extension of human consciousness beyond the space-time continuum—areas in which there has been considerable observation all through human history but which have been receiving both more widespread and more concentrated orderly attention in recent decades.

As one who in the last few years has become increasingly familiar with the literature in this field and has had some opportunity to become acquainted with the programs of empirical investigation and the various alternatives, hypotheses, and conclusions, I regard this field as one which should be taken quite seriously and hope for considerable extension of both scientific work and public information . . .* This was *before* the publicity in Toronto (so the nature of some of the response to public knowledge of my involvement there did not take me totally by surprise) and before the publication of my own *If This Be Heresy*, which, in Chapter 7, covers this very field.

In any case, Allen Spraggett came to Geneva in May of 1967 to cover our Center's Pacem in Terris II Conference for the Toronto *Star*. While there, he and I had an opportunity to share some personal experiences—in confidence—in the

* New York: New American Library, 1967, pp. xi–xii.

psi area. Allen learned there of the Cambridge events and of the chapter in my book, which was coming out in September, covering the subject in general.

Since his book also was due to be published in September, once back in Ontario, he and Charles Templeton, producer of the W-5 television series, thought of the idea of a program on which a medium would appear with the two of us to talk about this whole area and possibly to go into trance.

Now in connection with this occasion two questions arise: Were Allen Spraggett and Arthur Ford in cahoots in planning a "good show?" With or without Allen's knowledge and/or cooperation, had Arthur Ford done a rather extensive piece of research between the time he was invited and the day of the taping?

A "Yes" to either question contradicts the sense of genuine respect we have come to have for both of the gentlemen involved, each of whom Miss Kennedy and I have come to know fairly well in the course of this whole matter. But as important as intuitive responses are in evaluating persons, I recognize, of course, the subjective and unverified character of this assessment of Mr. Spraggett and the Rev. Mr. Ford. Somewhat more objective is the fact that the character of the material which came through does not very well support the research hypothesis.

As has already been suggested, the remote and private nature of some of the data would suggest the necessity of a team of investigators who are no ordinary gumshoes, but who operate on the level of successful sophistication we used to attribute to the CIA. On the other hand, paradoxically enough, had a program of investigation been mounted, it would seem that with regard to some of the subject matter, the most amateur detective could have done better. It would seem many facts could have been uncovered which had not been published and which would have been remote enough to appear impressive, yet would seem more directly connected with me and would be more accurate than those concerning the Rev. Mr. Seager, whom I have no recollection of meeting and who did *not* die in an automobile accident, and concerning Carol Rede's brother, whom Carol presumably believed to be living in Carmel but who in fact had died fairly soon after she did.

What I am saying is that it is difficult to believe that the content of the Toronto session is to be explained away on the assumption of a prior program of research because on that assumption some of it is too well done and some of it is too poorly done. But several months later we had an opportunity to confirm our conclusions as a result of two then unanticipated events.

Ψ

I was invited to WHY-TV (the educational station) in Philadelphia to appear early in December 1967 as a panelist for an hour's discussion of psychic phenomena. On the panel were to be persons of several disciplines representing the full gamut of the spectrum of belief and disbelief with regard to the subject matter. When I was told Arthur Ford was also to be on the program, I was glad, but made it clear I would appear only if it was understood that a televised séance would not form part of the program. The director reassured me by saying that Arthur Ford had made exactly the same request. Neither of us was eager for more publicity of the kind that had followed the Toronto program.

Confident, then, that this would not provoke a repeat of the Toronto aftermath, I agreed to take part. Along with Mr. Ford and me, the following people appeared: Mr. Karl Abraham, science writer, Philadelphia *Bulletin*; the Rev. Walter Houston Clark, Ph.D., Visiting Professor of the Psychology of Religion, Tufts University; Mr. Daniel Cohen, Editor of *Science Digest,* author of *Myths of the Space Age;* Mr. Donald Drake, Science Editor, Philadelphia *Inquirer;* the Rev. Edgar Jackson, Ph.D., pastoral psychologist; Carroll B. Nash, Ph.D., Professor of Biology, St. Joseph's College; Karlis Osis, Ph.D., Director of Research, American Society for Psychical Research; and Mr. David Prowitt, Science Editor of National Educational Television, who served as moderator.

Our discussion raised many of the questions which had been put to me through letters as well as in person, and—because of the diversity of backgrounds of the panelists—the responses were both stimulating and enlightening.

Miss Kennedy and I saw this occasion as an opportunity to assess more carefully Arthur Ford's gifts. We decided to request a private sitting with him following the television taping, and go with a list of questions pertaining to mysteries about both my son's death and Maren Bergrud's which we were virtually certain that Mr. Ford could not research. Moreover, we intended to steer the conversation by our questions and comments so that any information he might have gathered about other persons would figure very little. Also we felt that the degree of directness of the responses would give considerable indication as to whether there was genuine communication going on or not.

Miss Kennedy and I had made the appointment to sit with Mr. Ford following the television taping, and Diane arranged for a friend of hers in New York, Miss Jane Kingman, Executive Secretary of another foundation, to come down from New York and accompany us. Miss Kingman was the friend who had been able to help us pursue the lead given in the Toronto séance about Marvin Halverson, for it turned out she was working for the Foundation for Arts, Religion and Culture, which Mr. Halverson had served as the first director. Jane knew, then, something about Mr. Halverson's activities and patterns of life in the years immediately preceding his death. She knew, for example, that he had gone out to Berkeley after leaving his job at the Foundation in New York and had died there on February 24, 1967, more than a year *after* Jim's death. She knew he had been involved in the use of psychedelic drugs as well as having some other rather serious problems. She knew he had lived in Greenwich Village. And finally, quite by accident one day she learned from a Greenwich Village liquor dealer from whom she was buying a bottle of wine that on the day the news of Jim's death appeared in the New York papers, Marvin Halverson had come into his store and had commented, "I knew that boy." This all fit with Nan Lanier's statement in her letter later from London that Jim had talked to her about Marvin Halverson.

We felt if anything further were to come out about my son's connection with Halverson it would be well to have Jane there. Also, we wanted a third witness.

After the show Dr. Clark, who has studied intensively the psychology of mystical experiences, Father Rauscher, with whom I had corresponded but whom I had not had the pleasure of meeting until that day, Arthur Ford, Jane Kingman, Diane Kennedy and I had a leisurely lunch together. This gave us a chance to talk about the whole psi field at greater length. Then Father Rauscher (who agreed, before leaving for his rectory in New Jersey, to set up a tape recorder for us so we would have an exact transcript of the session), Mr. Ford, Diane, Jane and I went to the small apartment nearby in which Arthur Ford lives.

Ψ

Mr. Ford's apartment is pleasant but modest. One would not get the impression that he has become a wealthy man by being a medium. That fact in itself would almost eliminate the motive of financial gain from any hypothesis of fraud. We had not suspected that money was an incentive for Arthur Ford, however. In fact, we felt fairly certain that if fraud was involved in any of this it was only because of a sincere desire on the part of any of the three mediums with which I had been associated to minister to persons. It was clear that all three believed profoundly that persons survive death and are able to communicate. It would appear, then, that any researching done would have been in an attempt more fully to convince me of the veridical nature of such communication in order that I would "believe" and give testimony to my belief.

In motivation this would not be unlike a pastor who assures the bereaved person that his loved one lives on and is with God or Christ in heaven, without any actual proof that this is so—and sometimes with very little basis in the biography of the deceased to support an inference, within the terms of conventional theology, that there has been this blissful outcome. Nevertheless, he may *believe* it to be so and want the bereft one to have the comfort which such an assurance can give. In much the same way, a medium who *believes* in survival and communication might seek to give evidence to convince the sitter so that he might have the comfort of such belief too. Thus his (or her) *motives* could be of the highest nature, though he might resort to research and a kind of deception (the sitter is led to believe the information comes from his loved one) to bolster the total impression.

We did not suspect Arthur Ford of bad motives, but we had agreed it was possible he might have researched some of the information which came through in Toronto, and we knew for a fact that the publicity following that program had greatly increased interest in this whole field and had caused a considerable boom in the call for mediumship all over the country—not excluding, of course, Arthur Ford and George Daisley, with whom I was known to have had sittings. In any case, for one wanting to promote belief in survival and communication and to increase the credibility of his own profession, Mr. Ford had had something to gain by being as convincing as possible on the Toronto show.

But now we were in private. There were no TV lights and no audience. There would be no publicity. What kind of information would come through?

After some conversation, we settled down where each of us could be comfortable in the small room which obviously doubled as a living room and study. The tape recorder was on the desk, ready to record. Diane was seated by it; Jane was on a sofa; I took a chair directly in front of Mr. Ford, who seated himself in a large red leather chair. He explained that his chair reclined in order to make it easier for him to relax and go into a trance.

With no further explanation then, Arthur Ford covered his eyes as he had in Toronto, pushed his chair back into a reclining position, began his deep-breathing exercises and after several minutes seemed to go off into a trance. Father Rauscher addressed Fletcher and, on hearing a brief response, turned on the tape recorder, said "Fletcher, I'm going to leave you with your guests" and quietly left.

Ψ

We waited in silence for a moment or two.

Then came words purportedly from Fletcher: "I was there listening to some of the things this afternoon. [He was referring to the television taping, I presumed.] There were many more people looking on than there were taking part. I mean from our side. But I do not think anyone could have penetrated the barrier of negative thinking. I remember you, sir, you are the preacher I was talking to on the television one time. Is that right?"

"That's right," I answered.

"Glad to see you again. There's someone here I can see first of all—it's some boy I've seen before. I heard you people talking about him this afternoon. Well, I know who he is but—says to 'Tell my . . .' does he call you 'Dad'?"

"Right," I responded.

"Tell my dad that I'm always glad to—that I have been near him quite often and I don't think it will be too long before he can dispense with crutches like Ford because it is a matter of blending with you. It is easy in the spiritual body; the flesh presents no barrier. People on this side want to have a sympathetic cooperative person on the earthly side—it's very easy to merge the two bodies and then your own powers and gifts will be released and you'll realize . . ."

There was a pause, and it was reported that Jim seemed to be talking about his grandmother on his mother's side, whom he identified by giving her name (correctly—it is Alexandra). Concern was expressed about her and several comments which I knew to be relevant followed. None of this could have been researched, but perhaps it could have been pulled out of my unconscious by ESP.

Then Jim seemed to speak directly: "And I want to tell you that I'm sorry that I insisted on coming back alone." [Then, apparently from Fletcher:] "Or something like that."

Then I asked: "Coming back alone?" I didn't quite get the import of the words. The answer was "Yes."

"This time, you mean?" I was trying to figure it out. Then

Fletcher seemed to intervene to give some help: "Sounds like he was in some country with you and came back alone."

"Oh," I said. "Insisted he come back alone; he's sorry he did."

Now I understood that his reference was to coming back to the States alone in order to stop in New York City to see friends. I was being especially careful not to give away any information this time, as we wanted to know how much would come through. I was becoming aware of a process unlike what I had experienced before, except when the medium was not in trance and therefore made comments himself: it almost seemed as if Jim, Fletcher and I were in a three-way conversation, with Fletcher trying to make sure Jim got across his messages.

"Because I was doing all right with you and I felt that for the first time we had gotten to be close friends."

"Right," I responded. A sudden warmth came over me. Again I felt on an intuitive level the reality of the communication. Yet I tried to maintain an agnostic attitude, even a skeptical one.

"You'd been so busy that I never had enough chance to get acquainted with you. Too bad. You understand?"

"Yes." I did indeed.

"But I am happy that our relationship is on a good basis now."

"Yes," I replied, and, according to plan, I now took the initiative to push for further information. "I never quite figured out what happened when you hit New York. Two or three days and then this happened. You didn't get hold of anybody, people you'd said you wanted to see. It's a little mysterious in there."

The reply: "I got hold of something that wasn't good for me."

"Yes." I wanted to keep the conversation going without priming the pump too much. Then Fletcher again seemed to interject a comment.

"Was it whiskey, or drugs or something? It wasn't whiskey."

"No." I was sure it wasn't alcohol. Jim hadn't used alcohol much at all since he got on psychedelic drugs. And the New York medical examiner had reported that there were no signs of alcohol in the system.

Now Diane began a dialogue. "Was that a part of your plan, when you went to New York? Had you had that in mind?"

"No, I ran into some—not old friends—but some people I had known. I guess I was a little bit weak. But—"

"Who were they?"

"Do you remember?" I interjected. "What was that like in there? When you came over and were alone downtown?" We were pressing for specific information.

Then: "Remember what it was like? I was—" [Then Fletcher, seemingly:] "What's the word? Coming down, that fellow, he didn't jump out, but the idea is it was a high place and then he got into a low place, or something, and confused him. He wasn't normally a mental case."

"Right." I had a feeling that an attempt was being made to talk about what it feels like when a person is "coming down" from a psychedelic trip. If it were Fletcher coming through, the feeling probably wouldn't have been familiar to him, since he passed away long before the psychedelic era. This would account for the physical analogies to try to put across the idea.

"But he had something that depressed him, something that confused him. Tried to write it but couldn't make sense, you understand?" Ford's voice continued.

"Tried to 'write' it or 'ride' it?" I asked, I wasn't sure I had understood the word, and this time I didn't want to do my own filling in. I wanted to be sure I was getting this through the medium.

"Tried to *write* it but didn't make sense. Couldn't get his symbols right. You understand?"

"Yes, words were used, but not making sense." I was, of course, thinking of some incoherent notes which had been found in Jim's hotel room. The police had reported the fact of these notes, so this was something Arthur Ford could have known from the newspaper coverage of the suicide. But the words had not been quoted. In fact, although the handwriting was clear and real words were used, they didn't "add up." I pressed again for specific information:

"After you got over here, Jim—or Fletcher talking for Jim, or whatever—Jim, did you make contact with friends over here or did you move on into this with—"

"You mean after I got out of the body?" Ford's voice interrupted.

"After you got to New York," I responded.

"Yes, I met some friends from the West Coast."

"Here in New York?" I was puzzled. Also I forgot for the moment I was in Philadelphia, not New York.

"Yes, they were not friends; they were part of a crowd. You understand?"

Diane then entered the dialogue again. "How did you meet them, Jim?"

"Ran into them."

"Do you remember who they were?" she pressed.

The response to that question was very direct, and the conversation that followed gave us some remarkable leads which we have since followed up. The information is such that it can't be printed here, which is unfortunate from the standpoint of allowing the reader fully to appreciate the quite amazing nature of the data. However, suffice it to say that we were given specific names. One was that of a friend in Berkeley with a most unusual last name (there also came through the profession of his father) with whom Jim had been closest during the summer before he went to Cambridge. Then we were told that he (the friend) could "clear it all up" if he would. (Extended conversation with that friend—I got hold of him and invited him to Santa Barbara —later confirmed that he was indeed able to clear a lot up for me.) Jim—apparently it was he—was able to talk at length about his problems with close to the same degree of frankness we had enjoyed in Cambridge. He elaborated on Marvin Halverson's role in his life. He tied together events which occurred in England and Europe—and how they spoke to him about himself—with his final decision. In other words, he fit together many missing pieces in the puzzle, enabling me to understand his death better.

After a lengthy interchange Jim seemed to say, "I think if I had continued on the earth I would have caused you a lot of trouble."

"Possibly so," I responded, reflecting on all he had just purportedly said and all I knew of his difficulties. "But as you know now, nothing of this is such that we couldn't have worked out whatever might have been. I just wanted to be close to you in it—whatever. You know that."

In spite of my determination to remain skeptical throughout, I had a deep sense again of really talking to my son. All that had been said fit so perfectly the facts I knew and filled in a lot that I didn't know, that I actually felt I was in conversation. I was profoundly moved by the purported responses from Jim:

"I know that. I never knew it until six months before I

came here, and I am sorry that my actions have caused the things to happen since then that made you unhappy."

However one would precisely define the source of these words, they struck home. I was sorry to think that Jim had not known how much I cared until six months before his death. Had I only not been so busy . . . had I only recognized his deep needs sooner . . . had I only been able to relate as effectively and as helpfully to Jim as I had apparently been able to in counseling relationships with hundreds of others. I was filled with regret and remorse. But I couldn't deal with that in the context of the séance—and the damage had been irrevocably done, whatever I might wish were true; so I tried to comment with words which pointed to the future.

"We don't know yet, do we, what good will come from all of this? I think that good will come—not that I wouldn't have preferred that you hadn't—well, hadn't left *this* life. But many good things have already come, and you must, I think, see value, too, for it has been seeming that you know some of the things."

I thought back to that portion of the séance conversation in March when I read a very moving article about Jackie Robinson in the New York *Times* (March 10, 1968). His son had been arrested on a charge of possession of heroin. Robinson, who had himself become a hero to an entire generation of American boys because as one with baseball fame he had involved himself in work with boys' clubs and community organizations throughout the country, made this comment to newsmen about his son's arrest:

> Somehow we just couldn't reach Jack [his son]. My problem was my inability to spend much time at home. I guess I thought my family was secure, that at least we wouldn't have anything to worry about, so I went running around everywhere else. I guess I

had more of an effect on other people's kids than I had on my own.

As different as our circumstances have been, when I read that I felt a deep sense of empathy for Jackie Robinson and I admired his courage in pointing openly to what could be viewed as his own shortcomings in his family scene. It is not easy to face the fact that one has not been all that he might have been as a parent—especially when some tragedy befalls one's child. Yet I suspect there are hundreds of fathers who, like me, responded to Robinson's comments with a deeply felt "I know just what you mean."

Ψ

I raised an issue with Jim, if indeed it was he with whom I was in conversation in Arthur Ford's apartment, which had been brought up in a rather harsh criticism by a friend who had also been quite close to Jim. I told him that in a letter she had expressed concern that any of this had gotten to the press for fear that the public attention would hold him back in his spiritual progress. She had suggested that my attempts to be in communication would be a drag on Jim. There was a prompt response:

"No, it isn't that. I wanted to explain things. I wanted . . . like, if you can talk things over, then you can forgive yourself. So you have done me more, much more good than I can ever do for you."

"I think it's quite mutual," I countered.

"Anyway, you can't hold me back," came through next.

"I wouldn't have thought so," was my observation.

"Because of the law of progression," the voice went on, "I have definitely turned my face toward the light." I remembered his "trip" in Cambridge in which together we had searched for a lighted path while lost in the darkness on the way first entered upon.

Ψ

Then we moved on to Maren, to see what information might come through about her death. I asked if Jim had been in touch with Maren. Before a reply came, Maren herself appeared to break in:

"I have been right here listening and Jim and I have been holding each other up. But I feel like the old prophet whose mantle fell down and landed on . . ."

Fletcher purportedly re-entered the conversation for the first time in a long while. "Are you Diane?" was asked.

"Yes, I am," Diane answered.

Then: "Well, you carry on. Listen and I am sure I can give you a little guidance and push when you reach a point where you don't quite know which way to turn. Visualize the end; wait for the answer."

"With regard to what?" Diane was maintaining her approach of skepticism.

"Your work," was the response.

"She seems to feel [it seemed that Fletcher was interpreting] that more or less her mantle has fallen on you, or something."

"But I have a feeling, Maren, that I have a somewhat different idea about what direction the work should move in than you did," Diane said candidly.

Diane was suspicious of this word which purportedly came from Maren, for she had learned enough about her predecessor to know that they were interested in quite different facets of the Foundation's work: Maren had really hoped to develop a lecture agency out of it, eventually establishing her own business; Diane was interested in developing educational thrusts in the Foundation program.

Anyway, this was the response: "Well, that's probably right. Times change. Circumstances demand a different format. And so carry on. You are very open to—you are open to anything of—you are more open to illumination— You understand? Might be a form of inspiration. [This presumably from Fletcher, to be sure we were getting the message.] And we can use any method that is necessary with any person that is necessary and I don't feel at all out of the picture. I'm simply glad that things are just—well even better than they were when I was there."

Diane told me afterward that she had felt that whole section to be what we call "fluff"—that is, words that the sitter would probably like to hear, but which are not at all evidentiary and could easily apply to anyone. She did not receive them as coming from Maren—at least not during the séance.

Neither did I, but I was still wanting to press for details about Maren's death, so I didn't challenge it, but went right on.

"That's right, Maren, I—there is still an element of mystery, and I'm sure there is even with you, in the events of that early morning when you decided to go, to take your life. What really happened, I—"

The response came so quickly it interrupted.

"Well, I can tell you what happened. I was just tired and fed up, and the loneliness was too much."

"Maren," Diane said, "Joyce and Gertrude [referring to the secretaries in the New Focus office] have felt that this was something you had thought about doing for a long time. Is that right?"

"Yes," was the answer. "I was in a depressed mood periodically and it kept getting worse and worse."

"Had you prepared for that night?" Diane asked.

There seemed to be no direct response to Diane's question. It was as if Maren were caught up in another train of thought: "Anyway, when you feel that you are no longer anxious to carry on, and nothing seems to be worth while and you just sort of feel empty, well, I think that you have a right to . . ."

"Well, I would say—" I started to say something on the complicated question of a person's right to take his own life,* but there seemed to be an impatience to go right on:

"I don't know whether you knew it or not, but I was afraid of a certain growth. I was afraid of cancer."

"Yes, I knew you were—more than probably you needed to be," I commented. Maren had had two operations—each quite serious—to remove malignant growths, and she mentioned from time to time, when for any reason she didn't feel well, that she feared that the cause was a recurrence of cancer. She had been feeling quite ill for about ten days before her death. In fact, she had been in the Midwest and her condition delayed her return to work for several days.

"Well, I couldn't face it. [The response was relevant.] I hope you will forgive me."

"Of course you are forgiven," I replied. "I hope you will forgive my lack of perception with regard to your—your state."

"How can we expect the God that Jesus talked about to forgive us if we are not willing to forgive other people?" came next.

"Right," I said, without the need of much pondering. I hoped we weren't moving into platitudinous material.

* See James Hillman, *Suicide and the Soul* (New York: Harper & Row, 1964).

Then: "I firmly believe that I am going to see Jesus someday."

"Do you really?" I said in surprise. (Maren had not been a great believer in Jesus, though from her thorough Norwegian Lutheran background, she knew the Bible very well indeed.) "Do you hear about him?"

I received not only an answer, but an analysis: "No, he's just another person, been here longer, but I have been told that the people who have been here long enough to advance to a high plane or a high dimension can always come down to the lower plane to help us. But we who are just here have to earn the right to go up."

"Or to change," I suggested, interposing my own concept.

Expressed was not agreement or disagreement, but quite another thought: "I know one thing—Jim and I are in what we call the etheric body in the etheric plane. That is, it is in the in-between place. Do you understand?"

"Yes, I do," I said, thinking of the various books I had read on this subject by persons who felt that they had communicated with the dead.

The train of thought was continued: "And we will generally stay here, I am told, until the people we care about on the earth plane have either come here or somehow we are no longer concerned about them. As long as there is anyone on the earth plane that we care about and think we can help—we have all the time there is. And then we go on to the next one. But we are in no hurry."

Ψ

Then out of the blue, as from Jim, came a message: "Tell George Livermore—you'll be seeing him soon—that, as I get it, Caroline will be coming over soon. By the way, he is a great fellow and, as you know, a loyal backer of yours."

"Yes, I know that," I said somewhat casually—because my mind was on something else. I had the impression that "Caroline" was the first name of George Livermore's mother, but I wasn't sure, since I had always called her "Mrs. Livermore," rather than by first name. She was in her eighties and a great lady indeed. She had held any number of posts in the diocese; in fact she was the first woman in any American diocese to be elected to the Standing Committee (which, under our canon law shares the traditional episcopal functions with the bishop).

I saw no reason why I would be seeing George Livermore soon (though it was always a pleasure to: he had been indeed a great friend and himself carried on the tradition of taking various responsibilities in the diocese); and I doubted, even if I might have run into him, that on the basis of what I had just heard I would be announcing to him the impending death of his mother—or of a "Caroline" in case I found that was not his mother's first name, but the name of another member of the family. So the message dropped out of my mind, until—

At the Christmas Eve Midnight Eucharist in Grace Cathedral, I participated as a Canon, which honorary disignation I have had since no longer being the Diocesan. As the clergy moved out of the ambulatory to their places, preparatory to the festival procession, I was headed toward my stall in the last row of the south side of the Great Choir. The first person I saw sitting in the row ahead (stalls in the Great Choir not needed by those taking part in the service are often used on crowded occasions by lay worshipers) was George Livermore. In fact he was the first lay member of the diocese I had spoken to following the Philadelphia session. We smiled and quietly greeted each other. I had a chance to speak to him briefly afterward. I thought of saying something about what had come through, but just couldn't.

It was on February 2 that Myrtle Goodwin, my secretary at the Center, passed the word to me which she had just learned by phone from her successor as secretary to the Bishop of California, that Mrs. Livermore had died.

"Oh, I am so sorry . . . Myrtle, do you remember her first name?"

"It was Caroline," she answered.

Ψ

The communication then began to fade out. The Fletcher personality rambled over several rather disjointed messages, mentioning my mother by her full name—Pearl—and her never-used middle name, Agatha—and several other acquaintances. We tried to interject questions, but there seemed need for haste to get said what there was to say before "the current" ran out. A few comments were made to Jane Kingman about her future, and then silence.

Within a few moments, Arthur Ford was awake and sitting up in his chair. "Did you get anything?" he asked.

"We certainly did," I responded, feeling that all in all the material had been quite remarkable. "Thank you."

Ψ

As the three of us left we evaluated the material which had come through. Though that which had been said to Jane at the end and the opening remarks Maren had purportedly made to Diane seemed less than evidentiary—being of the "all too true" nature—the rest of the material gave us plenty to work on in order to verify it.

A careful item-by-item analysis of the transcript some time later revealed that far more factual and interpretive data of an evidentiary nature came through in this séance than in any other single sitting. The conversation had flowed easily and naturally, with few pauses or gropings for words. Answers to questions had been direct and instantaneous. The Fletcher personality figured very little once it appeared Jim was able to communicate well by himself. And all that had come through was consistent with what we already knew and what had been said in other séances.

We were convinced that the hypothesis of advance researching did not adequately explain Arthur Ford's mediumship. As far as we were concerned, only one of two explanations could account for the biggest part of the data which came out that day. What could not have been drawn out of my conscious thinking by ESP could not have been researched either, we felt sure. Therefore, Arthur Ford either had some direct knowledge of it—by normal means, through living persons who knew the full story—or something remarkable in the paranormal realm was going on: ESP at a distance, pulling information out of the minds of living persons, and/or drawing out of the collective unconscious by ESP and/or direct communication with deceased persons. We could not with finality settle which of the latter explanations accounted for this knowledge, but we were fully satisfied that the explanation wasn't fraud.

There was a segment of the material which was so evidentiary that I am not able to reveal it here. I regret that its nature makes it necessary to withhold it, for I should like my readers to be able to judge for themselves its quality. But I have shared a great deal in these pages and what has been told and the reader's assessment of it (and of me, too, I suppose) will serve to supply the facts part of the *facts + faith* formula in his accepting—or not accepting—this statement: that I have been able to verify nearly all of the facts that came through, thereby clearing up a number of unknowns about Jim's death.

Ψ

Any theoretical doubts about Arthur Ford's integrity were completely allayed by that sitting in December. After Toronto we realized that even if some of the material had been researched, or had been known by him consciously at one time or another, there was a great deal of it which would have been very, very difficult to find that way. Now the balance had shifted further: the percentage of what was even in theory researchable was very low indeed; the percentage requiring the recognition of paranormal gifts was very high.

We still weren't certain about Allen Spraggett's role—though once we were satisfied about Mr. Ford, the theoretical possibility that Mr. Spraggett had engaged in some planning, even well intentioned, was for all practical purposes eliminated. But we had an opportunity to test that out, too.

In February Allen called by phone from Toronto to say that he had learned of an outstanding "physical medium" (i.e., one who could purportedly produce both materializations and "direct voice," presumably from spirits, with or without the use of a "trumpet") and that he and several others, including an outstanding scientist who has published significant works in the psi field, were going to check him out. He invited me to join them if I wanted. Since it happened to be convenient to do so, Diane and I decided this would help round out our experience with psychic phenomena, so we accepted Allen's invitation.

Those particular sittings *did* prove to be fraudulent, though we have been unable to determine just *how* the medium produced a half-dozen "materializations" at the outset. But we were reassured on another score, for it was evident that Allen Spraggett was as skeptical, iconoclastic and agnostic as any of us. He put forth challenges to the medium in the sittings, was among the first to observe (having had a great deal of experience with mediums) that these purported communications were phony, and was involved in the second session in the exposure of the purported use of the trumpet by spirits. Not only that, he had been quite willing to agree —*before* they proved fraudulent—that nothing should be written about my participation in the series of séances without my explicit approval. So he was obviously not just out for a good story; he was genuinely interested in finding whether there are such things as veridical materializations.

Thus we gave up the option of fraud or conspiracy to explain the complex of events (recognizing of course that some individual items theoretically might have been "researched" or "planted"). Whatever other explanation there might be for the complex variety of phenomena I had observed and experienced in the past two years, we were left with no reason to doubt the motives or conduct of the persons who had been related to the events, nor could we find any evidentiary basis for inferring collusion among them.

Ψ

Both for personal and intellectual reasons I wanted to be very sure I wasn't being taken in. I am not naturally of a suspicious nature in personal relations, in spite of my training as a lawyer and service in World War II in Naval Intelligence. Yet I gave special attention to analyzing all possibilities of deception in this whole matter, not only because of the quite unusual character of all that had happened but also because, I must confess, I shared the quite widespread presumption against the honesty and/or stability of mediums and the like. In fact, more often than not when I found it appropriate to speak of such matters, I threw in a standard qualifier: "While I know there are charlatans, phonies, and self-deluded people operating in this field . . ."

But it began to dawn on me that—true as this iconoclastic clause is—to keep repeating it is a rather gratuitous insult. After all, I myself belong to two professions—the ministry and the law—each of which over many centuries has provided a vivid assortment of less than straightforward, noble and clearheaded practitioners! And I realized that I did not say, every time I referred to a clergyman or an attorney, or to a theological or legal matter, something like "While I know there are many charlatans, phonies and self-deluded people operating in this field . . ."

The purpose of the empirical method is to seek to sift out the false from the true. Hence it is very unscientific to dismiss a whole field of phenomena because some of what is claimed as veridical data may in fact not be such. This would be like closing all the law courts because some witnesses from time to time (intentionally or unintentionally) give testimony which is false. The long-standing recognition of this possibility has been the reason for the provisions of cross-examination, character testimony, expert witnesses, etc. Likewise, with regard to psychic phenomena: there is a *tertium quid* between uncritical gullibility and dogmatic rejection of all that pertains to the subject matter.

An easy way of escaping the need to deal with data which

do not fit one's system of thought about the universe is to brand as fraudulent those who uncover the data. But the data still remain, and if we are sincere about our search for truth we will seek to adjust our hypotheses to accommodate them.

By the end of March, then, Miss Kennedy and I had already gone quite thoroughly into the various theories that would more adequately account for such phenomena than a broadside dismissal on the assumption of fraud.

12

All our most real convictions are born and brought up in . . . personal experiences. Communication is always, of necessity, personal, so it is always incredible until personally experienced. Once realised, it is unforgettable and indestructible.

—*Robertson Ballard*

ESP research is providing us with one basic, easily verifiable principle of communication: That living beings interact at a deeper level than that which can be encompassed by the conscious mind—a *vibration channel* exists which allows the Inner Self of one person to communicate with the Inner Self of another, without the need of any verbal exchange. That channel is activated partly by the sound of the voice and partly by the touch of the hand. Helen Keller, for example, learned how to *see* by holding on to Anne Sullivan's hand until the vibrations that passed from one to the other finally could be understood by the deaf, dumb and blind girl as *thoughts* and *feelings*, then as words and ideas until finally an unspoken language of the spirit came to life.

—*Walker H. Westcott*

If psi-phenomena, as they are now often called, do *not* fit into the material-physical system then they must have a profound meaning for both religion and philosophy; they would not only throw light, either directly or indirectly, upon the vexed question of the mind-body relationship, but would break once and for all the supposed scientific grounds for the materialism which now grips the world. . . . This would alter the whole intellectual atmosphere and again admit the reality of a non-material, spiritual if you like, part of the universe in which the religious yearnings of man could find a place; it would be like supplying air to a fire which is now only dimly flickering for lack of it. The divine flame would burn again with a new light.

—*Sir Alister Hardy*

In this field, as in other areas involving the assessment of data presumably relating to a person, over and above the testing and assessment of the many particular items can be a compelling sense of the continuity between them, a sense of commonalty of causation. Intuitive, subjective—yes; but when combined with a careful screening of purported evidence and a consideration of all the possible hypotheses of explanation, neither the process nor the result is necessarily unscientific. In any case, it will be far less so than the attitude of those who, with little or no knowledge of either the considerable volume of data or the impressive quantity of scientific literature in this field, dogmatically pronounce that none of it can be so, that all of it is "nonsense." My impatience with this frequently expressed attitude is amplified by my having as a colleague at the Center for the Study of Democratic Institutions one [Dr. Linus Pauling] who has won a Nobel Prize in a field of science that deals with doing what I was taught in high school chemistry absolutely could not be done —namely, the changing of one element into another. That which had long been called alchemy is now called nuclear physics. The arrogance of the uninformed who pontificate with unexamined negatives is every bit as irritating as the naïveté and defensiveness of the overly credulous. There is a middle way.

—*J.A.P.* in SATURDAY REVIEW

What constitutes the normal and what the paranormal is rapidly becoming more and more difficult to discern. The more we learn about our universe, the more laws of nature we learn to use and work with, the less sure we are of the rigid and limiting notions about the how and why of it all which we used to hold in the past. Yet we are increasingly able to recognize pointers toward the unity of reality and to experience ourselves as integral parts of the nature of things—with the transcendence to see it all, to say it as it is and to take a more and more effective part in its further evolution and change.

Factual data, which amass at an almost incredible rate, force one continually to alter his world view to make room for more and more that is being discovered to be true. More new things have been discovered and developed in the last twenty-five years than in the previous forty-two thousand years of history since the appearance of our Cro-Magnon prototype. Such change—at an exponential rate—cannot help but outdate our systems of classification and of interrelationship—indeed, the whole way we look at things.

Take just one example: Not long ago astronomers in England and in the United States reported "radio emissions" from outer space. They described the pulsations as extraordinarily precise, recurring every 1.3372795 seconds, remaining observable for about a minute, vanishing for some three minutes, then reappearing. During the one minute plus of steady pulsing, the scientists observed a ten-fold variation in the intensity of the signal, from pulse to pulse. Furthermore, the observers recorded a difference in the pattern of the variations when observed at different frequencies. This much was in the category of facts.

What should be made of such facts is, however, a question of a different order, for no particular conclusion is entailed in the data—that is, strictly *required* by the data; no theory presently accepted by astronomers and astrophysicists is sufficient to account for the signals. Thus the scientists are forced to seek an explanation for the facts, and any explanation adopted will to some degree involve a "leap of faith"—that is, it will be the most plausible inference from the data, but not necessitated by them.

Perhaps a "white dwarf" or a neutron star is causing them, one British scientist suggested. But, although white dwarf (or "senile") stars have been identified in the sky, to date no one has found any clear-cut evidence of the existence of neutron stars (which would represent the final stage of collapse of a star, according to one theory). So to explain the strange signals by an unknown—an unverified theory—is not very helpful.

Other scientists have suggested the possibility of superior galactic communities which have been in communication with each other for millions of years and whose signals we are only now technologically able to pick up. The pulsations *could* represent, they assert, some kind of coded attempt by a distant civilization to reach us by "radio." This is also speculation. Verification will come only when and if we are able somehow to decode the "messages."

Ψ

Most astronomers and astrophysicists would prefer, however, to find what they have called a "natural" explanation. By that they mean, confusingly enough, one which does not require a higher form of intelligence, but rather has some "material" source, and so in order to refute ideas about an "artificial" source—such as intelligent creatures—they continue to search for an explanation which would fit a presently existent theory. Only a theory which can account for all of the data will be sufficient, however, and thus far there has been found no "natural" hypothesis sufficiently broad to merit its adoption.

The astronomer's discovery of signals from outer space (which have been dubbed LGMs—for "little green men"—until an explanation can be found) is comparable to the psychologists' investigations of extrasensory perception. All kinds of data have now been recorded, thousands of observations have been made and elaborate descriptions have been spelled out as to how ESP functions. To cover just a few points: Such functions seem to occur spontaneously (without preparations of any kind) as well as under controlled experimental conditions. ESP apparently operates at both the conscious and the unconscious levels. It does not seem to be limited to the here and now as far as time and space are concerned: precognition and retrocognition have empirical support of both the laboratory and the spontaneous variety, and communication is affected by distance only to a limited degree. ESP seems to operate more effectively when the sender and receiver are congenial with each other—and even more so when they are emotionally close.

There are many ways in which extrasensory perception defies all of our presently known and accepted laws of physics. For example, it does not diminish significantly in strength over distance as do most energy waves. Also, ESP transmissions can be passed from a hypnotizer to his hypnotized subject from the inside of one cabinet lined with thick lead (which excludes all electromagnetic energies) to the inside of another such cabinet.

Scientists are searching for explanations which can account for this paranormal communication. Some are working with the hypothesis that there are "natural" causes for extrasensory perception, meaning in this case that there are in the universe certain energies, of a generic character, which we have access to and can use, but of which we have been relatively unaware. It has also been suggested that, in the case of apparent communication from the dead, memory traces of an individual's life remain after he has died and that they can "break through" to us from a collective unconscious. Again, such explanations represent attempts by scientists to avoid the necessity of inferring from the data that "powers" exist which cannot be explained by presently established laws of physics, or that the source of verbal information should be an intelligence apart from human beings as we know them.

Some scientists have put forth the hypothesis that intelligent life on other planets could be invading our unconscious minds, and possibly even controlling us with superior modes of communication. Such a theory would explain apparently paranormal perception. (This hypothesis is so far unverified, and the evidence revealed in the parapsychological investigations would not appear to suggest superior intelligence, but rather finite understanding at our own level.)

A few attribute all apparently paranormal communication to the inner workings of the human psyche, using a combination of one or another component-personality theory with sundry variations of Dr. Carl G. Jung's concept of the collective unconscious. In our culture, which has been so profoundly influenced by the science of depth psychology in recent decades, such hypotheses are more likely to be accepted than are others. But in order to accept any form of this method of analysis, one would have to presuppose a most amazing selection process as "natural" to the medium. In other words, the medium would have to be endowed with an ability—in the middle of a dialogue or a séance—to select bits of information pertinent to the sitter's queries or comments or at least relevant to a particular deceased person out of the quintillions of items presumably contained in the collective unconscious. And this selection would have to be accomplished in a matter of seconds.

If we do talk about accepting conclusions without ironclad proof, the presupposition that a medium has such powers certainly requires as much faith as does the acceptance of the survival hypothesis.

Hence, it is not surprising that some scientists and philosophers infer from the data available that finite human beings live on after death and can be, from time to time, in communication with us. This hypothesis will probably never be "proved"—and, obviously, it cannot be *dis*proved. But it appears to many—and to me—to account for some data more adequately than any other hypothesis yet put forward. At the least by analogy it helps account for the matter of initiation, unity and continuity of communication in a way no other known theory really can do. Scientists and other thinkers continue, however, to search for adequate alternative explanations—and such efforts are entirely "on the side of the angels."

Ψ

There are many who would think that an amateur would be imagining things if he reported he was receiving radio signals from outer space on his homemade ham radio set. They would dismiss him as "obviously" engaging in wishful thinking or exaggeration, or assume that he was probably a little "off." Meanwhile, very few in this scientific era will call into question the data gathered by the highly specialized astrophysicists and astronomers, who—with powerful antennas and sensitive recording instruments—make the same report. On the other hand, if in the light of what is now the public knowledge of such scientific data, a ham radio operator today should say he has intercepted pulsations from outer space, the fair-minded person would probably say, "Well, maybe he has . . ."

Almost since the beginning of recorded history, ordinary men—many quite untutored—have been reporting paranormal experiences. Their phenomenal accounts have been received differently according to the given cultural preconceptions and biases of their times. In our cultural environment such reports tend to be dismissed as nonsense and as possible evidence of mental imbalance by many "liberals," and as probably true, but indubitably the work of the Devil, by many Biblical fundamentalists. It is my conviction, however, that as scientific research in the field of psi phenomena is expanded, intensified, subjected to full critique and more widely publicized, we will pay more and more attention to the isolated spontaneous experiences of common persons and their reports will be received in the realm of the "at least possible." I also believe that, at least as far as the "liberals" are concerned, there will be fewer and fewer dogmatic pejoratives.

It is only recently that scientists have had instruments to measure and record psi manifestations, such as electroencephalographs, computers, tape recorders and highly sensitive cameras. But as the scientific data keep piling up, public credence in the *fact* of such phenomena will inevitably increase and there will be fewer people who—when confronted with reports of paranormal experiences—will react as did the Rev. Dr. Frederick M. Morris, who said with a dogmatism typical of some "liberals" (plus a quaint adherence to the matter/energy dichotomy now abandoned by physicists).

When it comes to unseen and immaterial spirits moving visible, material objects about, one sees immediately the totally illogical aspects of it all and then the incredible absurdity of it. Matter requires the application of physical force to move it about and physical force must also be material. Whatever the force that moves matter, it must be discernible to some physical sense.

Instead, reports of personal, spontaneous experiences will be seen as compatible with experimentation carried on by reputable scientists, none of whom would declare to be incredible that which is. Even one as medieval as St. Thomas Aquinas averred that one cannot deny possibility in the face of actuality. Or, as Dr. Gardner Murphy has said:

It has long been recognized that telepathy cannot reasonably be explained in terms of physics (as we now know it)—for example, in terms of Sir William Crookes's "brain waves"—unless we are to neglect most of the facts of experimental and spontaneous telepathy. What is now known about radiant energy and the electromagnetic waves from living cells throws no light upon actual telepathic transmission, which neither observes the inverse square law nor functions as if there were a physical code by virtue of which thoughts could be transmitted through space in some definite system of dots and dashes or similar physical symbols. It is indeed true that we hope in time to understand the unity of the universe and to find that telepathy is in a very broad sense a form of energy, but if we are to take physics for what it is actually worth, we shall have to recognize that the type of energy involved in telepathy is utterly dissimilar to all the types of physical energy with which we are now acquainted, and of which we make use in radio or other types of long-distance communication.*

Ψ

It seems to be man's nature to resist the new. Seldom has an innovation in any field been received with unqualified enthusiasm, and many innovators have first been dismissed as "not well." Consider, for example, the reactions of specialists in their own or related fields—not to mention the general public—to such men as Copernicus, Galileo, Darwin, Fulton, Edison, Schweitzer, Einstein, Columbus, Wright, Freud. The list could go on and on, for almost any man whose creative capacity is great enough to conceive of a new hypothesis which embraces the available data and makes *more* sense out of it than the commonly accepted one, is likely to be heaped with scorn from his contemporaries. It is not easy to see things new, even if they can be more easily understood that way.

Today the challenge before all of us interested in knowledge of the paranormal is to seek a break-through to an undergirding hypothesis which can embrace, tie together and plausibly account for the wide variety of veridical data from the various psi fields. And certainly innovators are emerging more frequently as the gross amount of scientific experimentation and research continues to increase. Without attempting to be at all comprehensive,† the following are simply

* "An Outline of Survival Evidence," *Journal of American Society for Psychical Research*, vol. 39, p. 32 (January 1945).

† For those desirous of fairly complete coverage of the various types of laboratory experimentation and of carefully reported and investigated spontaneous phenomena, reference is made to the appended bibliography, especially to the scientific journals there listed. The same is true with reference to full treatment of most of the examples summarized in the text.

referred to as samples of recent explorations (with the recognition that by the time these pages are between covers, the author and/or the readers may well have heard of later experimental programs as interesting—or more interesting):

the hypnosis-ESP experiments (previously mentioned), with sender and receiver in Faraday cages, in the U.S.S.R.;

similar experimentation under the direction of Andrija Puharich, M.D. (this time with the receiver in a fully conscious state and with the Faraday cage carrying an electrical charge of twenty thousand volts direct current negative on the outer walls), with scores which could occur by chance four times in a million "tries," in the presence of an investigating committee of the Psychic Research Society, Massachusetts Institute of Technology;

also already discussed, the conditioning of subjects for psychedelic states, without drugs but with combination of EEG measurement of alpha-wave cycle and Pavlovian-conditioned response, at the University of California Langley-Porter Clinic;

experimentation at the Maimonides Hospital (Brooklyn) Dream Research Center with transmission by ESP of material into dream states of subjects during periods when the EEG records a sufficiently low alpha-wave level;

testing, with careful controls, under the auspices of the American Society for Psychical Research, of the correlation of distance with the accuracy of ESP transmission, with the differentials ranging from the room next door to halfway around the world;

under the same auspices, tests with groups of sitters to clarify the relationship of meditation experiences to the effectiveness of ESP transmission;

experiments in several places with the mental projection of pictures directly onto film in Polaroid cameras, with or without lenses, as in the case of the abundantly witnessed demonstrations at the University of Colorado Medical School;

correlation studies in Switzerland as to the relationship of psychedelic states and ESP;

laboratory experiments, under the direction of W. G. Roll, Ph.D., on the relationship of mental concentration to the movement of objects (in the field called telekinesis);

investigations in the correlation of trance, through hypnosis, and ESP ability;

use of hypnosis in place of anesthesia in surgery, with reduction of excessive blood-flow through hypnotic suggestion;

experiments with regard to the effect of telepathic activity on the growth of plants;

analysis of the role of ESP among animals with reference to group functioning, with special attention to the process of evolution, as developed by the Oxford zoologist Sir Alister Hardy in his recently published Gifford Lectures.

Ψ

In this book I have tried to analyze my own experiences, using, basically, the categories offered by others, both scientists and laymen, who are familiar with the field. I have found fault with the theories of some, have felt others could serve as partial explanations, and have felt a few to be quite adequate to explain given phenomena. But now the question must be faced: What does it all add up to? Where does one finally come out?

Any useful application of over-all theories to the large number of individual items experienced requires some consideration of the role of the several operative components—

principally mediums, sitters, visually observable happenings, and messages.

Ψ

Mediums are people. Therefore no two are alike. Truly here there are "diversities of gifts, . . . diversities of operations" (1 Cor. 12:4a, 6a). The seeming clarity of what "comes through" as between mediums—and with the same medium—can vary about as widely as FM stereo does from the old crystal set. Widely differing too are the proportions, in "the mix," of what—whatever the source—seem like kindly pastoral comments, advice and opinions, on the one hand, and what has the character of factual statements on the other. (The presence of some of the former does not mitigate against the possible truths of the latter; in fact, *during* a sitting, generally pastoral remarks "go down" well enough and not only do not break the continuity of apparently factual statements but can seem congruent with them. It is usually afterward that the distinction becomes more evident.) Bearing on the proportion of factuality is the wide range of difference, in sittings, in the directness of answers to questions. The ability to answer without hesitation and with explicitness conveys a conviction that whoever is talking knows what he is talking about—in contrast to vague answers, followed by an immediate change of subject.

When there are "hits" it is difficult to assess, in most instances, what process or processes might be involved: good guesswork, sensitivity to the sitter—his comments and behavior, direct ESP or depth ESP from the sitter, clairvoyance of impersonal information sources, clairaudience from a deceased person. When there are "misses" (and they are certainly not uncommon), the assessment is likewise difficult:

poor guesswork, lack of sensitivity to the sitter, weakness of transmission from "beyond," imprecise communication by the medium.

The few mediums I have had very much to do with have been fine, intelligent and genuine persons. But I gather from the literature that such qualities are not prerequisites to mediumistic gifts (leaving open what their nature may actually be). That is a conclusion surprising to those of us raised in, and conditioned by, a moralistic culture. But it is in line with the recognition, in the Catholic sacramental tradition, that the validity of a sacrament does not depend on the worthiness of the minister thereof.* The contrary notion—that good mediumship is connected with spiritual and moral quality—has been furthered by the connection of mediumistic activity with a religious denomination, the churches which center on "spiritualism" and bear the name Spiritualist. And there has been a widespread assumption in most Christian churches that clergymen are to be good and kind—indeed (illogically enough) better and kinder than the lay members of a given denomination. Many mediums are ordained ministers, though they are more often than not "worker-priests" in that their living does not come from a congregation; in fact, most hold no office in a congregation and many have no connection with one. The standards applied to other ministers tend to be held up for them, too, by many raised in the Church. Other persons with psi ability do not have nominally ecclesiastical connections, however.

A characteristic judgment is that handed down as to Mrs. Ena Twigg's character by the Rev. Dr. Frederick M. Morris. In his widely publicized and widely disseminated sermon, he

* E.g., Art. XXVI of the Anglican Articles of Religion.

says of Mrs. Twigg, a fellow Anglican, "The whole thing begins to be thoroughly ludicrous, as in the case of Bishop Pike's séances, . . . when the questionable Mrs. Twigg comes into the picture." Nor, for him, does "Mrs. Twigg give any evidence of spiritual stature or . . . special endowments of mind or soul." I know Mrs. Twigg and her work quite well as do other bishops, priests and laymen who hold her in high esteem. Dr. Morris has never met her and yet he feels free thus to denigrate her character. This is a good illustration of how far dogmatism on this subject will carry even persons who, like Fred Morris, generally seek to be fair in their assessment of fellow human beings. This vividly reminds me of the pattern of vilification of the character of Martin Luther which was prevalent in the Roman Catholic Church when I was being raised therein. His views were impossible—and threatening—and hence he had to be a bad man. Now, happily, his critique of late medieval teaching is being taken seriously by Roman Catholic scholars and teachers—and in parallel development, they are beginning to picture him as almost an admirable character (some even predict canonization!).

When it comes to socially acceptable behavior patterns, however, some of the most startling phenomena ever scientifically tested have been generated from one who, in his personal life, appears to be a quite unreliable alcoholic, frequently arrested and jailed and quite unreliable and undisciplined, the erstwhile Chicago bellhop, Ted Serios. Yet in the presence of numerous M.D.s and Ph.D.s—including psychiatrists, neurologists and psychologists—he has projected onto Polaroid film, pictures supplied by various of the witnesses but never seen by Ted Serios (they have been sealed in brown envelopes), using cameras (with or without lenses!) belonging to those conducting the investigations.*

But there is at least one quality—one not high in the priority scale of the self-appointed guardians of the morals of others, but actually pretty near to the top on the admiration thermometer of some of us—which would seem to have a bearing on the ability paranormally to produce information (whether from the mind of the sitter or from beyond): *sensitivity* to others and warmhearted, loving *concern.* Both common sense and empirical data† would seem to confirm this connection. This might appear obvious enough to be a cliché; but it is a correlation which has significance in the assessment we will attempt to make as to the here-and-now value of further activity in, and knowledge about, psi interconnections.

Ψ

These very qualities—sensitivity to and concern for others—are obviously not the peculiar possession of professional mediums. The same is true of other facets of personality make-up contributing to mediumistic manifestations. They are all among the natural potential capacities of the psyche. So just as there is no 100 per cent medium, there probably is no zero per cent medium anywhere among the world's human beings. In short, every person is to some extent a medium.

* Many samples of the photographs as well as a thorough presentation and analysis of the evidence—and of Mr. Serios—is provided in Jule Eisenbud, M.D., M.Sc.D., *The Strange Case of Ted Serios* (New York: William Morrow & Co., 1967).

† Preliminary (and as yet unpublished) data from a long-range laboratory study being conducted by the American Society for Psychical Research would seem to provide objective confirmation.

This likelihood would, of course, include the sitter in a séance. True, he seems to be simply "one of the audience" or a concerned inquirer: generally he is not conscious of playing any other part in the drama. As the almost universal experience of dreaming demonstrates, however, every person is capable of receiving into his conscious mind facts and feelings from his unconscious mind and possibly from beyond this apparently "personal" possession. This would mean that, in measure, we can all receive facts from the same sources which may be combining to supply the medium's messages: the collective unconscious, ESP, departed spirits. Therefore, it is unlikely that—in a situation in which the medium is uttering information he hadn't known before—the sitter is simply a cipher in the process. Anyone accepting the enormous weight of evidence supporting ESP would assume the sitter's participation in providing information through that channel. And to the degree the other routes mentioned are open to the medium, they are also open in principle to the sitter. In fact, there can be little doubt that, in various degrees, the sitter participates in the process, wittingly or not, during every sitting; and if such is the case, there is no reason why the medium's conscious mind, via his unconscious, could not be supplied with material from "outside" sources coming by ESP via the sitter's unconscious mind.

Even more obvious is another way in which the sitter can serve as a means of communication. By his responses even to a statement that might be a guess or an obvious assumption on the medium's part, the sitter can "give away" information which a sensitive person can build on (not necessarily by clever deception but as part of the natural reaction to the total intake).

As I became more knowledgeable in this field, I consciously sought to discipline myself in the transmitting of clues, but nevertheless I have been impressed, especially in the replay of tapes, with how much I have given out without realizing it. In spite of an intent to "clam up," two countervailing factors are operative. One is the spontaneous response to the "personal," whatever precisely its source or sources, which is cultivated and encouraged in our culture in everyday relations. The other is the apparent need in the conversational sense to say enough to keep the information coming.

Even the sitter, who on a given occasion acts as "the strong, silent type," will nevertheless contribute to the total picture (usually only in the silence of his own reflections and reactions during the sitting itself) that which *for him* (whatever it may be for the medium or anyone else present) provides the continuity or the context in which the various separate utterances assume a relevant, interconnected pattern. Without this, whatever might be true or informative about one item or another expressed by the medium, there would be no sense of relationship with a living personality.

Suggestive are analogies from the way life is, quite apart from the psi-factor dimension. The amnesiac cannot "locate" himself and his experiences no matter how much others tell him—about present or past—until there comes alive again in him the complex interlocking of impressions which *memory* provides. But we need not go that far afield. Even in ordinary communication with long-standing friends—let alone loved ones—it is never the specific words or actions that matter most but rather the whole cumulative pattern of relationship, restored at each new encounter by memory.

Here there are several implications for the process of interpretation in the psi field.

First, it is the pattern sensed by the receiver in a particular set of psi communications (taken as a whole) which determines the degree to which he is convinced of their reality. We shall have more to say about this later.

Ψ

Second, the receiver's role in a sitting is active enough to take into account the human mind's well-known, though forever surprising, capacity for distorting memories. In the psi field, this means we must allow for a significant possibility of error in the recall and the retelling of information received during a given sitting.

This capacity for distortion is frequently underscored in courses on Evidence at law schools, when the professor conspires with a few students to enact some unannounced episode during class and then asks the other students to write down an account of what happened. To say the least, these accounts invariably display a considerable range of variations. Not only that, but if the members of the class are invited to write out an account two weeks later, the variety in recall (and the disparity between the reports and the facts) is much magnified. This is not just due to the dimming of memory. In addition, something almost precisely opposite is operating: in most cases the students have told various persons about the classroom drama and all too often the narrative has become elaborated in the telling. So when it comes to the second write-up, the student generally records not what he saw (or even what he then thought he saw) but his memory of what he said when he last told the story.

Until I got down to work on this book I thought I had a quite clear recollection both of the details of the external happenings and of the oral content of the few séances which they occasioned. However, when I began to review the notes and the transcripts of tape recordings, I realized to my surprise that I too had come to remember various aspects of the whole complicated experience less in terms of what actually happened (or seemed to happen at the time) and more in terms of how I last told about it.

The natural reaction to this admission would be to use it as fuel for the all too commonly heard wish-fulfillment explanation. But my own experience is actually not supportive of that hypothesis. It is true that in some cases certain events or statements were in my memory shorn of their ambiguity; but it seems that even more frequently I had tended to forget things which would actually strengthen the case for the recognition, in instance after instance, that something paranormal was involved. In the case of the séances, reading straight through a transcript often brought to light what seemed to be important connections between successive statements which, when remembered in isolation, had seemed to be meaningless, trivial or platitudinous.

From such experiences came further support for a legal principle which I had not thought about for a long time: the *res gestae* exception to the hearsay rule. Contrary to the usual exclusion as evidence of the quotation of statements purportedly made by others than the witness on the stand, such statements may be tesified to if they were uttered very soon after and in the context of a dramatic event. Because of the rapid distortion of impressions in human memory, the exception does *not* apply if any considerable amount of time has elapsed after the happening to which the statement applies. This principle helps emphasize the importance of taking notes and making tape recordings of events in the psi field.

Third, the rather important role played by the sitter could well explain why certain members of the family seem to experience psi phenomena, whereas others do not—even when a deceased family member is the one seemingly trying to communicate. It is just possible that because of the openness (or open*ing*—by unusual external events) of some persons to participate in the process, in contrast to the reticence of others, communication is facilitated (granted the survival hypothesis) between the person on the other side and certain living members of his family.

Fourth, the sizable part the sitter or involved observer apparently plays in the whole picture would suggest that it might be worth while to consider him in connection with the poltergeist aspect of this case. But this I had not done, until two fortunate meetings—one with a man, and one with a book.

Ψ

Late in my analysis of my experiences with psi phenomena, I was fortunate enough to have the pleasure of meeting Dr. Ian Stevenson, Professor of Psychiatry and Neurology at the University of Virginia School of Medicine, in Santa Barbara in connection with a project in which we were mutually involved. In the course of the time we were together, I had an opportunity not only to learn a great deal about Dr. Stevenson's own special studies with regard to life after death (the careful investigation in various parts of the world by a team, operating under a grant, of objective evidence related to instances in which children purport to recall their previous existences, thus yielding scientific data which apparently point to reincarnation*), but also to consult with him regarding analysis of my own experiences. He made one of the most helpful (and to me also most surprising) remarks regarding an approach to the external, visible events of those

* See Dr. Stevenson's *Twenty Cases Suggestive of Reincarnation* (American Society for Psychical Research. Richmond: William Byrd Press, Inc., 1966).

ten days in Cambridge which I had been offered up to that point. He said, "Jim, it's just possible, you know, that you yourself were the source of the poltergeist phenomena."

I was reminded of the remark of a long-time friend and fellow bishop, Brooke Mosley, who, having heard my Cambridge experiences shared in confidence, asked, with matching confidence and an admixture of genuine concern, "Jim, did you see a doctor?" My response to Bishop Mosley's question was rather defensive: "What you're asking is, did I see a psychiatrist? Well, the answer is 'Yes'; as a matter of fact I did." I added that had there not been two witnesses for the various phenomena, I would have gone to see one right there in England. I then explained that before going to Cambridge, I had had over two years of Jungian analysis—both for better self-understanding and for the improvement of my top-priority role as *pastor pastorum*, the counseling of clergy and clergy wives—and that no psychoses or patterns of neurosis had come to light. Moreover, I revealed that almost immediately upon my return to San Francisco from Cambridge, I had arranged to see the psychiatrist with whom I had spent so much time previously, this time to consult him about these experiences—even though the presence of the witnesses made hallucination or self-delusion unlikely hypotheses. I reported, too, that Dr. John Perry was quite open to this whole field of phenomena;* and that in any case he had not suggested that what I had to tell him made appropriate even a tentative diagnosis of some kind of mental quirk either at the time of the happenings or at the time we were talking in his study.

I thought the answer was pretty conclusive; and, whether the then Bishop of Delaware agreed or not, he did not pursue

* Not uncharacteristic for a Jungian: see Dr. Jung's works and Dr. Perry's work cited in the bibliography.

the point. Nevertheless, while granting Bishop Mosley's good intentions, I must confess that I was somewhat "put off" by his question.

Now as Ian Stevenson turned the focus on me in connection with the Cambridge experiences, I thought back on my episcopal brother's question a year and a half before and realized that, taken literally, the question indeed might have something to it. My Virginia friend's query, I realized, was not based on the assumption that I must have been "ill" and have imagined such things, for he obviously took the external happenings very seriously. His was rather the question of a scientist searching for an adequate explanation for empirical—and apparently paranormal—data. This time my response was quite different.

"How do you mean?" I asked. "I'm sure I was not hallucinating, for there were witnesses. Moreover, I was handling my grief very well."

"That suggests all the more the possibility that the energies causing the disturbances were coming out of you—unwittingly, of course," Dr. Stevenson observed. Then he went on to report the various investigations into poltergeist phenomena with which he was familiar, indicating that it appeared that living persons (most frequently young girls entering puberty) were generally the source of the energies by which objects were moved. He suggested it was possible that because I was handling my grief relatively well at the conscious level, there may well have been suppressed or repressed emotions which might somehow have found expression in the poltergeist phenomena.

Ψ

Ian Stevenson's observations opened up a whole new possibility for me. None of the theories I had come across, or had even thought of, had been adequate to embrace the objective, physical phenomena which had occurred and which were responsible for my initial visit to a medium—except the survival hypothesis.

It was ironical, but it appeared now that Bishop Mosley had asked a good question. I was unable to receive the question except in the context of reality/delusion. But I had continued to search for an alternate explanation for the Cambridge phenomena; now it seemed possible I was on the track of at least one. And all the more so because of what seemed to be my vivid memory of a physical drain and dehydration noted by all three of us in Cambridge at the time of the many poltergeist phenomena—a possible sign that energy was being drawn out of us.

Very shortly after the weekend sessions with Ian Stevenson I had the pleasure, while down at U.C.L.A. for a public lecture, of meeting with Mrs. Marjorie Kern, secretary for the Southern California branch of the American Society for Psychical Research. When I told her of Dr. Stevenson's contribution to the analysis of my experiences, she offered to lend me from her extensive library a work which proved to be of inestimable help: *Can We Explain the Poltergeist?*, by A. R. G. Owen, Cambridge scientist (New York: Garrett Publications, 1964). Dr. Owen's book reports and analyzes at length the various types of external phenomena, the reality of which has been carefully established, but for which no normal explanation can be found. His conclusion is that it would appear that generally the poltergeist "focus" is a living person who is the source of a force or forces which are set in operation due to some kind of emotional upset or psychological or physical disorder.

Perhaps the analogy which would be best understood by most of us, in trying to grasp the process at work here, is the now well-established relationship between emotional or psychological upsets or disorders and physical illness. The person is no less sick because of the psychological origin of the sickness; but if he is to be understood (and hence cured, if this be possible), the cause must be properly classified. So here it would appear that the movement of external objects can be caused by an internal disordering—either psychological, physical or emotional—of energies which, not being dealt with directly, are mysteriously set loose "at random," so to speak. The disturbances can be stopped, then, by uncovering and dealing with the disorder in the person who is the poltergeist focus.

In my own case, it is possible that I was suppressing much of the grief connected with my son's death, for I was under a number of other pressures at the same time which were also placing heavy emotional demands upon me—not the least of which were the issue with some of my fellow bishops regarding heresy and my strong feelings about the need of maximum help in the Rhodesian situation, fired up by recent memories of my arrest, incarceration and expulsion. It may well be that on the conscious level I could deal only with the pressures most urgent in terms of timing and that, even though after I returned to Cambridge my mind naturally and frequently turned to Jim with whom I had shared so much there, the focus of my attention was on the several projects I had begun but not completed before the end of my sabbatical. If that was the case, I may have felt "forced" by the poltergeist phenomena to turn my attention back to Jim.

Now if I was indeed suppressing my grief reactions (which is certainly possible), it is likely that whatever energies might have been released at an unconscious level would have seemed to me at a conscious level to be related to Jim. This was in fact what happened: I grew increasingly to feel that Jim was somehow the source or cause of it all, and the only thing I could think of to do—if that were the case—was to try to seek communication with him to find out why.

Following this line of thought, then, my first visit to Ena Twigg could have represented a form of attention to my grief feelings, thus dealing more directly with those energies which had been diverted into poltergeist phenomena. This would explain, then, why the phenomena stopped after the appointment was made.

Ψ

There are several ways, however, in which this theory falls short in adequately accounting for the poltergeist events which I experienced. First of all, in classical cases it is very rare that the poltergeist focus is a person over forty. Usually the age range is from fourteen to thirty-five. Secondly, the most common type of phenomena is that of flying or moving objects observed by the persons present. In Cambridge only once did the three of us observe something in motion. Third, in nearly all classical poltergeist cases, the person who is the focus is present in the house when the phenomena occur—if not in the very same room. In Cambridge, objects were generally found moved after we had been *away* from the apartment—often miles away. Fourth, a very common manifestation in most recorded cases is noise of different kinds—often rappings or knockings. To my knowledge there were no noises out of the ordinary in the Cambridge flat.* And, finally,

* I am frankly perplexed as to where Dr. Morris got the impression (as reflected at least three times in his homiletical analysis of my experiences) that I thought I heard "table-tapping." Not even the most careless and garbled newspaper reports included references to any form of noise. This gratuitous addition to the data was hardly calculated to decrease its "sensational" character!

I have yet to read any account of poltergeist phenomena which includes such a large variety of events. Generally they seem to be repetitive, whereas in my case almost half of the varieties of poltergeist phenomena mentioned and analyzed by Dr. Owen apparently occurred: trance states, teleportation, movement, heating, fire-raising. Those which did not occur were: controlled ballistics, coded raps or other sounds, direct speech and writing.

So it would appear that if I was the poltergeist focus, I have a more imaginative unconscious than most—and a more powerful one, able to work at great distances. In fact, it would appear that from Santa Barbara, on the eve of August 1, 1966, I was able to be the source of energies which moved pins in the home of David Barr in San Francisco—at a distance of nearly four hundred miles. No small energy source, that. (Modesty forbids my claiming to be such a "powerhouse"!)

Nevertheless, it is difficult to dismiss any of the four explanations of the poltergeist offered by A. R. G. Owen as irrelevant in my own case. To the contrary, it would appear at least possible that all four were at work: that additional, and as yet unknown, forces in the universe which act in a regular fashion and do not contradict other laws of nature were somehow brought into action; that I, as the poltergeist focus (or some component of my personality) was the source of the energy; that Jim, as a disembodied entity, was using the persons present as "mediums" in order to manifest his activity; or that grief or anxiety or some other suppressed emotion evoked an otherwise submerged mediumistic capacity in me. It is also possible that the "disorder" explanation (with regard especially to bodily malfunctioning) could be applied as well to Mrs. Bergrud, who was not in good physical health.

In any of these cases—or in all—however, the phenomena

remain basically a mystery; for even these theories do not explain *how* the phenomena happen: they only hypothesize as to the source of the energy. And what *kind* of energy we cannot even imagine.

Poltergeist phenomena therefore remain the most difficult of my experiences to deal with when it comes to making inferences. The most I can say is that it is equally plausible to me—since neither hypothesis can be adequately explained or defined—that either my son was the source of the various phenomena or that the source was I myself (or either or both of my companions and I). There seemed to be a connection between the events in Cambridge and the messages which came through the various mediums, but of course I could have been the source of that information myself, the medium receiving it by ESP. The timing of the external phenomena was such that it almost suggested an outside source of initiation—but perhaps I underrate the creative power of my unconscious imagination.

If I was in fact the source of the poltergeist energy, then it is almost more interesting that I should have stumbled upon psychic communication—to which there is undoubtedly a profound reality under whatever hypothetical explanation—by such an unconscious route. At the least, this would seem to point to the inner-connectedness of all facets of our experiences, which is the most important of all conclusions to be drawn from such experiences anyway.

Ψ

The most veridical quality of the messages in my experience—and probably in the experiences of most people who have sat with mediums—has not been the specific content of given statements (though that has certainly not been unimportant), but rather the over-all consistency and unity of that which has come through. There are well-verified reports of series of messages which by their interlocked content—their congruence—seem almost to require an outside source of initiation and coordination.* However, in most cases the sitter makes his leap of faith regarding the source of the messages because of a body of material which *coheres* and which gives a distinct impression of personality consistent with the one known before death.

In the first two sessions with Mrs. Twigg, for example, the impression I received was that Jim (if indeed we can attribute it simply to him) deeply regretted that he took his own life. He was confused and suffering, and concerned about whether we would judge him for what he had done. It seemed that he felt his death to be an accident—"everything snapped." During the next year he seemed to move on to a new level where he felt more or less neutral about what the future might hold for him. He was particularly anxious to convince me (and, through me, the rest of the family) that he lives on, and he began to be able to show concern for others—both on the other side and on this. More and more he appeared to be actively concerned about my affairs and to want to be involved in them. As to his own death, he apparently began to be able to view it more philosophically: "Maybe it was meant to be," he purportedly said once, spelling out on that and other occasions what the resulting values were.

Finally, when almost two years had passed from the time of his death, he apparently had found a specific role on the other side ("I have been given the job of helping those who come over after having committed suicide—it's because I

* I am thinking especially of the numerous cross-correspondence cases. See, for example, Dr. Gardner Murphy's full accounts in *Challenge of Psychical Research* (New York: Harper & Bros., 1961), ch. 7.

understand"), and the need to be in communication with me seemed reduced. There were still indications of his interest in my work and thought, but the lessening of communication seemed to support the word that he had "moved on." He also seemed to be able to recall more of the details of the events which immediately surrounded his death, being quite specific in response to questions about the suicide. And finally, for the first time he was able to say he was genuinely happy—that he had found his role there, was learning a lot, and had worked through many of his problems.

Though it is possible that at each point the mediums could have been "guessing" where Jim would be in his development (since they knew when he died), it does seem remarkable that the concerns and comments should fit together so neatly, having come through three different mediums, the various sessions with them falling in random order. It is also possible that by sensitivity to my expectations, the mediums could have said what I wanted to hear. However, at each point I would have hoped that Jim might have progressed more rapidly than he appeared to have. But no matter whether the information about Jim's purported progress came out of the medium, out of me, or through the medium from the other side, I can only report that in *fact* the apparent progress, and continuity between reports, is one of the factors which gives the sitter the impression he is dealing with a living, growing personality.

As has been pointed out several times, this is a purely intuitive matter; but then, so is the whole of human relationships. After all, while Jim was alive, I knew him only in part: I knew him only during the direct encounters and periods of time we spent in each other's presence—including his words, his expressions and his responses to situations—but even then I saw only that part of Jim which he chose—or was able—

to reveal to me; I knew him from comments and observations by others who knew him, inside the family and out; I knew Jim through his own descriptions of himself, which I could only accept as his view of what was his internal life. The understanding of his personality I had to put together for myself, building on the assorted data I received. Each new impression helped make my understanding correspond more directly to the reality of who Jim was, but the Jim I say I knew is really the image I myself carried in my memory of my intuitive understanding of him. Thus, the statement that the data which came through the mediums seemed consistent with the Jim I knew is only a reflection of the same intuitive response.

This observation about the intuitive nature of the dynamics of human relationships can be confirmed by each reader if he will only reflect briefly on the instances in which he has had difficulty "believing" or "understanding" a friend or loved one because the friend's actions or words did not conform to his expectations. Each of us provides the continuity for our relationships by means of our memories of and about the people involved; the continuing revelation of new facets of personality corrects our image of the old to bring it more in line with reality, but it does not make the image any less subjective. That virtually the same process which operates in ordinary human relationships also functions in séances has contributed to the over-all meaning which I have, in the end, derived from my various experiences.

Ψ

It seems to me that the vast amount of data classified as psychic phenomena and the broader category of evidence pointing to the psi factor in the human personality refer us mentally *beyond these categories themselves*. Raised anew are two basic questions: What is the nature of the human person? and, What is the nature of the universe? In my striving in recent years toward a truer and more relevant theology for our times, I have been moving in a discernible direction—to put it briefly, toward the universality of truth and grace and toward the unity of reality.* My experiences with psi phenomena, as well as the extensive study that they have stimulated, have led me to be even more open to and to affirm tentatively an understanding of man and his universe that seems more adequate than the conventional Christian one or that of its near relative, Western secularism.

First of all, it would appear that we have perhaps been mistaken, in our culture, to conceive of persons as individuals. Sociologists, psychologists and anthropologists have long pointed to the tremendous influence that society has on the formation of an individual, and the school of psychological determinism has held that no man is in fact a free agent. Yet the predominant image has been one of a shape and reality to each human personality that is entirely and uniquely one's own, even though molded by external forces.

Perhaps what is really needed is a new way of looking at the human personality—a way in which we can at one and the same time take account of both the highly individuated, decision-making, conscious personal focus *and* the more diffuse but person-connected constellation of fluid factors from the individual's unconscious mind and from the collective unconscious. I grope for words to express such a view of personal reality, for our Western thought forms do not lend themselves readily to the expression of an outlook of

* For example, cf. *What Is This Treasure*, extended note on pp. 45–47 (written before the experiences described in this book), and *If This Be Heresy*, pp. 193–95 (written afterward).

this type. But if we are to encompass in our understanding such data as we have been dealing with in this book, then it would seem we must push ourselves to new images.

It is in the nature of the human personality that only a small portion of reality can be held "in focus"—that is, within our conscious attention—at any given time. We can concentrate on only a very limited portion of reality—whether past, present or projected future—during any given time span. We have "sequential" thought patterns, which in languages can be broken down into segments—paragraphs, sentences, words and even syllables. Selective perception operates during all waking moments and we "take in" by our five senses only that which is relevant to our concern at the time.

This of necessity means, on the one hand, that the largest portion of the reality to which we are exposed in each waking moment goes *unnoticed* at the conscious level (though not necessarily *unperceived*) and, on the other hand, that nearly all of what we have experienced in the past is temporarily "forgotten" as we confront the new. General impressions include more than those aspects of our experience which we have consciously taken in; if pressed, we can often hold the "general" in our conscious attention long enough to perceive and enumerate the "particulars." In much the same way, the past can be recalled—and again held in conscious focus—if it is stimulated and evoked by the process of association or by a current experience.

Most of what comprises the human personality—what makes us "who we are"—is at any given moment relatively inaccessible at the conscious, sensory level. It would appear that our five senses function in a manner somewhat like tape recorders and audio-video equipment. That is to say, the five senses seem to be devices through which impressions are received and recorded. One can be consciously aware of *some* of those impressions as they are received, but *all* are apparently recorded. Many can be recalled and "experienced" as memories.

Ψ

It has long been assumed that an individual's memories are "his own" and thus accessible only to him. Scientists have even suggested that the individual's memories are "recorded" in his own brain—that each "wrinkle" in the cortex is the *locus* of a single recorded experience or a series of experiences. This assumption has led to the recent speculation as to whether the transplant of a dead person's brain into a living person would not, in essence, be a transplant of the person.

However, making as much sense—or even more—is a quite different hypothesis: namely, that personhood really resides in the unconscious mind; that the conscious, sensory level of existence is a series (sometimes more like a scattering) of manifestations—momentary, or of relatively short duration—of an abiding personality at the unconscious, extrasensory level; and that at the unconscious level all persons participate in, contribute to and share in one vast reservoir of reality which is common to all. In other words, each of us receives sensory impressions and thinks conscious thoughts that are passed into the collective unconscious as an individuated addition to the whole. We have access to those contributions more readily if they are "our own," but each of us participates in the life of every other person at the unconscious level and can receive impressions from and through them by extrasensory processes, which provide additions to the sensory impressions we are already aware of in varying degrees.

Perhaps the most common experience of the latter is in the dream state. When we fall asleep, our conscious, sensory-level activity is reduced to an absolute minimum—an apparent necessity for our refreshment and the restoration of energies—yet our unconscious activity goes on, and occasionally some of it makes a vivid "impression" on us, just as our conscious activity is reawakening us. This impression can then be recalled, just as other experiences entirely in the waking state can be recalled.

It should be noted, however, that those who do recall dreams find that a dream "produces" the same kind of dramatic interaction of personalities and of environmental facets as events which occur at the conscious level. The difference is that in a dream state the full drama is produced unconsciously. For such remarkable plays, where are the producer, the scenario writer, the designer of sets, the wardrobe mistress, the director? Have those who have categorized psychic phenomena and even ESP as incredible nonsense ever pondered *that* mystery? How does the dream get put together into a dynamic production when the dreamer, unconscious, is "out of it"?

Sounds, colors, odors, tastes and tactile sensations can be as vivid as waking reality—the individual, in his recall of the dream, is usually as "involved" in the drama as he would have been in a waking state, even in regard to experiencing the same emotions. The only difference is that he is not consciously aware of his role until after the event—that is, when he wakes up.

Instead of perceiving the dream state as a "private production" of the individual that principally reveals his own internal order or disorder (as many in the various fields of depth psychology have tended to view it), it is more likely that each individual has free access to a *larger* scope of reality while asleep than he has in his ordinary, conscious, waking state; yet his participation at that unconscious level is no less "real" than his sensory-level, conscious activity.

Ψ

It would appear that sleep numbs sensory perception and conscious controls sufficiently to give the unconscious freer play. The same can result from hypnosis, trance states, hallucinogenic drugs and meditation processes.

Perhaps a helpful analogy would be to conceive of the collective unconscious, i.e., the whole of reality, as a giant computer, constructed and programed in such a way as to allow any personality to feed material (information) into it according to his own filing system (his own language, thought forms, images, etc.) and to receive out whatever information he wishes. The ability to receive information from the computer is limited by the degree to which the individuated (or conscious) person insists that the information conform to his own filing system. He receives "new" ideas, that is, ideas not directly related to or implied in information he himself fed in, only to the extent that he is open to receiving "raw data" to be classified later. Any person would, of course, have considerably more ready access to the material he himself put in the computer, since he would know his own filing system and would know what to expect to find there.

It is possible, however, for a person to open himself to data which can come to him not only from the conscious, sensory level, but also from the unconscious, extrasensory level, which does not fit his own—or even his culture's—preconceived filing system, images and concepts. Such a person is generally deemed by his society to be creative, eccentric, free, strange, prophetic, psychotic, non-conformist (used pejoratively or as a compliment); a seer, an escapist, a mystic, a dreamer or a genius—or he might be called a medium. I am convinced that the processes of sensitivity (as, for example, the types encouraged by sensitivity training), mystical experience, spiritual healing, hypnosis, extrasensory perception and psychic communication are all, at the deeper level, of the same nature. We need more experience and/or more consciousness of what we already experience. We need more understanding of these already operative processes, so that this whole dimension of communication and energizing can be more effectively used in our lives.

It would seem that the goal is to become more and more open to reality so we might more fully participate in it and contribute positively to its becoming. We should be open to that part of our personal history which has been fed into the grand computer as well as to others around us at both the conscious, sensory level and at the unconscious, extrasensory level, to have freer traffic between our conscious minds (via our unconscious minds) to the collective unconscious. And finally, through all these routes, we should be able to experience more and more fully a continuity between our ego-centers and the great Ego, the One, the All.

The result of all such growth should be increased harmony between the conscious and the unconscious at both the individual and social levels, and thus increased freedom, serenity and love—to magnify our ability to respond sensitively to all within and around us.

It is in this latter regard that psychedelic drugs seem to fall far short. Though for some they evidently bring a sense of unity and harmony for the duration of the effects of the hallucinogenic, the apparent result for most is not a unity of the unconscious and the conscious, but rather a greater dichotomy between them. Indeed, in some cases the dichotomy can express itself in a psychotic break. Moreover, those who have been consistently on hallucinogenics often feel themselves to be alienated from other persons at the conscious (social) level, even though at one with them in the depth of the collective unconscious. Far more beneficial would be a non-conformist subculture which, by the development of internal openness and sensitivity, would enable its participants to experience both personal and social unity and harmony.

Thus, I hope more and more people will leave themselves open to such experiences as I have described in this book. I feel that they, together with a fast-accumulating amount of other kinds of data, point to the possibility that most of us are operating like ordinary record players, whereas in reality we all have not only hi-fi but also stereo built into us. Thus, we are playing monaural records when we should be using nothing but stereo. Further psychic research may well improve sensitivity and human communications and develop human potential more fully *here and now*. In any case, it is certain that to close one's mind even to the evident data is to preclude new insight into the nature of our own psyches.

Suppose Rip Van Winkle had awakened in the electronic age. Suppose he had been instructed to ask a computer a question, had fed in the question, received the answer, and then been asked, "How do you think you got that information?" Surely his answer would have been something like, "A man in there must have looked it up quickly." Nothing in his previous experience would have enabled him to conceive of what are actually the inner workings of such an electronic device.

Ψ

In much the same way, I cannot really imagine what processes are at work when a medium goes into a trance and material comes through which is apparently directly related to, and associated with, my son Jim in such a way as to have unity of personality. I have no other words to use than those of my conscious experiences and expression. Thus, I say the communication seems personal and appears to be Jim in the same general sense that I "knew" him before he died. It is not unrealistic to say, "The sun rose at six this morning," though what is involved is a much more complex process. Similarly, it is not unrealistic (in fact, it is considerably less unrealistic) to say, "Jim said . . ." Yet, I have nowhere thus far in these pages used such a form of affirmation. Could I have? Can I now?

Until we have more understanding and better concepts and words to use to talk about the experience (and, for that matter, about the daily interpersonal relationships with which we are more accustomed), and in the light of all that has been said here, in response to the oft-asked questions—the ones the reader also no doubt has in mind—"Do you believe in ongoing personal life?" and "Do you believe you have been in touch with your son?" (since asked is not "Do you *know* . . . ," but "Do you *believe* . . ."), my answer is *Yes, I do.*

AFTERWORDS*

After finishing the final chapter in Israel, passing through London I had an opportunity to sit once more with Mrs. Ena Twigg. A portion of the transcript of the tape-recorded séance, at which there were an additional three witnesses, seems more than appropriate for the closing of the record and analysis which have been the aim of this book.

At a session early in May with the Rev. Mr. Daisley, Jim (I can so speak in the light of the qualifications and affirmations made in the preceding pages) said he was "now studying philosophy." This was the first time since his death that he had used the word "philosophy." But he used it again at the session a month later with Mrs. Twigg in London, and he expanded on the theme. My son, through Mrs. Twigg in trance:

I'm going to do my best to use this opportunity to tell you

* NOTE TO REVIEWERS (and others if they wish to read it): As one who has written quite a few book reviews in various publications, I know how tempting it would be, especially in a case like this in which the book is of some length and considerable complexity, to turn right to this page and summarize, giving the impression that this last short section represents the gist of the whole matter.

Such an approach would be understandable but, in the case of this book, quite wrong and misleading. I am hoping that material from these last pages will not be quoted except in close connection with the relevant portions of all that precedes. The words here reproduced—remarkable as they seem in relationship to the whole—can in no wise alone carry the weight of what seems the soundest interpretation of this whole matter. They are nevertheless included because I felt that they would be quite meaningful to those who, with a reasonable degree of attention, had read thus far from the beginning—as indeed they were meaningful to me, having experienced all that is recorded in this book.

the pattern as I see it . . . I'm so excited at the fact you are going on with what we have found together. Oh, this is the treasure. This is the treasure. We want to give you the next piece of the pattern . . . I want to tell you that we are conveying to you a tremendous amount of guidance and help, in order that you would not become involved in the less necessary things—not the unnecessary things—the less necessary things . . . You know I came over here in a state of mental confusion and great—not antagonism toward the world, but in a state of not understanding and being almost afraid to trust many people. You knew that. And I had to come to terms with the situation. And when I came over here they said, "Now, come along. Academic qualifications won't help you here. Let's get down to the basics," you see; and we tried to find out what are the things that really matter—to have compassion, and understanding and to be kind—yes, they are wonderful things, but not as things. You have to put them into operation. You have to relearn how to think, how to really understand and be able to put yourself in the other guy's place to see how you would work out in the same circumstances. And gradually I began to get a sense of pattern, you know. I began to feel that this was one way of release. This was religion, without somebody forcing God and Jesus down my throat. And I find that by working this way I could find a philosophy that religion hadn't been able to give me . . . Dad. You see, I found when I came over here, I thought, if they all come to me, all the blessed saints, all come trooping in I'll have none of it—I'll have none of it. I couldn't accept it on those terms. And I didn't think that they would want me to, because they knew me, didn't they? Those invisible people knew me. So they cater for the individual need and lead you so gently, so kindly. They show you things that are essential and they put the things that are not essential on one side.

So I gradually began to get a sense of belonging again. And one great thing that was a stimulus and great help was to know that I have got this one foot on earth and I could reach you. Do you see? And I thought, whatever this lifeline is—you know, Dad, the cord that joins the mother to the child, don't you? . . . Well, it's . . . it's . . . it's an analogy, something like that you see. It's like having a lifeline to the earth because you have got love for those who are still there, and want to understand how you are—do you see? And that's what I wanted to say to the family: I am all right, don't worry. Do you see? But what's more, I wanted to tell you my story—what I am doing . . . [In answer to the question, "Have you heard anything over there about Jesus, or a Jesus?"] *I told you before. I am telling you again. You know I told you. Oh, it is difficult. I'm afraid I might hurt you. I might hurt you. This is what I was telling you: people must have an example, you know. People must have an example. And I have questioned my teachers, and they have said, Jim, you are not in a position to understand—*YET*! You are not in a position to understand yet. I haven't met him. They talk about him—a mystic, a seer, yes, a seer. Oh, but, Dad, they don't talk about him as a savior. As an example, you see? . . . You see, I want to tell you, I would like to tell you, Jesus is triumphant, you know? But it's not like that. I don't understand it yet. I don't understand it yet. I may, sometime I may, but right now I have got as much to comprehend as I can. You don't want me to tell you what I don't know . . . not a savior, that's the important thing—an example . . .*

But what I want to tell you is just to learn that everybody's not going to like us. You know, I will tell you something . . . As soon as you start to shine a light and give peo-

ple truth, the tremendous forces of darkness gather up. They say "put out the light, put out the light." This is what they have done with John [Kennedy]. *This is what they have done with Bobby* [Kennedy]. *This is what they have done with* [Medgar] *Evers, and this is what they have done with Martin Luther King—and that is put out the light . . . But all they have done is put out the flicker. Oh, yes, they don't know what happens over here. They don't know what happens over here. It burns even brighter. Their cause will not wither. It will gain strength. People are seeking to free themselves, and the best way to understand this is to become involved . . . in trying to help people to free themselves where they have not learned how to free themselves already . . . Do it by literature, do it by talking, do it by an example. I was not much of an example . . . It's a damn fine thing when you have got to die before you know what's true, isn't it? . . . Well, there is no need, is there? . . . It's a wonderful world; it's full of—just full of opportunity . . . I want to tell you this.* [To a college-age witness:] *Learn all you can about this, because you don't know at what juncture in your life you can put it to some use and find a great sense of purpose in so doing. It is the greatest thing that God ever made.*

Don't you ever believe that God can be personalized. He is the Central Force and you all give your quota toward it. Do you agree with me, Dad? . . . I want you to know it's exciting, it's exciting. Do you know how exciting it is to come back? To be dead—but we are not the dead ones, you are the dead ones, you are the dead ones, because you are only firing on two cylinders. I want so much to tell you about a world where everybody is out to create a greater sense of love and harmony. A world in which music and color and poetry are all interwoven, making a majestic pattern—and to be kind of sure, as we hunger so we can absorb some of this quality and harmony. And then, in gratitude, we want to repay. We want to give back to the Central Force some of that love that has been developed in us, that we didn't know we had the capacity to contain . . . I hope one day that I shall understand to the point where I don't have to clutch at my own identity so much . . . You see, we have to be selfless. This creates freedom. It's a paradox . . . Yes, and also by not possessing, one possesses; by loving, one gets a return of love. You see, so many things seem to be in a paradoxical way. I am learning. I am learning. I'm trying very hard . . . And this is the process of evolution. This is man cleansing himself, gradually and continuously, and he evolves and becomes more enlightened. He throws away his props and his shackles, and he works to what is essential. This is what I've discovered.

. . . grant them continued growth in thy love and service . . .

. . . grant that, increasing in knowledge and love of thee, they may go from strength to strength, in the life of perfect service, in thy heavenly kingdom . . .

. . . having opened to him the gates of larger life . . . receive him into thy joyful service; that he may win, with thee and thy servants everywhere, the eternal victory . . .

THE BOOK OF COMMON PRAYER

SELECTED BIBLIOGRAPHY

This listing is intended to provide a variety of levels, ranging from the technical to the popular. In order to have a balanced view of the psi field one really should read representative books from all the various categories.

Included in those listed under POPULAR WORKS are descriptions of spontaneous cases which if taken alone would not carry much weight. Their significance depends on their consistency with data gathered in carefully controlled experimentation or with reliably observed phenomena.

Learned journals and other publications in the psi field are listed in the directory of organizations, which follows this bibliography.

PSYCHICAL RESEARCH–SUMMARIES AND ANALYSES

Beard, Paul, *Survival of Death: For and Against*, with foreword by Leslie Weatherhead. London: Hodder and Stoughton, 1966.

Broad, C. D., D.Litt. (Cantab.), F.B.A., Fellow of Trinity College, Cambridge, *Lectures on Psychical Research*, The Perrott Lectures, Cambridge University. New York: The Humanities Press, 1962.

Crookall, Robert, D.Sc., Ph.D., former Principal Geologist, H.M. Geological Survey, London, *The Supreme Adventure: Analyses of Psychic Communications*. London: James Clarke & Co., 1961.

Ducasse, C. J., Ph.D., Professor Emeritus of Philosophy, Brown University, *The Belief in a Life After Death*. Springfield, Ill.: Charles C. Thomas, 1960.

Eddy, Sherwood, *You Will Survive After Death*. Evanston: Clark Publishing, 1950.

Fodor, Nandor, Ph.D., LL.D., *Encyclopaedia of Psychic Science*. New Hyde Park: University Books, 1966.

Hansel, C. E. M., Professor of Psychology, University of Wales, *ESP—A Scientific Evolution*. New York: Scribners, 1966.

Hardy, Sir Alister, M.A. (Oxon.), D.Sc., Professor Emeritus of Zoology, Oxford, and President of the Society for Psychical Research, *The Divine Flame*. London: Collins, 1966.

Hart, Hornell, Ph.D., former Professor of Sociology, Duke University, *The Enigma of Survival*. Springfield: Charles C. Thomas, 1959.

Heywood, Rosalind, *The Sixth Sense*. London: Pan Books, 1959.

Johnson, Raynor C., M.A. (Oxon.), D.Sc., Master of Queen's College, University of Melbourne, *Nurslings of Immortality*. New York: Harper & Brothers, 1957.

——, *Psychical Research*. London: The English Universities Press, 1955.

Laubscher, B. J. F., M.D., *Where Mystery Dwells*. London: Bailey Bros. & Swinfen, 1963.

Murphy, Gardner, Ph.D., Director of Research, Menninger Foundation, and President of American Society of Psychical Research, *Challenge of Psychical Research: A Primer of Parapsychology*. New York: Harper & Brothers, 1961.

——, *Three Papers on the Survival Problem:* "An Outline of Survival Evidence," "Difficulties Confronting the Survival Hypothesis," and "Field Theory and Survival," reprinted from *J. Am. Soc. Psych. Res.*, Jan., July, Oct., 1945. New York: American Society for Psychical Research, 1945.

Myers, F. W. H., *Human Personality and Its Survival of Bodily Death*, ed. by Susy Smith with a foreword by Aldous Huxley. New Hyde Park, N.Y.: University Books, 1961.

One Hundred Cases for Survival After Death, ed. by A. T. Baird. New York: Bernard Ackerman, Inc., 1944.

Osis, Karlis, *Deathbed Observations by Physicians and Nurses*, Parapsychological Monographs #3 (1961). Available at the Parapsychology Foundation, Inc., 29 West 57 Street, New York, N.Y.

Rosher, Grace, *Beyond the Horizon*. London: James Clarke & Co., 1961.

Salter, W. H., *Zoar: The Evidence of Psychical Research Concerning Survival*. London: Sidgwick & Jackson, 1961.

Tyrrell, G. N. M., *Science and Psychical Phenomena and Apparitions*. New Hyde Park: University Books, 1961.

William James on Psychical Research, ed. by Gardner Murphy, Ph.D., and Robert Ballou (an anthology of James' writings on the subject). New York: The Viking Press, 1960.

EXTRASENSORY PERCEPTION

Ehrenwald, Jan, M.D. *Telepathy and Medical Psychology.* New York: W. W. Norton, 1948.

Extrasensory Perception, Ciba Foundation Symposium. Boston: Little, Brown & Co., 1956.

Gudas, Fabian, *Extrasensory Perception.* New York: Scribner's, 1961.

Hardy, Sir Alister, M.A. (Oxon.), D.Sc., Professor Emeritus of Zoology, Oxford, and President of the Society for Psychical Research, *The Living Stream,* Gifford Lectures. New York: Harper & Row, 1965.

Heywood, Rosalind, *Beyond the Reach of Sense: An Inquiry into Extrasensory Perception,* with intro. by J. B. Rhine, Ph.D. New York: E. P. Dutton & Co., 1961.

Karagulla, Shafica, M.D., Neuro-psychiatrist, and President and Director of Research of Higher Sense Perception Research Foundation, Beverly Hills, California, *Breakthrough to Creativity.* Los Angeles: De Vorss & Co., Inc., 1967.

Mangan, Gordon L., *A Review of Published Research on the Relationship of Some Personality Variables to ESP Scoring Level,* Parapsychological Monographs #1. New York: Parapsychology Foundation, Inc., 1958.

Phantasms of the Living, Cases of Telepathy Printed in the Journal of the Society for Psychical Research During Thirty-five Years; and *On Hindrances and Complications in Telepathic Communication,* bound in one volume with *Phantasms of the Living,* by Edmund Gurney, F. W. H. Myers, and Frank Podmore, abridged and edited by Eleanor Mildred Sidgwick, intro. by Gardner Murphy, Ph.D. New Hyde Park: University Books, 1962.

Puharich, Andrija, M.D., *The Sacred Mushroom: Key to the Door of Eternity.* Garden City: Doubleday, 1959. (In addition to the psychedelic data implied by the title, the book covers laboratory experiments in the field of ESP, including clairvoyance, retrocognition, and precognition.)

Rhine, J. B., Ph.D., and Pratt, J. G., Ph.D., *Extrasensory Perception After Sixty Years.* New York: Henry Holt, 1940.

——, *Parapsychology: Frontier Science of the Mind.* Springfield: Charles C. Thomas, 1957.

Rhine, Louisa E., *Hidden Channels of the Mind.* New York: William Sloane Associates, 1961.

Schmeidler, G. R., and McConnell, R. A., *ESP and Personality Patterns*. New Haven: Yale University Press, 1958.

Sinclair, Upton, *Mental Radio*, rev. 2d ed., intro. by William McDougall, preface by Albert Einstein. Springfield: Charles C. Thomas, 1930 and 1962.

Soal, S. G., Ph.D., formerly lecturer in Pure Mathematics, University of London, and F. Bateman, *Modern Experiments in Telepathy*. New Haven: Yale University Press, 1954.

Tyrrell, G. N. M., *The Personality of Man*. Baltimore: Penguin Books, 1947.

——, *Apparitions*. New York: Collier Books, 1963.

PSYCHOKINETIC PHENOMENA

Owen, A. R. G., Ph.D., Fellow of Trinity College, Cambridge, and lecturer in Genetics at the University, *Can We Explain the Poltergeist?* New York: Garrett Publications, 1964.

See also chapters in works listed under PSYCHICAL RESEARCH and EXTRASENSORY PERCEPTION.

NEW FRONTIERS OF CONSCIOUSNESS

Andrews, Donald Hatch, Ph.D., Professor Emeritus of Chemistry, Johns Hopkins University, *The Symphony of Life*. Lee's Summit, Mo.: Unity Books, 1966.

Bucke, Richard Maurice, M.D., *Cosmic Consciousness*. New York: E. P. Dutton & Co., 1964.

deChardin, Pierre Teilhard, *The Phenomenon of Man*. New York: Harper & Brothers, 1959.

Eiseley, Loren, Ph.D., *The Immense Journey*. New York: Vintage Books, Random House, 1957.

Eliade, Mircea, Ph.D., Professor of History of Religions, University of Chicago, *Cosmos and History*. New York: Harper Torchbooks, 1959.

Johnson, Raynor C., M.A. (Oxon.), D.Sc., Master of Queen's College, University of Melbourne, *The Imprisoned Splendour*. New York: Harper & Row, 1953.

Loomis, W. Farnsworth, M.D., Rosenfield Professor of Biochemistry, Brandeis University, *The God$_B$ Within*, with foreword by James A. Pike. New York: October House, 1967.

Martin, P. W., *Experiment in Depth*. New York: Pantheon Books, 1955.

Osborn, Arthur W., *The Meaning of Personal Existence*, with foreword by Ian Stevenson, M.D. Wheaton, Ill.: The Theosophical Publishing House, 1967.

THEOLOGICAL WORKS

Baillie, John, D.Litt., *And the Life Everlasting*. New York: Scribner's, 1948.

Boros, Ladislaus, S.J., Lecturer in Theology, University of Innsbruck, *The Mystery of Death*. New York: Herder and Herder, 1965.

Cullmann, Oscar, Th.D., Professor of the Theological Faculty of the University of Basel, and of the Sorbonne in Paris, *Immortality of the Soul or Resurrection of the Dead?* London: The Epworth Press, 1958.

Forsyth, P. T., late Principal of Hackney College, Hampstead (Divinity School of the University of London), *This Life and the Next*. Boston: The Pilgrim Press, 1948.

Grant, Frederick C., Th.D., Professor Emeritus of Biblical Theology, Union Theological Seminary, *Can We Still Believe in Immortality?* New York: The Cloister Press, 1944.

Hocking, William Ernest, Ph.D., late Alford Professor of Philosophy, Harvard University, *The Meaning of Immortality in Human Experience*. New York: Harper & Brothers, 1957.

Immortality and Resurrection–Death in the Western World: Two Conflicting Currents of Thought, including lectures by Professors Oscar Cullmann, Harry A. Wolfson, the late Werner Jaeger, and Henry J. Cadbury. Krister Stendahl, Ph.D., Dean of the Harvard Divinity School and Frothingham Professor of Biblical Studies, is editor and co-author. New York: Macmillan, 1965.

McLeman, James, *Resurrection Then and Now*. London: Hodder & Stoughton, 1965.

Perry, Michael C., lately Senior Scholar of Trinity College, Cambridge, *The Easter Enigma: an Essay on the Resurrection with Special Reference to the Data on Psychical Research*, with an intro. by Austin Farrer, D.D., Fellow of Trinity College, Oxford. London: Faber & Faber, 1959.

Robinson, Bishop John A. T., Ph.D., *In the End God*. New York: Harper & Row, 1968.

Weatherhead, Leslie D., Ph.D., late Minister Emeritus of the City Temple, London, *After Death*. New York: Abingdon-Cokesbury Press, 1936.

——, *The Christian Agnostic*. Nashville: Abingdon Press, 1965.

POPULAR WORKS

Behind the Five Senses, ed. by Eileen J. Garrett. New York: J. B. Lippincott, 1957.

Cerminara, Gina, *The World Within*. New York: William Sloane Associates, 1957.

Cohen, Daniel, *Myths of the Space Age*. New York: Dodd, Mead & Co., 1965, 1966, 1967.

Dingwall, E., and Langdon-Davies, J., *The Unknown–Is It Nearer?* New York: New American Library, 1956.

Edsall, F. S., *The World of Psychic Phenomena*. New York: David McKay Co., 1958.

Ford, Arthur, with Margueritte Harmon Bro. *Nothing So Strange*. New York: Harper & Row, 1958.

——, *Unknown but Known*. New York: Harper & Row, 1968.

Harlow, S. Ralph, Ph.D., retired Professor of Religion, Smith College, *A Life After Death*. Garden City: Doubleday, 1961.

Haynes, Renée, *The Hidden Springs*. New York: The Devin-Adair Co., 1961.

Holzer, Hans, *ESP and You*. New York: Hawthorn Books, 1967.

Kelsey, Denys, and Grant, Joan, *Many Lifetimes*. Garden City: Doubleday, 1967.

Lehmann, Rosamond, *The Swan in the Evening*. New York: Harcourt, Brace & World, 1967.

Montgomery, Ruth, *A Gift of Prophecy*. New York: William Morrow & Co., 1965.

——, *A Search for the Truth*. New York: William Morrow & Co., 1967.

Oursler, Will, *The Healing Power of Faith*. New York: Hawthorn Books, 1957.

Smith, Alson J., *Religion and the New Psychology*. Garden City: Doubleday, 1951.

——, *Immortality–the Scientific Evidence*. Englewood Cliffs, N.J.: Prentice-Hall, 1954.

Smith, Susy, *ESP*, with intro. by Professor C. J. Ducasse, Ph.D., Brown University. New York: Pyramid Books, 1967.

Spraggett, Allen, *The Unexplained*, with foreword by James A. Pike. New York: New American Library, 1967.

Stearn, Jess, *Edgar Cayce, the Sleeping Prophet*. New York: Doubleday, 1967.

——, *The Search for the Girl with the Blue Eyes*. Garden City: Doubleday, 1968.

Sugrue, Thomas, *There Is a River: the Story of Edgar Cayce*. New York: Dell Publishing Co., 1967.

White, Stewart Edward, *The Betty Book*. New York: E. P. Dutton & Co., 1937.

COGNATE FIELDS

MYSTICISM

Ancelot-Hustache, Jeanne, *Master Eckhart and the Rhineland Mystics*, trans. by Hilda Grael. New York: Harper Torchbooks, 1957.

Clark, J. M., *The Great German Mystics*. Oxford: Blackwell, 1949.

The Cloud of Unknowing, trans. into modern English with intro. by Clifton Wolters. Baltimore: Penguin Books, 1961.

Dodds, E. R., Regis Professor of Greek (Emeritus), Oxford, *Pagan and Christian in the Age of Anxiety: Some Aspects of Religious Experience from Marcus Aurelius to Constantine*, The Wiles Lectures at Queen's University, Belfast. Cambridge: University Press, 1965.

Goodenough, Erwin R., Ph.D., late John A. Hoober Professor of Religion, Yale University, *The Psychology of Religious Experiences*. New York: Basic Books, 1965.

James, William, Ph.D., late Professor of Psychology, Harvard, and former President of the Society for Psychical Research, *The Varieties of Religious Experience*, Gifford Lectures. New York: The Modern Library, 1902; Brooklyn: The Fontana Library, 1960.

Laski, Marghanita. *Ecstasy: A Study of Some Secular and Religious Experiences*. Bloomington: Indiana University Press, 1961.

Maslow, Abraham H., Ph.D., Professor of Psychology, Brandeis University, *Religions, Values and Peak Experiences*. Columbus: Ohio State University Press, 1964.

The Protestant Mystics, ed. by Anne Fremantle, with intro. by W. H. Auden. Boston: Little, Brown & Co., 1964.

The Religious Experience, ed. with intro. by George Brampl. 2 vols. New York: George Braziller, 1964.

The Three Pillars of Zen, Teaching Practice in Enlightenment, ed. and trans. with intro. by Philip Kapleau. New York: Harper & Row, 1966.

Underhill, Evelyn, *Mysticism*. New York: E. P. Dutton & Co., 1955.

Watts, Alan W., *Behold the Spirit: A Study in the Necessity of Mystical Religion*. New York: Pantheon Books, 1947.

Zen Buddhism, selected writings of D. T. Suzuki, ed. by William Barrett. Garden City: Doubleday, 1956.

"OUT OF BODY" EXPERIENCES

Crookall, Robert, D.Sc., Ph.D., Former Principal Geologist, H.M. Geological Survey, London, *The Theory and Practice of Astral Projection*. London: Aquarian Press, 1960.

——, *More Astral Projections*. London: Aquarian Press, 1964.

CRYOGENICS

Ettinger, Robert C. W., *The Prospect of Immortality*. New York: MacFadden-Bartell Corporation, 1966.

SPIRIT PHOTOGRAPHY

Eisenbud, Jule, M.D., M.Sc.D., Associate Clinical Professor of Psychiatry, University of Colorado Medical School, *The World of Ted Serios*. New York: William Morrow & Co., 1967.

GLOSSALALIA

Hoekema, Anthony A., Th.D., Professor of Systematic Theology, Calvin Theological Seminary, *What About Tongue Speaking?* Grand Rapids, Mich.: William B. Eerdman, 1966.

Kelsey, Morton T., *Tongue Speaking: An Experiment in Spiritual Experience*. Garden City: Doubleday, 1964.

SPIRITUAL HEALING

Frost, Evelyn, Ph.D., *Christian Healing*. London: A. R. Mowbray & Co., Ltd., 1940.

Gross, Don H., Ph.D., *The Case for Spiritual Healing*. New York: Thomas Nelson & Sons, 1958.

Hutton, J. Bernard, *Healing Hands*. New York: David McKay Co., 1966.

PSYCHEDELIC AND OTHER HALLUCINOGENIC DRUGS

Braden, William, *A Private Sea: LSD and the Search for God.* Chicago: Quadrangle Books, Inc., 1967.

Cohen, Sidney, *The Beyond Within.* New York: Atheneum, 1964.

DeRopp, Robert S., *Drugs and the Mind.* New York: Grove Press, 1957.

Huxley, Aldous, D.Litt., *Doors of Perception.* New York: Harper & Row, 1954.

———, *Heaven and Hell.* New York: Harper & Row, 1956.

The Marihuana Papers, ed. by David Solomon. New York: New American Library, 1966.

Watts, Alan W., *The Joyous Cosmology: Adventures in the Chemistry of Consciousness.* New York: Pantheon Books, 1962.

REINCARNATION

Reincarnation: An East-West Anthology, ed. by Joseph Head and S. L. Cranston. New York: The Julian Press, 1961.

Stevenson, Ian, M.D., Professor of Neurology and Psychiatry, University of Virginia School of Medicine, *Twenty Cases Suggestive of Reincarnation.* American Society for Psychical Research. Richmond: William Byrd Press, Inc., 1966.

SUICIDE

Hillman, James, *Suicide and the Soul.* New York: Harper & Row, 1964.

THE COLLECTIVE UNCONSCIOUS

Jacobi, Jolan, *The Psychology of Jung,* with foreword by the latter. New Haven: Yale University Press, 1943.

Jung, C. G., M.D., foreword to *The I Ching,* the Richard Wilhelm edition, trans. by Carl F. Baynes, Bollingen Series XIX. New York: Pantheon Books, 1920.

———, *Psychological Types,* trans. by H. G. Baynes. London: Kegan-Paul, 1933.

———, *Memories, Dreams, Reflections,* ed. by Aniela Jaffé. New York: Vintage Books, Random House, 1961.

Perry, John, M.D., *The Lord of the Four Quarters.* New York: George Braziller & Co., 1966.

Westman, H., *The Springs of Creativity: The Bible and the Creative Process of the Psyche.* New York: Atheneum, 1961.

DREAMS

Kelsey, Morton T., Th.D., *Dreams: The Dark Speech of the Spirit.* New York: Doubleday, 1968.

ORGANIZATIONS FOR RESEARCH AND INFORMATION

INSTITUTE OF PARAPSYCHOLOGY
College Station
Durham, North Carolina 27708
Journal of Parapsychology—$8.00 a year. (Louisa E. Rhine and Dorothy H. Pope, Editors; J. B. Rhine, Consultant)

PSYCHICAL RESEARCH FOUNDATION, INC.
Post Office Box 6116
College Station
Durham, North Carolina
Theta—$1.50 a year. (W. G. Roll, Editor)

AMERICAN SOCIETY FOR PSYCHICAL RESEARCH, INC.
Dr. Gardner Murphy, President
880 Fifth Avenue
New York, New York 10021
Journal of American Society for Psychical Research—$1.50 per copy.
Proceedings of American Society for Psychical Research (for members) (Mrs. Laura A. Dale, Editor)
5 West 73rd Street
New York, New York 10023

PARAPSYCHOLOGY FOUNDATION
Eileen J. Garrett, President
29 West 57 Street
New York, New York 10019
International Journal of Parapsychology—$6.00 a year

SOCIETY FOR PSYCHICAL RESEARCH
31 Tavistock Square
London, W.C. 1
Journal of the Society for Psychical Research Proceedings of the Society for Psychical Research
1 Adam and Eve Mews
London, W.8

THE COLLEGE OF PSYCHIC SCIENCE, Ltd.
Mr. Paul Beard, President
16 Queensberry Place
London, S.W. 7
Light–13/8d a year

THE CHURCHES' FELLOWSHIP FOR PSYCHICAL AND SPIRITUAL STUDIES
The Rev. E. Garth Moore, President
5/6 Dennison House
Vauxhall Bridge Road
London, S.W.1
Churches' Fellowship for Psychical and Spiritual Studies Quarterly Review–25¢ per issue

SPIRITUAL FRONTIERS FELLOWSHIP
The Rev. William V. Rauscher, President
800 Custer Avenue
Evanston, Illinois 60202
Gate Way: Journal of the Spiritual Frontiers Fellowship (Laurence L. Tunstall Heron, Editor)

HUGH LYNN CAYCE FOUNDATION and
ASSOCIATION FOR RESEARCH AND ENLIGHTENMENT, INC.
Mrs. David Kahn, President
215 67th Street
Virginia Beach, Virginia
(Deals with subjects treated in Edgar Cayce's readings) *The A. R. E. Journal* (Quarterly for members)
Box 595
Virginia Beach, Virginia 23451